AF560021

William Golding

LORD OF THE FLIES

William Golding

LORD OF THE FLIES

[Edited with Introduction, Author's Information, Complete Text, Summary and Analysis and Study Questions]

Misha Kandhari
M.A., M. Phil. English,
Delhi University

ANMOL PUBLICATIONS PVT. LTD.
NEW DELHI - 110 002 (INDIA)

ANMOL PUBLICATIONS PVT. LTD.

H.O.: 4374/4B, Ansari Road, Darya Ganj,
New Delhi-110 002 (India)
Ph.: 23278000, 23261597

B.O.: No. 1015, Ist Main Road, BSK IIIrd Stage
IIIrd Phase, IIIrd Block
Bangalore - 560 085 (India)
Visit us at: www.anmolpublications.com

Lord of the Flies

First Published, 2009

PRINTED IN INDIA

Printed at Mehra Offset Press, Delhi.

Contents

Preface

William Gerald Golding was born on September 19, 1911 in Cornwall England. His father was a schoolmaster and his mother was a suffragette. His parents had wanted him to study science, so he did from grammar school until the second year of college. After his second year of college, he abandoned the study of science in favor of English literature. He wrote poetry and worked in amateur theater for a while before becoming a teacher where he was at the beginning of World War II. At the start of World War II, he entered the Royal navy and served with distinction on mine sweepers, destroyers, and rocket launchers. He believed that the horrors of World War II can be based on some innate evil which he explores in Lord of the Flies. After the war, he returned to teaching and writing, although had little success getting published. He was able to get Lord of the Flies published and it experienced great success

Author

Chapter 1

Introduction

Sir William Golding composed Lord of the Flies shortly after the end of WWII. At the time of the novel's composition, Golding, who had published an anthology of poetry nearly two decades earlier, had been working for a number of years as a teacher and training as a scientist. Golding drew extensively on his scientific background for his first narrative work. The novel's plot, in which a group of English boys stranded on a deserted island struggle to develop their own society, is a social and political thought-experiment using fiction. The story of their attempts at civilization and devolution into savagery and violence puts the relationship between human nature and society under a literary microscope. Golding's allusions to human evolution also reflect his scientific training.

The characters discover fire, craft tools, and form political and social systems in a process that recalls theories of the development of early man, a topic of much interest among many peoples including the mid-century Western public. The culmination of the plot in war and murder suggests that Golding's overarching hypothesis about humanity is pessimistic, that is, there are anarchic and brutal instincts in human nature. Ordered democracy or some other regime is necessary to contain these instincts.

As an allegory about human nature and society, Lord of the Flies draws upon Judeo-Christian mythology to elaborate on the novel's sociological and political hypothesis. The title has two meanings, both charged with religious significance. The first is a reference to a line from King Lear, "As flies to wanton boys, are we to gods." The second is a reference to the Hebrew name Ba'alzevuv, or in its Greek form Beelzebub, which translates to "God of the Flies" and is synonymous with Satan. For Golding however, the satanic forces that compel the shocking events on the island come from within the human psyche rather than from an external, supernatural realm as they do in Judeo-Christian mythology.

Golding thus employs a religious reference to illustrate a Freudian concept: the Id, the amoral instinct that governs the individual's sense of sheer survival, is by nature evil in its amoral pursuit of its own goals. The Lord of the Flies, that is, the pig's head on a stick, directly challenges the most spiritually motivated character on the island, Simon, who functions as a prophet-martyr for the other boys. Published in 1954 early in the Cold War, Lord of the Flies is firmly rooted in the sociopolitical concerns of its era. The novel alludes to the Cold War conflict between liberal democracy and totalitarian communism.

Ralph represents the liberal tradition, while Jack, before he succumbs to total anarchy, represents the kind of military dictatorship that, for mid-century America and Great Britain, characterized the communist system. It is also notable that Golding sets the novel in what appears to be a future human reality, one that is in crisis after atomic war. Golding's novel capitalizes on public paranoia surrounding the atom bomb which, due to the arms race of the Cold War, was at a high. Golding's negative depiction of Jack, who represents an anti-democratic political system, and his suggestion of the reality of atomic war, present the novel as a gesture of support for the Western position in the Cold War.

In addition to science, mythology, and the sociopolitical context of the Cold War, Lord of the Flies was heavily influenced by previous works of speculative fiction. In particular, Golding's novel alludes to R. M. Ballantyne's 1857 *The Coral Island*, which tells the story of three boys stranded on a desert island. Golding, who found Ballantyne's interpretation of the situation naive and improbable, likely intended Lord of the Flies to be an indirect critique of *The Coral*

Island. Golding preserves the names of two of Ballantyne's characters, Ralph and Jack, to force the two texts into deeper comparison. While the boys of Coral Island spend their time having pleasant adventures, Golding's characters battle hunger, loneliness, and the deadly consequences of political conflict after they are deserted. The pessimistic character of Golding's story reflects the author's emphasis on the necessity of democratic civilization. Critics also have noted the relationship between Lord of the Flies and Joseph Conrad's canonical 1902 Heart of Darkness, which follows a soldier's excursion into marginal African civilizations. Reflecting some biases, Heart of Darkness depicts these parts of Africa as places where social order is absent and anarchy rules, breeding death and disorder; the novel sees the same problem as an issue within the individual human soul. Like Conrad's work, Golding's novel emphasizes the brutal and violent human impulses that arise in the absence of political order.

Lord of the Flies, with its dystopian and speculative characteristics, established Golding as a solid author with an interest in the science-fiction literary genre that was popular in the 1950s. The novel depicts ostensibly realistic characters, but the plot, which follows a small group of humans isolated within an alien landscape, employs or alludes to the conventions of popular science fiction novels of the time. Golding's subsequent works saw him moving even further into the science fiction genre. *The Inheritors,* heavily influenced by H. G. Wells's *Outline of History,* imagines life during the dawn of man and is considered a modern classic of speculative fiction. Lord of the Flies was not an instant success, selling fewer than 3,000 copies before going out of print in 1955. Shortly thereafter, however, the novel became a bestseller among American and British readers who, as the arms race intensified, likely saw in Golding's wartime dystopia a grim prediction of their own future.

By the 1960s the novel was required reading for many high school and college courses, where it has remained to the present day. The enduring popularity of the novel inspired two film adaptations, one by Peter Brook in 1963, and the second by Harry Hook in 1990. Golding's original novel, however, remains the best-known version of the tale. In 2005, *Time Magazine* named the novel one of the 100 best English-language novels since 1923.

A continuing controversy surrounding the political message of the novel and its view of human nature has led some readers to challenge its status as a book suitable for children. The American Library Association thus positioned Lord of the Flies at number 70 on its list of the 100 most challenged books of 1990-2000. Among literary critics of the late twentieth and early twenty-first centuries, however, Lord of the Flies has been revisited less as an allegory of human evil than as a literary expression of Cold War ideology. This historicizing does not do justice to the novel. But in terms of reception history, contemporary critics are right to note that the novel's position at the centre of many English curricula across America and Great Britain during the Cold War illustrates how the pedagogy of literature has been used to bolster national identity and ideology.

Chapter 2

Biography of William Golding

William Golding (1911-1993)

Sir William Gerald Golding was born in 1911 in Saint Columb Minor in Cornwall, England, to Alec Golding, a socialist teacher who supported scientific rationalism, and Mildred Golding (née Curnroe), a supporter of female suffrage. As a child, William Golding was educated at the Marlborough Grammar School, where his father worked, and later at Brasenose College, Oxford. Although educated to be a scientist at the request of his father, the young Golding developed an interest in literature, becoming devoted first to Anglo-Saxon texts and then to poetry, which he wrote avidly.

At Oxford he studied natural science for two years and then transfered to a programme for English literature and philosophy. Following a short period of time in which he worked in various positions at a settlement house and in small theater companies as both an actor and a writer, Golding became a schoolmaster at Bishop Wordsworth's School in Salisbury. During the Second World War he joined the Royal Navy and was involved in the sinking of the German battleship Bismarck, after which he returned to Bishop Wordsworth's School, where he taught until the early 1960s.

In 1954, Golding published his first novel, Lord of the Flies, which details the adventures of British schoolboys stranded on an island in the Pacific who descend into barbaric behaviour. Although at first rejected by twenty-one different publishing houses, Golding's first novel became a surprise success. E.M. Forster declared Lord of the Flies the outstanding novel of its year, while Time and Tide called it "not only a first-rate adventure story but a parable of our times." Golding continued to develop similar themes concerning the inherent violence in human nature in his next novel, IThe Inheritors, published the following year. This novel deals with the last days of Neanderthal man.

The Inheritors posits that the Cro-Magnon "fire-builders" triumphed over Neanderthal man as much by violence and deceit as by any natural superiority. His subsequent works include Pincher Martin , the story of a guilt-ridden naval officer who faces an agonizing death, Free Fall , and The Spire , each of which deals with the depravity of human nature. The Spire is an allegory concerning the protagonist's obsessive determination to build a cathedral spire regardless of the consequences. In addition to his novels and his early collection of poems, Golding published a play entitled The Brass Butterfly in 1958 and two collections of essays, The Hot Gates and A Moving Target . Golding's final works include Darkness Visible , the story of a boy horribly injured during the London blitz of World War II, and Rites of Passage . This novel won the Booker McConnell Prize, the most prestigious award for English literature, and inspired two sequels, Close Quarters and Fire Down Below . These three novels portray life aboard a ship during the Napoleonic Wars.

In 1983, Golding received the Nobel Prize for literature for his novels which, according to the Nobel committee, "with the perspicuity of realistic narrative art and the diversity and universality of myth, illuminate the human condition in the world of today." In 1988 he was knighted by Queen Elizabeth II. Sir William died in 1993 in Perranarworthal, Cornwall. At the time of his death he was working on an unfinished manuscript entitled "The Double Tongue," which focused on the fall of Hellenic culture and the rise of Roman civilization. This work was published posthumously in 1995.

Early Years and Jobs

William Gerald Golding was born in Cornwall, England, in 1911. His mother, Mildred, was a strong supporter of the

British suffragette movement. His father, Alec, was a schoolteacher and an ardent advocate of rationalism, the idea that reason rather than experience is a necessary and reliable means through which to gain knowledge and understand the world. Alec's anti-religious devotion to reason was the legacy of such scientific rationalists as T.H. Huxley and H.G. Wells. This rationalist viewpoint was not tolerant of emotionally based experiences, such as the fear of the dark that Golding had as a child. His father wielded a tremendous influence over him, and, in fact, until leaving for college, Golding attended the school where his father taught.

Education

Golding began attending Brasenose College at Oxford in 1930 and spent two years studying science, in deference to his father's beliefs. In his third year, however, he switched to the literature programme, following his true interests. Although his ultimate medium was fiction, from an early age, Golding dreamed of writing poetry. He began reading Tennyson at age seven and steeped himself in Shakespeare's work. While still at Oxford, a volume of Golding's poems was published as part of Macmillan's Contemporary Poets series. Later in life, Golding dismissed this work as juvenile, but these poems are valuable in that they illustrate his increasing distrust of the rationalism he had been reared on, mocking well-known rationalists and their ideas. In 1935, he graduated from Oxford with a Bachelor of Arts in English and a diploma in education.

Jobs

From 1935 to 1939, Golding worked as a writer, actor, and producer with a small theater in an unfashionable part of London, paying his bills with a job as a social worker. He considered the theater his strongest literary influence, citing Greek tragedians and Shakespeare, rather than other novelists, as his primary influences.

In 1939, Golding began teaching English and philosophy in Salisbury at Bishop Wordsworth's School. That same year, he married Ann Brookfield, with whom he had two children.

With the exception of five years he spent in the Royal Navy during World War II, he remained in the teaching position until 1961 when he left Bishop Wordsworth's School to write full time. Golding died in Cornwall in 1993.

Chapter 3

Major Works of William Golding

Major Works

The five years Golding spent in the navy (from 1940 to 1945) made an enormous impact, exposing him to the incredible cruelty and barbarity of which humankind is capable. Writing about his wartime experiences later, he asserted that "man produces evil, as a bee produces honey." Long before, while in college, he had lost faith in the rationalism of his father with its attendant belief in the perfectibility of humankind. While Golding's body of fiction utilizes a variety of storytelling techniques, the content frequently comes back to the problem of evil, the conflict between reason's civilizing influence, and mankind's innate desire for domination.

Novels

In Lord of the Flies, which was published in 1954, Golding combined that perception of humanity with his years of experience with schoolboys. Although not the first novel he wrote, Lord of the Flies was the first to be published after having been rejected by 21 publishers. An examination of the duality of savagery and civilization in humanity, Golding uses a pristine tropical island as a protected environment in which a group of marooned British schoolboys act out their worst impulses. The boys loyal to the ways of civilization face persecution by the boys indulging in their innate aggression. As such, the novel illustrates the failure of the rationalism espoused by Golding's father.

A fast, intense writer, Golding quickly followed Lord of the Flies with The Inheritors , a depiction of how the violent, deceitful Homo sapiens achieved victory over the gentler Neanderthals. Although this novel is the one readers have the most difficulty understanding, it remained Golding's favourite throughout his life.

Pincher Martin followed in 1956. Like Lord of the Flies, it concerns survival after shipwreck. Navy lieutenant Christopher Martin is thrown from his ship during combat in World War II. He finds a rock to cling to, and the rest of the story is related from this vantage point, detailing his struggle for survival and recounting the details of his life.

Golding uses the flashback technique of Pincher Martin more extensively in his next novel, Free Fall . Unlike his first three novels, Free Fall is told with a first person narrator, an artist named Samuel Mountjoy. The novel takes as a model Dante's La Vita Nuova, a collection of love poems interspersed with Dante's own commentary on the poems. Golding uses the character Mountjoy to comment on the conflict between rationalism and faith.

Issues of faith are addressed in The Spire as well. A fourteenth-century Dean of Barchester Cathedral decides that God wants a 400-foot-high spire added to the top of the cathedral, although the cathedral's foundation is not sufficient to hold the weight of the spire. The novel tells the story of the human costs of the spire's construction and the lessons that the Dean learns too late.

The Pyramid provides an examination of English social class within the context of a town ironically named Stilbourne. A primary issue in this story is music, and the novel utilizes the same structure as the musical form sonata.

Golding's next publication was a collection entitled The Scorpion God: Three Short Novels . Each story explores the negative repercussions of technological progress—an idea that was in sharp contrast to the technology worship of the space age. One of the novellas had been originally published in 1956; Golding then turned the story into a comedic play titled The Brass Butterfly, which was first performed in London in 1958.

Golding's next novel, Darkness Visible, appeared in 1979. It addresses the interdependence of good and evil, exemplified in the two main characters: Sophy, who plots to kidnap a child for ransom, and Matty, who gives his life to prevent it.

Golding's 1984 publication, The Paper Men, was condemned by reviewers as his worst work, partly because the novel seemed to condemn literary critics. The plot concerns an elderly novelist trying to elude a young scholar who wants to write his biography.

One of Golding's most ambitious works is The Sea Trilogy, three full-length novels that follow the emotional education and moral growth of an aristocratic young man named Edmund Talbot during an ocean voyage to Australia in 1812. Rites of Passage shows Talbot's spiritual growth, Close Quarters depicts his emotional and aesthetic development, and Fire Down Below covers his political enlightenment.

Other Works

Golding's work is not limited to fiction: He published three collections of essays which are often comic and expand upon or illuminate his novels. The Hot Gates and Other Occasional Pieces was published in 1966; A Moving Target appeared in 1982; and An Egyptian Journal followed in 1985.

Honors and Awards

Following the publication of his best-known work, Lord of the Flies, Golding was granted membership in the Royal Society of Literature in 1955. Ten years later, he received the honorary designation Commander of the British Empire (CBE) and was knighted in 1988. His 1980 novel Rites of Passage won the Booker Prize, a prestigious British award. Golding's greatest honour was being awarded the 1983 Nobel Prize for Literature.

Chapter 4

Context of Lord of the Flies

Context

A plane evacuating a party of English boys from a nuclear war in Britain is shot down over a deserted tropical island. Stranded, the boys decide to elect a leader and to find a way to be rescued. They choose Ralph because he has a certain charisma and with the aid of Piggy impressed them by using a conch shell to call the first assembly.

Jack was the main opposition to Ralph, being the leader of the choirboys, and Ralph shows his diplomatic skills by making Jack responsible for hunting and maintaining the signal fire at the top of the island.

The group is roughly divided into boys of around the age of six who are called littluns, and biguns who are aged between ten and twelve.

Ralph's aim is to form a society similar to the one they have left behind and at an early date he establishes rules regarding the conduct of meetings, shelters, fresh water and latrines.

Ralph, Jack and Simon set off on an expedition to explore the island. When they return, they decide on the best position for a signal fire, and they use Piggy's glasses as a means of lighting the fire. However, many of the boys only wish to play and they use the excuse of hunting in order to avoid the building of shelters and the gathering of fresh water. On one occasion the signal fire is not watched and it burns out of control igniting the forest, which results in one of the littluns being burned to death.

So far the hunters have failed to catch a pig, and many of them are being absorbed by the bloodlust of the hunt. After a few days a ship is seen passing on the horizon and Ralph and Piggy realise that the signal fire has burned out. Furious, Ralph confronts Jack, but the hunter has just returned with his first pig and all the boys are gripped with a strange frenzy, dancing and re-enacting the pursuit of the pig. Piggy criticizes them for being immature and Jack slaps him across the face, breaking one of his lenses.

Ralph becomes increasingly concerned at the lack of discipline and using the conch shell, he calls another meeting. He vents his anger on the boys in an attempt to restore discipline. One of the littluns, who are all troubled by recurring nightmares, says he has seen a beast lurking on the island. The bigger boys try to placate him, saying that if such a beast did exist they would have seen it during the daytime hunts, but the littlun responds by saying that the beast lives in the sea during the day. This sows a seed of doubt for all the boys, which is to grow to dramatic proportions as the novel progresses. The fear that the boys have for this mythical beast roaming the island is the catalyst, which ignites the power struggle between Ralph and Jack, between civilization and the primitive, savage world.

One night the nuclear war comes close to the island and one of its casualties, a parachutist, floats down, coming to rest on the mountaintop. His parachute is snagged and as the wind inflates the canopy, it causes his body to rise and fall. The signal firewatchers awake to see this terrifying sight and they rush down from the mountain to tell the rest of the boys that the beast does exist and it has not been imagined by the littluns.

As a result of the chaos, which ensues, Jack starts to form his own following. As he now seems the best person to lead them in their fight against the beast, he ends up with most of the boys following him with the exception of Piggy, Simon, Samneric and a few littluns who stay loyal to Ralph. It is easy to see the attraction, which Jack offers, getting to hunt pigs, wearing camouflage face paint made up of clay and charcoal and performing frenzied tribal dances. Jack soon has them out on a hunting party and they find an easy prey in a sow suckling her young, which the tribe slaughter and mutilate placing the pig's head on a stake which provides their tribe with an idol to worship, and also a symbol to placate the beast. This idol becomes the Lord of the Flies and has been positioned outside Simon's hiding place who is suffering from hallucinations and thinks that the pig's head is speaking to him, warning him not to spoil the fun which is to be had on the island.

Simon is the only boy who has the courage to go back up the mountain and find out the true nature of the beast, and he discovers the truth. He realizes that the beast, which they are all frightened off, is not a creature lurking in the jungle, but a primordial, evil buried in everyone's sub-conscious. Exhausted, Simon decides to go back to Jack's camp to tell them the truth, but they mistake him for the beast in disguise and brutally murder him.

There are now only a handful of boys in Ralph's camp, but they have the ability to make fire, whereas Jack's group have to steal burning branches in order to have a pig roast. When Ralph decides to let the fire burn out, Jack's tribe raid Ralph's party and steal Piggy's glasses. When Ralph confronts Jack and his tribe in an attempt to obtain the glasses back so that they can maintain the signal fire, Piggy is killed and the conch he is holding is smashed, the last symbol of civilization on the island. Jack, leaving Ralph to fend for himself on the island, captures the rest of the boys.

Roger, Jack's lieutenant tortures Samneric in order to persuade them to join Jack's tribe. He was also the one responsible for the death of Piggy and the tribe is now held together by fear, not just of the beast, but also from Jack, Roger and the oldest boys.

Jack decides to mount a manhunt to track down and kill Ralph and they set light to the jungle in order to flush him out. The smoke that this generates attracts a passing ship and a British Naval Officer, who is amused to see the boys having such fun, playing like primitive cavemen, saves Ralph from certain death. Ralph breaks down when he considers what has happened to them all since they were marooned.

Chapter 5

List of Characters

Character List

Ralph

The protagonist of the story, Ralph is one of the oldest boys on the island. He quickly becomes the group's leader. Golding describes Ralph as tall for his age and handsome, and he presides over the other boys with a natural sense of authority. Although he lacks Piggy's overt intelligence, Ralph is calm and rational, with sound judgment and a strong moral sensibility. But he is susceptible to the same instinctive influences that affect the other boys, as demonstrated by his contribution to Simon's death. Nevertheless, Ralph remains the most civilized character throughout the novel. With his strong commitment to justice and equality, Ralph represents the political tradition of liberal democracy.

Piggy

Although pudgy, awkward, and averse to physical labour because he suffers from asthma, Piggy—who dislikes his nickname—is the intellectual on the island. Though he is an outsider among the other boys, Piggy is eventually accepted by them, albeit grudgingly, when they discover that his glasses can be used to ignite fires. Piggy's intellectual talent endears him to Ralph in particular, who comes to admire and respect him for his clear focus on securing their rescue from the island. Piggy is dedicated to the ideal of civilization and consistently reprimands the other boys for behaving as savages. His continual clashes with the group culminate when Roger murders Piggy by dropping a rock on him, an act that signals the triumph of brute instinct over civilized order. Intellectual, sensitive, and conscientious, Piggy represents culture within the democratic system embodied by Ralph. Piggy's nickname symbolically connects him to the pigs on the island, who quickly become the targets of Jack's and his hunters' bloodlust—an association that foreshadows his murder.

Jack Merridew

The leader of a boys' choir, Jack exemplifies militarism as it borders on authoritarianism. He is cruel and sadistic, preoccupied with hunting and killing pigs. His sadism intensifies throughout the novel, and he eventually turns cruelly on the other boys. Jack feigns an interest in the rules of order established on the island, but only if they allow him to inflict punishment. Jack represents anarchy. His rejection of Ralph's imposed order—and the bloody results of this act—indicate the danger inherent in an anarchic system based only on self-interest.

Simon

The most introspective character in the novel, Simon has a deep affinity with nature and often walks alone in the jungle. While Piggy represents the cultural and Ralph the political and moral facets of civilization, Simon represents the spiritual side of human nature. Like Piggy, Simon is an outcast: the other boys think of him as odd and perhaps insane. It is Simon who finds the beast. When he attempts to tell the group that it is only a dead pilot, the boys, under the impression that he is the beast, murder him in a panic. Golding frequently suggests that Simon is a Christ-figure whose death is a kind of martyrdom. His name, which means "he whom God has heard," indicates the depth of his spirituality and centrality to the novel's Judeo-Christian allegory.

Sam and Eric

The twins are the only boys who remain with Ralph and

Piggy to tend to the fire after the others abandon Ralph for Jack's tribe. The others consider the two boys as a single individual, and Golding preserves this perception by combining their individual names into one ("Samneric"). Here one might find suggestions about individualism and human uniqueness.

Roger

One of the hunters and the guard at the castle rock fortress, Roger is Jack's equal in cruelty. Even before the hunters devolve into savagery, Roger is boorish and crude, kicking down sand castles and throwing sand at others. After the other boys lose all idea of civilization, it is Roger who murders Piggy.

Maurice

During the hunters' "Kill the pig" chant, Maurice, who is one of Jack's hunters, pretends to be a pig while the others pretend to slaughter him. When the hunters kill a pig, Jack smears blood on Maurice's face. Maurice represents the mindless masses.

Percival

One of the smallest boys on the island, Percival often attempts to comfort himself by repeating his name and address as a memory of home life. He becomes increasingly hysterical over the course of the novel and requires comforting by the older boys. Percival represents the domestic or familial aspects of civilization; his inability to remember his name and address upon the boys' rescue indicates the erosion of domestic impulse with the overturning of democratic order. Note also that in the literary tradition, Percival was one of the Knights of the Round Table who went in search of the Holy Grail.

The Beast

A dead pilot whom Simon discovers in the forest. The other boys mistake him as a nefarious supernatural omen, "The Beast." They attempt to appease his spirit with The Lord of the Flies.

The Lord of the Flies

The pig's head that Jack impales on a stick as an offering to "The Beast." The boys call the offering "The Lord of the Flies," which in Judeo-Christian mythology refers to Beelzebub, an incarnation of Satan. In the novel, The Lord of the Flies functions totemically; it represents the savagery and amorality of Jack's tribe.

Naval Officer

The naval officer appears in the final scene of the novel, when Ralph encounters him on the beach. He tells Ralph that his ship decided to inspect the island upon seeing a lot of smoke (the outcome of the forest fire that Jack and his tribe had set in the hopes of driving Ralph out of hiding). His naivete about the boys' violent conflict—he believes they are playing a game—underscores the tragedy of the situation on the island. His status as a soldier reminds the reader that the boys' behaviour is just a more primitive form of the aggressive and frequently fatal conflicts that characterize adult civilization.

Chapter 6

Lord of the Flies: Synopsis

Form, Structure, and Plot

The Lord of the Flies contains twelve titled chapters. The plot is simple and rarely splits into more than one plot lines, although it does sometimes. Occasionally, the story separates from the general group and follows one child. For example, the story followed the first of Jack's hunts into the jungle, and also Simon's wanderings to be alone. One of the techniques he uses in organizing plot is foreshadow. Through the use and manipulation of many symbols, he gives the reader and idea of what is to come foreshadowing future events.

Outline of Events

Exposition-The exposition is basically all of chapter 1 and the first part of chapter 2. The characters are introduced and so is the problem. The readers learn that because of the war, the children was taken to be transported someplace by plane when the place was attacked and crashed on the island. Ralph is made the leader of the entire group and Jack is made the leader of the hunting party. Piggy tries to maintain order. This takes the period of 1 day.

Rising action-The rising action starts in the middle of chapter 2 where the boys attempt to make a signal fire but it rages out of control. One of the boys are lost. After this, order is slowly lost and chaos slowly takes its place.

Climax/Crises-The climax occurs when order is completely lost, the conch is crush, and Piggy is killed. Jack takes over the group.

Falling action-The falling action is the brief period between the time where Jack takes over and the officer arrives. We see the innate evil within the boys which is a reflection of the evil within the entire mankind.

Resolution-The jungle catches fire and a naval ship spots the smoke. An officer comes ashore just as Ralph is being hunted by the other boys and all are rescued and taken back into society.

Point of View

Golding write the novel in the third person perspective. There is one omniscient narrator. Although the book generally follows Ralph, it occasionally breaks off and follows another character for a time. This entire book is autobiographical in that it tells us something the author wants to show us. Golding tries to teach us and warn us of the evil nature of mankind. He says through the book that we are evil and that it is only society that keeps us from committing crimes.

Character

Golding's characters have a depth and are believable for the somewhat unbelievable situation they are put in. Each character has his own fully developed personality. He does this while maintaining a certain symbolism in the characters. Each characters, while being their own person, symbolizes some idea, but not to the point where the characters are flat.

Ralph-Ralph is 12 and one of the older boys on the island. He is the leader throughout most of the book being determined, rational, and understanding. He is dressed as in a typical school uniform, but not as the choir boys. He tries to understand the problem and the people on the island trying to give rational solutions. However, psychologically, he loses faith in the boys and decides that he has little hope to restore order into the island. His purpose is to show the reader through his eyes the degradation of the society on the island, and thereby show the innate evil within man. "This expresses his understanding and caring side."

Jack-Jack is also one of the older boys and about Ralph's

age. He starts as the leader of the choir boys, and develops into the leader of the hunters eventually taking over everyone on the island. He is dressed nicely in a choir boy outfit. He is strong, villainous, and proud perpetuating the crimes committed by the boys on the island. He cares only for his own power and not for the common good. He disregards order and in him the reader clearly sees the innate evil of man since he was the one that cast off society earliest. He becomes Ralph's most powerful antagonist because of this. "I ought to be chief because I'm chorister and head boy. I can sing C sharp."

Piggy-Piggy is slightly younger than Ralph and in the weakling in the group being overweight and suffering from asthma. He is dressed similar to Ralph in a typical school uniform and ears glasses. He is weak, smart, and friendly. While is put down by the other boys, he is necessary on the island as a source of intelligence and insight. His insights are often ignored because of his weak appearance and he is killed by the Jack and his savages. "My auntie told me not to run on account of my asthma."

Simon-Simon is the saint in the story. He is skinny and dressed similar to Ralph in the school uniform. He is kind, caring and sincere. In the novel, he serves to bring a certain insight into the story. He is the one that seems to best understand the inner evil, and the first to understand the beast. He takes care of the littluns. Sadly, his insight is lost among the boys as he is killed being mistaken for the beast. "Simon, sitting between the twins and Piggy, wiped his mouth and shoved his piece of meat over the rocks to Piggy, who grabbed it. The twins giggled and Simon lowered his face in shame."

Setting

The Lord of the Flies takes place on an island during World War II. This is significant since the isolation forms a sort of civilization and community, a sort of microcosm to the real world. At the same time, the island lacks a society and the societal laws and rules allowing for the boys to run wild and show their true, ugly, inner selves. Since the island is a microcosm, Golding uses it to reflect our world and give comments on our world and his view of human nature. In this book, the setting is used less to create a mood than to put the characters in a particular situation

Themes

- This book traces the faults in society to the faults in the individual person. Golding says that each person has in evil inner nature poorly covered by society. If the society is taken away, then the inner nature comes out and chaos and lawlessness erupt.
- Each person has an evil nature and is capable of committing heinous crimes. In this book, virtually every person fell to the level of Jack's savagery except those that were able to see that evil such as Ralph, Simon, and Piggy.
- The beast is human. In the beginning of the book, a littlun told the others that he saw a beast in the jungle starting everyone's fears. However, it turns out that the beast is actually a parachutist and human, symbolizing that what they should be scared of is not some evil creature, but their own selves and other humans.

Style

Golding makes his novel come alive with a significant use of symbolism, physiological development, and general truths. His writing style is simple but the subject matter is deep. He uses a rather comparatively simple story to convey a weighty idea.

Diction

In The Lord of the Flies, Golding's language is neutral. However, it is simple and it is as if he is telling the story himself rather than writing prose. The vocabulary and sentence structure are simply and easy to understand. Golding uses a lot of imagery and symbolic devices.

Passage 1-"The three boys walked briskly on the sand. The tide was low and there was a strip of weed-strewn beach that was almost as firm as a road. A kind of glamour was spread over them and the scene and they were conscious of the glamour and made happy by it. They turned to each other, laughing excitedly, talking, not listening. The air was bright. Ralph, forced by the task of translating all this into an explanation, stood on his head and fell over. When they had done laughing, Simon stroked Ralph's arm shyly; and they had to laugh again."

Passage 2-"When you're done laughing, perhaps we can get on with the meeting. And if them littluns climb back on the twister again, they'll only fall off in a sec. So they might as well sit on the ground and listen. no. You have doctors for everything, even the inside of your mind. You don't really mean that we got to be frightened all the time of nothing? Life," said Piggy expansively, "is scientific, that's what it is. In a year or two when the war's over they'll be traveling to Mars and back. I know there isn't no beast-not with claws and all that, I mean-but I know there isn't no fear, either."

Passage 3-"Ralph looked at him dumbly. For a moment he had a fleeting picture of the strange glamour that had once invested the beaches. But the island was scorched up like dead wood-Simon was dead-and Jack had.... The tears began to flow and sobs shook him. He gave himself up to them now for the first time on the island; great, shuddering spasms of grief that seemed to wrench his whole body. His voice rose under the black smoke before the burning wreckage of the island; and infected by that emotion, the other little boys began to shake and sob too. And in the middle of them, with filthy body, matted hair, and unwiped nose, Ralph wept for the end of innocence, the darkness of man's heart, and the fall through the air of the true, wise friend called Piggy."

Golding's writes in a simple neutral style. His language is not complicated or flowery. At the same time, it is not too informal. He uses a lot of imagery as can be seen in his description of the "weed-strewn beach" that was "as firm as a road" in passage one. The dialogue in passage two is not at all flowery and sounds like typical speech for a 12 year old, except that Piggy seems to show an amount of wisdom greater than your typical 12 year old. Passage 3 is written clearly and nicely shows emotion while still narrating in an neutral tone without too much involvement from the narrator.

Syntax

Most of the sentences in The Lord of the Flies are simple. There are sentences that are complex and the occasional compound sentence. Most characters speak simply and clearly. Often, they speak fragments and string together fragments and ramble suck as in passage 2. All the speech is written as if it were speech. The first passage contain mostly simple sentences. One example of a compound sentence is, "when they had done laughing, Simon stroked Ralph's arm shyly; and they had to laugh again." The second passage contains both simple and complex sentences. In this passage, the speech is somewhat rambling and contains several fragments. However, this sort of speech conveys the idea that Piggy was thinking while he was speaking. The third passage contains mostly simple and complex sentences. The writing style here gives the feeling of desperation and loss of hope. The reader feels how Ralph feels and understands what he understands about the "loss of innocence."

Imagery

Golding frequently uses imagery to describe the scenery and the setting. A good example occurs in the first passage where Golding's writes, "there was a strip of weed-strewn beach that was almost as firm as a road. A kind of glamour was spread over them and the scene and they were conscious of the glamour and made happy by it."

Symbolism

Golding uses a lot of symbolism in The Lord of the Flies. The entire book is symbolic of the nature of man and society in general as the island becomes a society metaphorical to society as a whole and the hunt at the end of the book symbolic of the war. A symbol Golding uses throughout the book is the conch. It represents authority and order. The person holding the conch had the power, and it created order and rules since when it was called, everyone had to listen. Another symbol is Piggy's glasses. It symbolized knowledge and insight. While Piggy had them, he was able to give advice to the group, such as that of the signal fire. It was the glasses that created the fire. However, after the glasses are broken, the group loses what insight they had. The war paint is also a symbol. It symbolized the rejection of society. In a way, when they put on the mask of war paint, they took off the mask of society and revealed their true inner selves which was savage.

Figurative Language

Personification-Golding uses little personification in this book. He does use it, however, during the conversation between the dead pig head and Simon. The head is personified and given able to speak to Simon. Although it is dead, it is proud and defiant in its speech. Simile-Golding occasionally uses simile. One occasion occurs in the first passage when Golding compares the sand with a road saying, "there was a strip of weed-strewn beach that was almost as firm as a road."

Metaphor-Golding often uses metaphor in this book. In fact, all symbolism is a type of metaphor since they compare two unlike things. Other metaphors in the book was when Golding described the choir boy at the beginning of the book as a dark creature crawling along the sand. Allusion-Golding has several allusions in the book. The title itself is an allusion to the Bible since "The Lord of the Flies" was a title given to Beelzebub. Simon's name in the book is also an allusion to the disciple Simon Peter.

Ironic Devices

There are several cases of irony in this book. Usually, the meaning is straightforward. However, I did find a case of verbal irony. That case is when Ralph and Piggy are discussing Simon's death. Ralph says, "I wasn't scared. I was-I don't know what I was."

Tone

Golding's tone is that of a lecturer. Through his book he

tries to teach us and warn us about our own evil. This tone is carried through the novel. The tone is maintain more through the events and the characters in the story than by syntax or writing style. An example is the discovery of the parachutist. The writing style at this part remained just as neutral as the rest of the book, but the event of finding the parachutist as the beast teaches us that it is not some mystical monster we have to be worried about but ourselves.

Memorable quotes

"'I ought to be chief,' said Jack with simple arrogance, 'because I'm chapter chorister and head boy. I can sing C sharp." This shows the early signs of the tension between Jack and Ralph, and it also shows Jack's pride.

"Ralph stirred uneasily. Simon, sitting between the twins and Piggy, wiped his mouth and shoved his piece of meat over the rocks to Piggy, who grabbed it. The twins giggled and Simon lowered his face in shame." This quote shows that Simon is kind and sincere. "Kill the pig. Cut her throat. Bash her in." These expresses the increasing intensity of the boys' savagery. "It was dark. there was that — that bloody dance. There was lightning and thunder and rain. We was scared!" This describes how the boys' have gone beyond the point of fun and games. They are no longer boys playing on the island but a bunch of savages.

Additional Comments and Analysis

I greatly enjoyed this book. The story without the symbolism was intricate and emotional. Golding does a good job showing the emotional states of Ralph and Jack. We can see Ralph gradually losing hope and understanding the evil, and we can see Jack become power hungry and savage. The murders add a nice touch to the story since they are both dramatic and moving. The symbolism add another level to the enjoyment of the story since I can compare the ideas developed in the story to my own life and my own beliefs.

Chapter 7

Background

William Golding wrote the novel Lord of the Flies with the intent to include certain elements of moral behaviour for readers to absorb. He utilized specific symbols found scattered in the novel to portray his intended message to all those who read his work of Literature. The author builds his message into the novel in the form of adventure. The actions done by characters in the novel eventually create Golding's message to the reader.

It can be said that Golding describes the moral of the book in relation to the scientific mechanics of society. This is found as a major theme in the book, which is actually fear. The boys on the island view this ideal in the form of the "beastie". The "beastie" is an unseen figure on the island, which is symbolized of the dead parachutist. This fear, however, represents the potential evil found in humans. Yet, this evil is only brought about amongst specific environmental conditions, which Golding synthesized in the book.

The most interesting aspect and probably the most influential characteristic of the story is found to be the age of the characters. The author successfully attempts to show how capable the aspect of evil is among human beings. However, Golding perfects this idea as he used children, who represent purity and innocence in a normal society. Through the use of children, the reader finds that barbarity and savagery can exist amongst even the smallest and most innocuous form of human beings. One can interpret that Golding is trying to represent human nature in its entirety. It is obvious that Golding is showing all levels of human capability in terms of psychology and science. The reader sees that humans exist in higher levels, such as present day activity, as well as the lowest form, which is represented by Lord of the Flies. The author creates a situation, which includes factors that are capable of forcing humans to fall into lower forms of mentality.

A very important concept of the story is the fact that in the society which was created on the island, order is a needed tool for existence. The concept of order is found to be a key issue as the society which Golding created contained no order. This book accurately shows how the absence of order results in an alteration of moral behaviour. In Lord of the Flies, morals can be seen in the form of aggressive behavioral actions. Such actions include the murder of Piggy. Obviously children would never come to such decisions or actions against one another under normal societal conditions. However, Golding creates a barbaric civilization in which children do such actions.

Lord of the Flies can be considered a classical novel. A classic in the respect that the author creates special circumstances under which abnormal actions and functions mutate into everyday activity. All of these concepts and ideals are generated by Golding to finally produce a novel of both perplexity and perfection.

Everything about Lord of the Flies is thematic. The story revolves around a question: Is unshackled freedom a good thing? Golding's obvious answer is the need for civilization, its rules, laws, and expectations. (Ironically, the nearly blind Piggy was the one boy who could "see" this most clearly.) Yet, while Ralph personifies law, cooperation and democratic choice, it is Jack's reliance on charisma, brute force and authoritarian rule that wins out on the island.

Chilling words from Golding's Notes reveal the final irony of this book: "The officer, having interrupted a man-hunt, prepares to take the children off the island in a cruiser which will presently be hunting its [own] enemy in the same implacable way. And who will rescue the adult and his cruiser?

Chapter 8

Major Themes of Lord of the Flies

Civilization vs. Savagery

The overarching theme of Lord of the Flies is the conflict between the human impulse towards savagery and the rules of civilization which are designed to contain and minimize it. Throughout the novel, the conflict is dramatized by the clash between Ralph and Jack, who respectively represent civilization and savagery. The differing ideologies are expressed by each boy's distinct attitudes towards authority. While Ralph uses his authority to establish rules, protect the good of the group, and enforce the moral and ethical codes of the English society the boys were raised in, Jack is interested in gaining power over the other boys to gratify his most primal impulses. When Jack assumes leadership of his own tribe, he demands the complete subservience of the other boys, who not only serve him but worship him as an idol. Jack's hunger for power suggests that savagery does not resemble anarchy so much as a totalitarian system of exploitation and illicit power.

Golding's emphasis on the negative consequences of savagery can be read as an clear endorsement of civilization. In the early chapters of the novel, he suggests that one of the important functions of civilized society is to provide an outlet for the savage impulses that reside inside each individual. Jack's initial desire to kill pigs to demonstrate his bravery, for example, is channeled into the hunt, which provides needed food for the entire group. As long as he lives within the rules of civilization, Jack is not a threat to the other boys; his impulses are being re-directed into a productive task. Rather, it is when Jack refuses to recognize the validity of society and rejects Ralph's authority that the dangerous aspects of his character truly emerge. Golding suggests that while savagery is perhaps an inescapable fact of human existence, civilization can mitigate its full expression.

The rift between civilization and savagery is also communicated through the novel's major symbols: the conch shell, which is associated with Ralph, and The Lord of the Flies, which is associated with Jack. The conch shell is a powerful marker of democratic order on the island, confirming both Ralph's leadership-determined by election-and the power of assembly among the boys. Yet, as the conflict between Ralph and Jack deepens, the conch shell loses symbolic importance. Jack declares that the conch is meaningless as a symbol of authority and order, and its decline in importance signals the decline of civilization on the island. At the same time, The Lord of the Flies, which is an offering to the mythical "beast" on the island, is increasingly invested with significance as a symbol of the dominance of savagery on the island, and of Jack's authority over the other boys. The Lord of the Flies represents the unification of the boys under Jack's rule as motivated by fear of "outsiders": the beast and those who refuse to accept Jack's authority. The destruction of the conch shell at the scene of Piggy's murder signifies the complete eradication of civilization on the island, while Ralph's demolition of The Lord of the Flies-he intends to use the stick as a spear-signals his own descent into savagery and violence. By the final scene, savagery has completely displaced civilization as the prevailing system on the island.

Individualism vs. Community

One of the key concerns of Lord of the Flies is the role of the individual in society. Many of the problems on the island-the extinguishing of the signal fire, the lack of shelters, the mass abandonment of Ralph's camp, and the murder of Piggy-stem from the boys' implicit commitment to a principle of self-interest over the principle of community. That is, the boys would rather fulfill their individual desires than cooperate as a coherent society, which would require that each one act for the good of the group. Accordingly, the principles of individualism and community are symbolized by Jack and Ralph, respectively. Jack wants to "have fun" on the island and satisfy his bloodlust, while Ralph wants to secure the group's rescue, a goal they can achieve only by cooperating. Yet, while Ralph's vision is the most reasonable, it requires work and sacrifice on the part of the other boys, so they quickly shirk their societal duties in favour of fulfilling their individual desires. The shelters do not get built because the boys would rather play; the signal fire is extinguished when Jack's hunters fail to tend to it on schedule.

The boys' self-interestedness culminates, of course, when they decide to join Jack's tribe, a society without communal values whose appeal is that Jack will offer them total freedom. The popularity of his tribe reflects the enormous appeal of a society based on individual freedom and self-interest, but as the reader soon learns, the freedom Jack offers his tribe is illusory. Jack implements punitive and irrational rules and restricts his boys' behaviour far more than Ralph did. Golding thus suggests not only that some level of communal system is superior to one based on pure self-interest, but also that pure individual freedom is an impossible value to sustain within a group dynamic, which will always tend towards societal organization. The difficult question, of course, is what individuals are willing to give up to gain the benefits of being in the group.

The Nature of Evil

Is evil innate within the human spirit, or is it an influence from an external source? What role do societal rules and institutions play in the existence of human evil? Does the capacity for evil vary from person to person, or does it depend on the circumstances each individual faces? These questions are at the heart of Lord of the Flies which, through detailed depictions of the boys' different responses to their situation, presents a complex articulation of humanity's potential for evil.

It is important to note that Golding's novel rejects supernatural or religious accounts of the origin of human evil. While the boys fear the "beast" as an embodiment of evil similar to the Christian concept of Satan, the novel emphasizes that this interpretation is not only mistaken but also, ironically, the motivation for the boys' increasingly cruel and violent behaviour. It is their irrational fear of the beast that informs the boys' paranoia and leads to the fatal schism between Jack and Ralph and their respective followers, and this is what prevents them from recognizing and addressing their responsibility for their own impulses. Rather, as The Lord of the Flies communicates to Simon in the forest glade, the "beast" is an internal force, present in every individual, and is thus incapable of being truly defeated. That the most ethical characters on the island-Simon and Ralph-each come to recognize his own capacity for evil indicates the novel's emphasis on evil's universality among humans.

Even so, the novel is not entirely pessimistic about the human capacity for good. While evil impulses may lurk in every human psyche, the intensity of these impulses-and the ability to control them-appear to vary from individual to individual. Through the different characters, the novel presents a continuum of evil, ranging from Jack and Roger, who are eager to engage in violence and cruelty, to Ralph and Simon, who struggle to contain their brutal instincts. We may note that the characters who struggle most successfully against their evil instincts do so by appealing to ethical or social codes of behaviour. For example, Ralph and Piggy demand the return of Piggy's glasses because it is the "right thing to do." Golding suggests that while evil may be present in us all, it can be successfully suppressed by the social norms that are imposed on our behaviour from without or by the moral norms we decide are inherently "good," which we can internalize within our wills.

The ambiguous and deeply ironic conclusion of Lord of the Flies, however, calls into question society's role in shaping human evil. The naval officer, who repeats Jack's rhetoric of nationalism and militarism, is engaged in a bloody war that is responsible for the boys' aircraft crash on the island and that is mirrored by the civil war among the survivors. In this sense, much of the evil on the island is a result not of the boys' distance from society, but of their internalization of the norms and ideals of that society-norms and ideals that justify and even thrive on war. Are the boys corrupted by the internal pressures of an essentially violent human nature, or have they been corrupted by the environment of war they were raised in? Lord of the Flies offers no clear solution to this question, provoking readers to contemplate the complex relationships among society, morality, and human nature.

Man vs. Nature

Lord of the Flies introduces the question of man's ideal relationship with the natural world. Thrust into the completely natural environment of the island, in which no humans exist or have existed, the boys express different attitudes towards nature that reflect their distinct personalities and ideological leanings. The boys' relationships to the natural world generally fall into one of three categories: subjugation of nature, harmony with nature, and subservience to nature. The first category, subjugation of nature, is embodied by Jack, whose first impulse on the island is to track, hunt, and kill pigs. He seeks to impose his human will on the natural world, subjugating it to his desires. Jack's later actions, in particular setting the forest fire, reflect his deepening contempt for nature and demonstrate his militaristic, violent character. The second category, harmony with nature, is embodied by Simon, who finds beauty and peace in the natural environment as exemplified by his initial retreat to the isolated forest glade. For Simon, nature is not man's enemy but is part of the human experience. The third category, subservience to nature, is embodied by Ralph and is the opposite position from Jack's. Unlike Simon, Ralph does not find peaceful harmony with the natural world; like Jack, he understands it as an obstacle to human life on the island. But while Jack responds to this perceived conflict by acting destructively towards animals and plant life, Ralph responds by retreating from the natural world. He does not participate in hunting or in Simon's excursions to the deep wilderness of the forest; rather, he stays on the beach, the most humanized part of the island. As Jack's hunting expresses his violent nature to the other boys and to the reader, Ralph's desire to stay separate from the natural world emphasizes both his reluctance to tempt danger and his affinity for civilization.

Dehumanization of Relationships

In Lord of the Flies, one of the effects of the boys' descent into savagery is their increasing inability to recognize each other's humanity. Throughout the novel, Golding uses imagery to imply that the boys are no longer able to distinguish between themselves and the pigs they are hunting and killing for food and sport. In Chapter Four, after the first successful pig hunt, the hunters re-enact the hunt in a ritual dance, using Maurice as a stand-in for the doomed pig. This episode is only a dramatization, but as the boys' collective impulse towards complete savagery grows stronger, the parallels between human and animal intensify.

In Chapter Seven, as several of the boys are hunting the beast, they repeat the ritual with Robert as a stand-in for the pig; this time, however, they get consumed by a kind of "frenzy" and come close to actually killing him. In the same scene, Jack jokes that if they do not kill a pig next time, they can kill a littlun in its place. The repeated substitution of boy for pig in the childrens' ritual games, and in their conversation, calls attention to the consequences of their self-gratifying behaviour: concerned only with their own base desires, the boys have become unable to see each other as anything more than objects subject to their individual wills. The more pigs the boys kill, the easier it becomes for them to harm and kill each other. Mistreating the pigs facilitates this process of dehumanization.

The early episodes in which boys are substituted for pigs, either verbally or in the hunting dance, also foreshadow the tragic events of the novel's later chapters, notably the murders of Simon and Piggy and the attempt on Ralph's life. Simon, a character who from the outset of the novel is associated with the natural landscape he has an affinity for, is murdered when the other children mistake him for "the beast"-a mythical inhuman creature that serves as an outlet for the children's fear and sadness. Piggy's name links him symbolically to the wild pigs on the island, the immediate target for Jack's violent impulses; from the outset, when the other boys refuse to call him anything but "Piggy," Golding establishes the character as one whose humanity is, in the eyes of the other boys, ambiguous. The murders of Simon and Piggy demonstrate the boys' complete descent into savagery. Both literally (Simon) and symbolically (Piggy), the boys have become indistinguishable from the animals that they stalk and kill.

The Loss of Innocence

At the end of Lord of the Flies, Ralph weeps "for the end of innocence," a lament that retroactively makes explicit one of the novel's major concerns, namely, the loss of innocence. When the boys are first deserted on the island, they behave like children, alternating between enjoying their freedom and expressing profound homesickness and fear. By the end of the novel, however, they mirror the warlike behaviour of the adults of the Home Counties: they attack, torture, and even murder one another without hesitation or regret. The loss of the boys' innocence on the island runs parallel to, and informs their descent into savagery, and it recalls the Bible's narrative of the Fall of Man from paradise.

Accordingly, the island is coded in the early chapters as a kind of paradise, with idyllic scenery, fresh fruit, and glorious weather. Yet, as in the Biblical Eden, the temptation toward corruption is present: the younger boys fear a "snake-thing." The "snake-thing" is the earliest incarnation of the "beast" that, eventually, will provoke paranoia and division among the group. It also explicitly recalls the snake from the Garden of Eden, the embodiment of Satan who causes Adam and Eve's fall from grace. The boys' increasing belief in the beast indicates their gradual loss of innocence, a descent that culminates in tragedy. We may also note that the landscape of the island itself shifts from an Edenic space to a hellish one, as marked by Ralph's observation of the ocean tide as an impenetrable wall, and by the storm that follows Simon's murder.

The forest glade that Simon retreats to in Chapter Three is another example of how the boys' loss of innocence is registered on the natural landscape of the island. Simon first appreciates the clearing as peaceful and beautiful, but when he returns, he finds The Lord of the Flies impaled at its centre, a powerful symbol of how the innocence of childhood has been corrupted by fear and savagery.

Even the most sympathetic boys develop along a character arc that traces a fall from innocence (or, as we might euphemize, a journey into maturity). When Ralph is first introduced, he is acting like a child, splashing in the water, mocking Piggy, and laughing. He tells Piggy that he is certain that his father, a naval commander, will rescue him, a conviction that the reader understands as the wishful thinking of a little boy. Ralph repeats his belief in their rescue throughout the novel, shifting his hope that his own father will discover them to the far more realistic premise that a passing ship will be attracted by the signal fire on the island. By the end of the novel, he has lost hope in the boys' rescue altogether. The progression of Ralph's character from idealism to pessimistic realism expresses the extent to which life on the island has eradicated his childhood.

The Negative Consequences of War

In addition to its other resonances, Lord of the Flies is in part an allegory of the Cold War. Thus, it is deeply concerned with the negative effects of war on individuals and for social relationships. Composed during the Cold War, the novel's action unfolds from a hypothetical atomic war between England and "the Reds," which was a clear word for communists. Golding thus presents the non-violent tensions that were unfolding during the 1950s as culminating into a fatal conflict-a narrative strategy that establishes the novel as a cautionary tale against the dangers of ideological, or "cold," warfare, becoming hot. Moreover, we may understand the conflict among the boys on the island as a reflection of the conflict between the democratic powers of the West and the communist presence throughout China, Eastern Europe, and the Soviet Union. (China's cultural revolution had not yet occurred, but its communist revolution was fresh in Western memory.) Ralph, an embodiment of democracy, clashes tragically with Jack, a character who represents a style of military dictatorship similar to the West's perception of communist leaders such as Joseph Stalin and Mao Zedong. Dressed in a black cape and cap, with flaming red hair, Jack also visually evokes the "Reds" in the fictional world of the novel and the historical U.S.S.R., whose signature colors were red and black. As the tension between the boys comes to a bloody head, the reader sees the dangerous consequences of ideological conflict.

The arrival of the naval officer at the conclusion of the narrative underscores these allegorical points. The officer embodies war and militaristic thinking, and as such, he is symbolically linked to the brutal Jack. The officer is also English and thus linked to the democratic side of the Cold War, which the novel vehemently defends. The implications of the officer's presence are provocative: Golding suggests that even a war waged in the name of civilization can reduce humanity to a state of barbarism. The ultimate scene of the novel, in which the boys weep with grief for the loss of their innocence, implicates contemporary readers in the boys' tragedy. The boys are representatives, however immature and untutored, of the wartime impulses of the period.

Chapter 9

Complete Summary and Interpretation

Chapter 1

Summary

Lord of the Flies opens with Ralph meeting Piggy. Their conversation provides the background of their situation: In the midst of a nuclear war, a group of boys was being evacuated to an unnamed destination. Their plane crashed and was dragged out to sea, leaving the boys stranded on an unfamiliar island. Because of the atom bomb's devastation, it's likely that no one knows the boys' whereabouts.

Ralph is delighted to be on a pristine tropical island without adults, but Piggy is less pleased. The two boys make their way out of the jungle and onto the beach. Ralph is not much interested in Piggy and does not request an introduction in turn when Piggy asks Ralph's name. Piggy confides his hope that the boys on this island won't call him Piggy as they did back home.

On the beach, Ralph investigates a large platform of pink granite overlooking a long pool that had formed in the beach. After demonstrating his swimming skills, Ralph spies a conch, which Piggy identifies as a valuable shell that can be blown as a trumpet. Piggy urges Ralph to blow into the shell, using it to summon any other survivors to the beach.

Soon boys between ages 6 and 12 come streaming out of the jungle onto the beach, assembling on the platform near

Ralph. Last to arrive are Jack and the choirboys. Despite the tropical heat and their own exertions in following the conch blasts, the boys from the choir still wear their black caps and long black cloaks and are clearly overheated when they reach the platform.

The assembled boys discuss their situation and vote on a chief, choosing Ralph over Jack. Ralph suggests that Jack remain in charge of the choirboys, designating them hunters. Jack is mollified by this seemingly small gift of command. As the assembled boys identify themselves, Ralph reveals Piggy's nickname before Piggy can establish his real name.

Ralph forms a search party to establish that they are, in fact, on an island. In agreeing to go along, Jack reveals with a flourish that he owns a large sheathed knife. Piggy is hurt to be excluded from the search party, and Ralph placates him by giving him the job of taking the names of all the boys who remain behind at the platform.

Ralph, Jack, and Simon confirm that the island is uninhabited. They enjoy their jaunt into the wild, experiencing the thrill of adventure and the new friendship forming between them. On their return, they encounter a piglet trapped in jungle vines, testing Jack's hunting skills and nerve. Jack pulls his knife but falters, and the pig gets away; he vows fiercely that next time he will follow through.

Commentary

In Chapter 1, Golding introduces the novel's major characters as well as its theme: that evil, as a destructive force in man, society, and civilization, is present in us all. To illustrate this theme, Golding uses several major motifs: civilization versus savagery; humanity versus animality; technology versus nature; hunters versus gatherers; men versus women; adults versus children; and the intellect versus physicality. As the characters interact with each other and with their environment, so do the forces they represent. Using the characters to embody these forces allows Golding the opportunity to compare and contrast with rich shadings of meaning rather than with simplistic oppositions.

The novel opens with a description of the "long scar smashed into the jungle," a reference to the snake-like damage done by the plane as it crashed into the island. Here civilization with its technology has dealt a blow to nature; nature counters by sweeping the wreckage out to sea. Yet the conflict is not so simple. While the jungle may represent nature, the beach provides the conch and the platform, both of which symbolize institutionalized order and politics (civilization).

True to the dynamics of democratic politics, Ralph is elected leader for superficial reasons. He is a personable and handsome boy who appears to be in charge because of his use of the conch, which functions for him at the moment of his election (and throughout the novel) as the symbol of authority. Although it was Piggy's quick thinking to use the conch to summon the others, hampered by asthma, he must allow Ralph to do the summoning. And while Jack clearly has some experience in exerting control over others, making his choirboys march to the assembly through the tropical heat in floor-length black cloaks, the sheer arrogance of his open grab for power probably puts off some of the boys, raised as they have been in a society that values politeness and decorum. Therefore, the boys choose Ralph for his charisma and possession of the compelling conch over Piggy, who lacks the physical stature or charsima of a leader despite his intelligence, and Jack, who is "ugly without silliness" and possesses a less civil manner.

With his calm, self-assured manner and the poise with which he allows Jack to retain control of the choir and places Piggy in charge of names, Ralph is much more of a diplomat than Jack or Piggy. While allowing Jack control of the hunters turns out to be political (and almost personal) suicide ultimately, Ralph himself is still under the spell of polite society, looking more to make friends than to lead strategically. In later chapters, he learns that, as a leader, he must be prepared to take a hard line with his friends if he is to achieve his goals for the group. In Chapter 1, however, Ralph engages in play—standing on his head, blowing jets of water while swimming, rolling a boulder downhill, gleefully scuffling with

Simon—which he has no time for once he is leader of the group. Note that the talents that set Ralph apart from the others (acrobatics and swimming) serve no practical purpose in the jungle, while Jack's recreational activity as choir leader serves him as a leader in training. Jack's warlike nature is evident from the start, as a choirboy who carries a knife and volunteers his choir to be the army, amending its role to hunters at Ralph's direction. While Ralph entertains others with his trick of standing on his head, Jack successfully practices authority: "With dreary obedience" his choir votes for him as chief. He uses to his advantage here his authority, not his ability to sing a C sharp.

From his first appearance as a dark creature, leading his group from the jungle, making them march in columns until Simon faints, Jack is represented as evil. When the creatures turn out to be "a party of boys, marching approximately in step in two parallel lines and dressed in strangely eccentric clothing," Golding is connecting not only the uniformed military with the frightening dark side of humanity but tacitly identifying Jack as an outspoken representative of aggression.

Naturally Jack has a strong and vocal aversion to Piggy, who represents thorough domestication in contrast to the savagery lying just beneath Jack's surface. Piggy is no fan of Jack's, being "intimidated by [Jack's] uniformed superiority and the offhand authority in [his] voice." With his poor eyesight, weight problem, and asthma, Piggy is a boy who could survive only in a civilization that offers the dual protection of medical treatment and cultural affluence—a society wealthy enough to provide food, shelter, and purpose for its physically weaker members. In England, Piggy would be valued ultimately for the contribution of his intelligence, despite his lack of physical ability or social skills. On this uninhabited island, however, Piggy is the most vulnerable of all the boys, despite his greater mental capabilities.

Although Ralph treats Piggy badly because Piggy lacks a spirit of adventure, he understands that Piggy has a realistic grasp of their situation. Piggy points out that the atom bomb killed everyone who might know of the boys' whereabouts.

While Ralph still speaks of his father in the present tense, telling Piggy that his father will come rescue them soon, Piggy describes his aunt in the past tense, realizing that she is gone. Her voice lives on in his head, however, as the voice that ordered his world and represents the protected domesticity he needs to survive and thrive. His frequent invocations of "my auntie says" provide the only female voice in the book, although he never gets to finish the phrase and reveal what his auntie did say. With only Piggy as her ineffectual mouthpiece, from this first chapter, the auntie's perspective is rendered invalid among the primitive conditions of the environment and the savage demagoguery of Jack.

By quoting his aunt, Piggy also establishes himself as a representative of the adult world. The boys have an ambivalent relationship to adults, viewing them sometimes as providers and protectors and sometimes as punishers and limiters. While Ralph is initially delighted at the lack of grownups on the island, he is at the same time relying on his father's naval expertise to facilitate their rescue. As the adult voice, Piggy tries to communicate the reality that his father is probably dead, a concept that twelve-year-old Ralph has difficulty grasping. Events later in the book reveal Piggy as the voice of reason again—his adult logic contrasting with the other boys' childishly emotional responses, such as in Chapter 2, when he scolds them for starting the fire before building shelters. Yet his logic holds no ground when confronted with the emotions running high in this primitive environment.

Jack and Ralph hold another, more fundamental election between themselves in this chapter. While exploring, they encounter a distinct trail in the jungle. In guessing what made the trail, Ralph offers "'Men?' Jack shakes his head. 'Animals.'" Without realizing it, each boy is casting a vote for who and what they will ultimately represent.

Glossary

- Creepers any plants whose stems put out tendrils or rootlets by which the plants can creep along a surface as they grow.

- Home Counties the counties nearest London.
- Stockings closefitting coverings, usually knitted, for the feet and, usually, much of the legs.
- Half here, considerably; very much.
- Garter an elastic band, or a fastener suspended from a band, girdle, etc., for holding a stocking or sock in position.
- Sucks to your auntie a British slang expression of derision or contempt; here, "forget your auntie" or "your auntie be damned."
- Gib., Addis abbreviations for Gibraltar and Addis Ababa, respectively; refueling stops the evacuation plane made before crashing on the island.
- Matins orig., the first of the seven canonical hours, recited between midnight and dawn or, often, at daybreak; here, a morning church service at which the choir sang.
- Precentor a person who directs a church choir or congregation in singing.
- Shop here, conversation about one's work or business, esp. after hours.
- Head boy an honorary title given to a student who has made the best all-around contribution to student life and maintains exemplary conduct.
- Wacco [Brit. Slang] excellent.
- Wizard [Brit. Informal] excellent.
- Smashing [Informal] outstandingly good; extraordinary.

Chapter 2

Summary

Summary: Ralph, Jack, and Simon return from their reconnaissance in the late afternoon. Ralph blows the conch to call the other boys back to assembly and describes the results of the exploration. Jack interrupts almost immediately to declare the importance of an army for hunting pigs. So that only one person will speak at a time in the assembly, Ralph makes the conch rule: Only the boy holding the conch can speak, and only Ralph can interrupt the one who holds the conch. Thus, a process for order and civil discourse is established.

Piggy takes the conch so he can make the point that no one knows the boys' location, meaning that they may be on the island a long time. Ralph points out the bright side, the adventure inherent in their situation. At this point the group of littlest boys push a representative forward to describe the "beastie" he saw in the woods the night before; the older boys are quick to assure the littluns that there is no beastie. Ralph offers reassurance that they will definitely be rescued, mentioning that they'll need a signal fire to attract passing ships and planes. At the word fire, Jack immediately takes over the group, leading a charge up the mountain to start a fire. Ralph attempts to maintain order, but everyone rushes after Jack, so he follows, too. Piggy follows last, angry at the impulsive behaviour.

On the mountaintop, the boys find a huge patch of dead wood and start a fire, using Piggy's eyeglasses. A massive bonfire that quickly burns itself out results. Jack volunteers his hunters to maintain a signal fire. Suddenly, in the midst of a complaint that no one will let him talk, Piggy sees that they've started a forest fire. He scolds the other boys for their lack of foresight in not first building shelters for the approaching night before racing up the mountain in defiance of Ralph. He further reprimands them for causing not only the waste of so much firewood but also the probable death of some of the littlest boys, since some of them had been playing in the area consumed by the rapidly moving fire. In the face of this news, Ralph attempts to first blame Piggy for not keeping better track of the little boys and then to convince himself and the others that the little ones might have just gone back to the platform. No one is convinced, but all are reluctant to face the reality.

Commentary

This chapter continues with and develops the themes

established in Chapter 1. Of particular importance to Ralph is his new experience with control over his electorate in the face of political and social dynamics. Initially the boys are quite impressed with him, as he finds he has a natural capacity for public speaking. His promise of rescue seems farfetched given the nuclear war that precipitated the boys' evacuation, but it is a promise he delivers well and believes himself. Even Piggy has faith in Ralph's ability to understand and communicate the issues, although he may be giving him too much credit. When Piggy grabs the conch and says "You're hindering Ralph. You're not letting him get to the most important thing," it's not clear from Ralph's hesitant response that he was in fact going to cover the likelihood that no one knows the boys' location.

Piggy's loyalty to Ralph stems from Piggy's logical mentality—it's logical to follow the leader's command and assume that he is in control of the situation. The rest of the boys are more emotional. They are quickly swayed from the chief they so respected moments before. Once on the mountain, they are very much impressed by Jack, with his seemingly generous offer to have his hunters take on the fire tending duties, just as they had been enamored of Ralph earlier.

Such a loyalty shift is part of the dynamics of politics. Golding sums up the status of those who assume a leader's role when he describes the littlest boys' shy representative as "warped out of the perpendicular by the fierce light of publicity." Once an individual such as Jack comes forth and makes himself heard over the rest of the crowd, the crowd views him as larger than life and expects big things—both good and bad. Leaders often attain a level of celebrity, at which point both their faults and their virtues are magnified by publicity's distorting lens so that their smallest mistakes may be viewed by the public with the same importance granted their greatest achievements. This syndrome springs from the emotional reaction that leaders invoke.

Piggy is missing this emotional connection. He may be attempting to present the most beneficial plan of action for the group, but, because he lacks rapport with the other boys, he cannot make himself heard. Seeing that the boys pay attention to Ralph when he repeats what Piggy has already tried to communicate, he protests "'That's what I said! I said about the meetings and things and then you said shut up—.' His voice lifted into the whine of virtuous recrimination. They stirred and began to shout him down." Piggy realizes the effect he has on the boys but not the cause of it, placing too much faith in the logical approach. Truth is not always obvious, and logic is seldom universal. Not until Piggy loses his temper can he get the boys' attention and reveal the priorities he had in mind before they raced up the mountain. He points out that the island gets cold at night and that they should have built shelters before nightfall, his reason expressed too late for their emotional deeds.

Piggy also relies too heavily on the power of the conch, on the social convention that holding the conch invests him with the right to be heard. He believes that upholding social conventions gets results. "How can you expect to be rescued if you don't ... act proper?" Piggy asks. He is partially right but is overlooking the dynamic of the crowd, the emotionality of mob rule. When Piggy screams, "You'll break the conch!" he is in essence protesting "you'll break the covenant," the agreement that everyone will behave in a certain way and follow established rules. The rules are more immediately necessary for him than for the other boys who can rely on their physical skills to survive.

Jack's rush up the mountain shatters the power of the conch rule, which is meant to ensure civil, rational conversation. Jack asserts that the conch has no power once they are on the mountain, but clearly it didn't have that much power on the platform either: Ralph shouted for order while holding the conch but lost the crowd in the excitement, foreshadowing how later he loses his authority completely. The impulsive dash with which Jack leads the boys away from the platform symbolizes the ease with which humanity's emotional, savage nature overwhelms its rational and civilized tendencies. To represent the evil that is part of human nature, Golding uses the beastie described by the littlest boys. At night, they report, the beast lurks in the jungle hunting and looking to devour them; by day it disguises itself as the creeper vines that hang innocently in the trees. Here the vines are like human nature in the daylight of civilization; in the darkness of a primeval environment their true predatory nature emerges. During the forest fire, the little boys shriek at the burning creeper vines "Snakes! Snakes! Look at the snakes!" This allusion is to the serpent in the Garden of Eden who stole innocence and introduced humanity to its own physicality.

Obviously on a conscious level, the boys perceive this beast as an actual animal rather than as the conceptualization of the evil inherent in humanity. Yet these littlest boys have an immediate and instinctive recognition of the island as a threat to them: They realise that they lack the domesticity that protected them back home. The older boys ostensibly reject the little boys' fear, presenting the logical explanation that the island is too small for large predators. Ralph is vehement on this point: "Something he had not known was there rose in him and compelled him to make the point, loudly and again. 'But I tell you there isn't a beast!'" He is denying that there exists a dark side to humanity.

The fire on the mountain has tremendous symbolic meaning. First, it represents hope and aspirations for the future, a gift from the gods, a tool that separates humankind from the animals. Just as the beach platform and the untamed jungle represent the duality in humanity's behaviour, the fire, also, represents both savagery and hope: "On one side the air was cool, but on the other the fire thrust out a savage arm of heat." Golding could be describing here how societies and individuals contain these conflicting yet complementary forces. In some individuals, the savage side runs closer to the surface, as with Jack, but it exists in everyone. The boys' fire shows that one entity can contain hot and cold, good and evil, civility and savagery.

The fire expresses another duality as well, a before and after for Ralph's perception of their situation and his role. This first bonfire is an act of communal play for all the boys, topped off with Ralph standing on his head to mark their triumph.

The fire becomes more like serious work when they make plans for specific teams to tend it. Later, with the probable deaths of some of the little boys, Ralph begins to realise that the group's disregard for his authority can and will have grim consequences. Before the fire, the boys take time for play, a luxury available only to those protected by a civilization, not for those engaged in a fight for survival.

Ultimately, the fire is about savagery: For the boys rushing around for firewood, "Life became a race with the fire," a phrase that quietly foreshadows Ralph's flight for his life at the end. And while fire starting was one of the first technologies to separate humanity from the animals, to start this fire, the boys adopt a primitive use of force in taking Piggy's glasses from him, making him an unwilling Prometheus.

Note that on this first day together, the group has already banded together to physically overwhelm Piggy—a show of physicality over intellect. It is also an uprising of children against an adult figure. Although Piggy is in the same age group as the other boys, he nonetheless holds the role of "martyred ... parent who has to keep up with the senseless ebullience of the children." On this island, for the first time in their lives, the boys experience sheer autonomy. "This is our island ... Until the grownups come and fetch us, we'll have fun," Ralph says, in an utterly failed and foolish prophecy.

By now the reader is aware of many of the developing symbols in the story Ralph, the responsible leader who attempts to organize the boys for their survival and rescue. He appears practical, capable of using Piggy's advice, able to avoid superstition and fear, and capable of developing processes for advancing their limited society. Jack, the evil that lurks within humankind, the one most in tune with his primitive urges and instincts.

Piggy, the intellectual who is physically inept, the least capable of surviving on this island under these circumstances.

Simon, the artistic, sensitive mystic. The conch, representing authority and civil debate.

The snake-like images (the scar left by the passenger tube,

the "creepers" [vines] that are encountered throughout), representing aggression, fear, and evil.

Glossary

- Treasure Island Robert Louis Stevenson's 1883 novel about a heroic boy's search for buried gold and his encounter with pirates.
- Swallows and Amazons the first of a series of adventure books by Arthur Ransome, about a group of children on vacation.
- Coral Island Robert Ballantyne's 1857 adventure tale about three boys shipwrecked on a Pacific island and their triumph over their circumstances.
- Caps of maintenance caps bearing a school insignia.
- Altos the boys who sing in the vocal range between tenor and soprano.
- Trebles the boys who sing the highest part in musical harmony.

Chapter 3

Summary

Jack, alone on a pig hunt, has clearly learned some tracking techniques. Frustrated that his day's hunt has ended yet again without a kill, he returns from the jungle to the area where Ralph and Simon work on building shelters. Ralph expresses his frustration: Although all the boys have agreed to help build shelters, only Simon actually puts in the time and effort alongside Ralph. All the other boys are off playing, bathing, or hunting with Jack, even though Jack and his hunters have failed so far to produce meat.

Ralph emphasizes the need for sturdy shelters, while Jack insists that he and the other boys need meat and tries to explain his compulsion to hunt. This difference—and the undercurrent of rancor—makes both boys uncomfortable given the relationship that had sprung up between them on the first day's exploring adventure.

Also in this chapter, a new side of Simon is revealed. He

has a secret place in the jungle, a sort of hut formed by vines, boulders, and trees. After helping Ralph with the shelters all day, he sneaks off to this shelter, pausing first to help the littluns gather some choice fruit and making sure that he hasn't been followed.

Commentary

In the first two chapters, Golding established regulated speech as a hallmark of civilization, as the boys set up the platform as a site for assemblies ordered by the conch. Ralph uses the conch to mimic the practice of "hands up," which all the boys know from school, the very place where literacy and verbal communication is systematically developed. In this chapter, Golding further develops this theme: Whereas verbal language is the sole property of civilization, silence is a property of nature. As Jack hunts in the "uncommunicative forest," he finds the "silence of the forest was more oppressive than the heat."

Ironically, when, in this chapter, Jack encounters Ralph at the shelters, Ralph comments on the uselessness of talk, railing about the abandoned resolutions to work everyone voices at the assemblies. "Meetings. Don't wc love meetings?" Ralph says bitterly, confused by the assemblies' lack of efficacy. He had been counting on the meetings to provide both framework and impetus for focused action but has found that, of a crowd, only a few actually follow through. Ralph's vision of order is one most of the other boys share but lack the self-discipline to carry out. With language as his only tool, Ralph's authority lacks the threat possessed by parents and schoolmasters to enforce the rules and resolutions. Although he doesn't like building huts any better than any of the others, he is able to control his impulses and do what is necessary.

Jack could serve as an enforcer of rightful authority and necessary discipline, but he does not share Ralph's civilized vision. He is fast losing the traces of civilization and tuning into his animal self: crouched "dog-like" and reacting to a sudden bird cry with "a hiss of indrawn breath ... ape-like among the tangle of trees." Jack seems to be losing his powers of rational thought, as well: Not only does he not share Ralph's priority on rescue, he "had to think for a moment before he could remember what rescue was." In trying to explain his feeling of being hunted while on the hunt, he finds verbalizing his experiences a great effort. The ability to express himself verbally is a skill necessary to civilization, not to hunting. His efforts go now to communicating with the nonverbal jungle, reading the signs left by the pigs. Where as Ralph can control his impulses for the good of the community, Jack puts all his focus on developing his impulses—in this case, his need to hunt. Furthermore, neither boy can communicate his perspective to the other, and neither considers the other's viewpoint. This lack of communication underlies innumerable conflicts, and the lack of understanding frequently has more to do with unwillingness on the listener's part than on the speaker's. Ralph and Simon's reactions to Jack's revelation about feeling hunted while hunting are true to form for both of them.

When Jack tries to convey his experience of the beast, he meets with resistance from Ralph. As the representative of reasonable society, Ralph is "incredulous and faintly indignant" that Jack could be granting any credit to the idea of a beast. Ralph is either unable or unwilling to acknowledge the existence of a beast. In contrast, the mystic visionary Simon is "intent" on understanding how Jack's feeling corresponds with the intuitive knowledge Simon has of human nature. Like the littluns, Jack's sense of the beast is formless and inarticulate; his domain is the emotions, which rule and fuel his animal nature. In truth, Jack is being hunted, in a sense, and both he and Simon, to varying degrees, recognize this. Ralph can't acknowledge this and continue to believe in what he believes in and relies on: the basic civility of man.

This chapter reveals Simon as the mystic. While Golding doesn't specify why Simon has a secret place or what he does there, clearly Simon feels the need to be sheltered from the other boys. "He's queer. He's funny," says Ralph of his only work partner, which is the reaction mystics typically provoke from mainstream society. Simon is different from the other boys not only due the physical frailty of fainting spells but also in his consistently expressed concern for the other more vulnerable boys. In the previous chapter, he sticks up for Piggy when Jack verbally attacks him for not gathering firewood, pointing out that the fire was started with Piggy's glasses. In this chapter, Simon takes the time to pluck from the trees the choice fruits that the littluns can't reach and passing them down "to the endless, outstretched hands," an almost saintly image. Simon's role as a visionary is alluded to in this chapter not only by his hidden place of meditation but also by Golding's description of his eyes: "so bright they had deceived Ralph into thinking him delightfully gay and wicked." While Piggy has the glasses, another symbol of vision, Simon has the bright eyes that later in the novel see the truth about the beast.

To highlight Ralph's growing disenchantment with Jack and disillusionment with being a leader, Golding brings back together, in this chapter, the three boys who went exploring that first day. Caught up in the glamour of newness and adventure, the three seemed to become instant friends. By now, however, Ralph cannot overlook that Jack's priority on hunting is undermining his own efforts to create a home for the boys, that Simon is not the mischievous prankster Ralph perceived him to be, and that the boys in general quickly forget their promises to work toward a common goal when faced with the more immediate gratification of eating and playing. Ralph has come to the realization that "people were never quite what you thought they were."

Glossary

- Batty [Slang] crazy or eccentric.
- Crackers [Slang, Chiefly Brit.] crazy; insane.
- Queer differing from what is usual or ordinary; odd; singular; strange.

Chapter 4

Summary

The chapter opens with a general description of the

island's changes throughout the day and the boys' responses to each day's cyclical progression. The focus narrows to the littluns' subculture and three of the littluns interacting as they play with one of their sandcastles. Then Roger and Maurice emerge from the jungle and deliberately destroy some of the sandcastles on their way to the beach.

Jack gathers the hunters to reveal his new hunting strategy: using colored clay and charcoal to camouflage their faces. Jack commands all his hunters, including Samneric who are on fire-maintenance duty at the time, to join in a hunt.

Ralph spots a ship in the distance and is confident that the ship's crew will spot the boys' smoke signal. But, unknown to Ralph, the fire has gone out, being left unattended. When Simon points out that there is no smoke, he and Ralph and Piggy hurry up the mountainside. By the time all three have reached the dormant fire site, the ship is gone.

Meanwhile, Jack and his hunters are triumphant, marching up to the fire site with the carcass of a pig. Jack and Ralph face off about the desertion of the fire for the sake of the hunt. Jack apologizes but Ralph remains angry. Tensions ease somewhat as the boys eat roast pig. The hunters reenact the kill as a sort of celebratory dance. In response, Ralph announces an assembly on the platform immediately.

Commentary

As the most fundamental of all cycles, the daily experience of morning's promise followed inevitably by night's menace is a microcosm of larger cycles. Golding's opening description of the island's daily rhythm is evocative of the many cycles that govern humanity: the life of an individual from birth to death, the development and disintegration of cultures, the rise and fall of great civilizations.

Even among this small group of boys, subcultures have sprung up. The littluns spend their days among themselves, following their own priorities and interests; "their passionately emotional and corporate life was their own." Within the littluns are further distinctions based on size and temperament, either of which can provide an immediate advantage to one littlun over another: "Henry was a bit of a leader this afternoon, because the other two were Percival and Johnny, the smallest boys on the island." Yet Johnny has the upper hand over the sensitive Percival due to his inclination to bully. In addition, while Johnny may be one of the smallest, he is also "well built." With no adults to control their activities, Henry and Johnny join in picking on Percival because they enjoy the thrill of mastery over another creature and because it keeps boredom at bay.

The boys focus on the most entertaining possibilities of the island, such as hunting, playing, and eating, to the detriment of such mundane but necessary tasks as building shelters. They are free to set their own priorities and agenda on an individual basis, allowing some of the boys the chance to develop the application of their own worst impulses. Henry, for example, assumes a dictatorial manner, experimenting further with mastery over other creatures as he traps tiny transparent beach scavengers in his footprints. His experience is a microcosm of another kind: Describing how Henry "became absorbed beyond happiness as he felt himself exercising control over living things," Golding alludes not only to Henry and Johnny's persecution of Percival but also to Jack's compulsion to hunt and to the probable cause of the nuclear war that landed the boys on this island.

The link between Henry's activities and Jack's is further strengthened by the image of Henry's attempt to verbally control the transparent creatures—"He talked to them, urging them, ordering them"—which evokes the image of Jack in the previous chapter staring at the traces of the pig trail "as though he would force them to speak to him." Both boys try to force their verbal communication on nonverbal entities, an effort doomed to failure. Henry cherishes what little control he feels he has and does not mind that his orders go unheeded. His efforts at mastery over another are still in the play stage, although cruel nonetheless to the vulnerable Percival. Jack, on the other hand, has a much more difficult time tolerating resistance. When the boys are forced to rebuild the fire in a different spot because Ralph silently refuses to move from the site of the original fire, Jack is furious. Ralph uses a means of control over the group that is nonverbal and nonviolent, ensuring that neither the rhetorical skills nor the physical superiority of the hunters can be used against him. In the face of passive resistance, Jack is powerless to stop Ralph from imposing his will on the group and asserting his authority.

As the biguns Roger and Maurice torment the littluns by destroying their sandcastles, they still hear in their heads the reprimanding adult voices of the civilization they left behind. Roger throws rocks at Henry, but he throws them so that they'll miss, surrounded as Henry is by "the protection of parents and school and policeman and the law. Roger's arm was conditioned by a civilization that knew nothing of him and was in ruins."

Even Jack still feels the influence of his former life, laughing while he describes the great amounts of blood spilled in the hunt but shuddering at the same time. His distaste is followed quickly by acceptance, however, as he wipes his bloody hands on his shorts. Golding implies a certain relief for Jack in the phrase "able at last to hit someone, [Jack] stuck his fist into Piggy's stomach." His entire life had been moderated by rules set by adults against hitting other children or physically acting out his aggression; now on the island, only the conditioning he received while still in civilization holds him back, and the imprint of that conditioning is fading fast from his character.

Most societies judge character to a great extent by how an individual behaves, how thoroughly a person has internalized the mores and ethos of civilized society. British culture, in particular, places a high value on maintaining civility even under adverse circumstances, the mask of good manners concealing strong emotions and impulses. Jack discovers the other side of a mask's power—the power to liberate—when he applies the clay and charcoal camouflage: "the mask was a thing on its own, behind which Jack hid, liberated from shame and self-consciousness."

While the masks of polite society leash our evil nature, Jack's mask of colored clay unleashes it. The mask—or the transformation it invokes—frightens the hunter Bill, who initially laughs but then backs off into the jungle, and it compels the twins to abandon their fire tending duties, a symbol of how they are being drawn away from all of the civilized domesticity and communal hope for rescue represented by the fire. Jack refers to the mask as "dazzle paint," the camouflage used in warfare, clearly linking his new identity as a shameless killer with those adults fighting the war. When the ship is sighted, Ralph remains calmly in place while the other boys present blunder around in excitement. Yet, when he realizes that there is no smoke signal for the ship to sight, he loses the calm that has so far characterized his behaviour—the mask over his emotions.

Now he rushes heedlessly up to mountain to the fire site, "savaging himself" on the bushes, reaching the top only to see that the fire is out and the ship is leaving. He loses control at this point: "his voice rose insanely. 'Come back! Come back!' … Ralph reached inside himself for the worst word he knew. 'They let the bloody fire go out.'" His use of a profanity indicates strong emotion not yet displayed; his anger compels him to break with the decorum so important to his culture. In the midst of this crisis, even Piggy, who is most closely linked with adult perspectives, "whimper[s] like a littlun" when he reaches the mountain top and, in the next chapter, also uses a vulgarity when Simon suggests that there may be a beast.

Under duress, some of the boys break with the social decorum expected of the offspring of proper civility, letting their baser emotions rule. Others of the boys go further, abandoning rational thought or civil communication. Jack has begun to think like an animal, as when he explains his rationale for the dazzle paint. His speech pattern becomes simplistic, mimicking the impressionistic understanding of animals: "They see me, I think. Something pink, under the trees." His group of hunters doesn't have the mechanism of the conch to regulate their discourse; they talk over each other when describing their successful hunt. When Jack as leader wants to make himself heard, he interrupts and takes the floor by force of personality rather than by an established, polite precedent.

Jack's shortsightedness has cost the boys a rescue while at the same time bringing them the immediate victory of a kill. Firmly rooted in their respective worlds, neither Ralph nor Jack can understand the other's position. "There was the brilliant world of hunting, tactics, fierce exhilaration, skill; and there was the world of longing and baffled common-sense." When Ralph denounces Jack for not keeping his agreement to maintain the fire, he is mourning not merely the lost opportunity for rescue but the loss of the world they've left behind in England. Because Jack has already lost interest in that world of politeness and boundaries, he feels no compunction to keep the fire going or to attend to any of the other responsibilities of a domestic life. He uses the device of an apology as a tool to end the conflict with Ralph, more of an instinctive political maneuver than an expression of regret. This apology pleases the crowd but infuriates Ralph, who perceives the apology as a "verbal trick" distracting everyone from the tragedy that had just occurred. Rhetoric triumphs for Jack despite the harm he has caused with his negligence and misplaced priorities.

Later, after Simon rebukes Jack for refusing Piggy a share of the meat, Jack lists all he has done to bring the boys meat in an effort to gain their full appreciation for his accomplishment and for what he's going through in his metamorphosis from choirboy to killer. The others do not fully comprehend Jack's message. He "looked round for understanding but found only respect." Although he does not get understanding, he does get respect, which is all that is required for a demagogue. Jack also discovers that the ritualistic face-painting and dancing further separates him from the constraints of his civil training and that involving his hunters in the dancing and chanting of the mock hunt after the meal has a powerful bonding effect, bringing the hunters more strongly under his influence.

Ralph is envious of this influence and of the victory Jack has brought to the group. He has not been able to provide such a decisive triumph for the boys, dependent as his agenda is on the external event of rescue and on the maintenance of cultural norms alien to their current environment. When he announces an immediate assembly, he is calling the boys not only to the platform but back to all that it symbolizes.

Glossary

- Dazzle paint British term for camouflage; the disguising of troops, ships, guns, etc. to conceal them from the enemy, as by the use of paint, nets, or leaves in patterns merging with the background.
- Accent a distinguishing regional or national manner of pronunciation; here, Piggy's manner of speech, characterized by his use of double negatives and informal contractions.
- Bloody [Vulgar Brit. Slang] cursed; damned.
- Ha'porth contraction of "a halfpenny's worth," meaning a very small amount.
- One for his nob a hit on his head.
- Give him a fourpenny one hit him on the jaw.

Chapter 5

Summary

Ralph calls the assembly and reminds everyone of their agreement to maintain fresh water supplies, observe sanitation measures, build shelters, and keep the signal fire going. He then addresses the growing fear that he knows is beginning to overwhelm many of the boys by opening up the floor for discussion. Meanwhile, darkness is falling.

Jack takes the conch to point out that if a beast were on the island, he would have seen it during his hunting trips. Piggy adds that the field of psychology can be used as a tool to explain logically the experience of fear, thereby invalidating it. When a littlun comes forward to describe a large creature he saw in the jungle the night before, Simon reveals that it was only he, going to his special place. Percival suggests that a beast could arise from the sea, then falls asleep on the platform from the effort of his revelation.

Simon attempts to explain that the boys themselves, or something inherent in human nature, could be the beast they fear. His unsuccessful explanation leads to talk of ghosts, so Ralph holds a vote to see who fears ghosts. This vote sparks an outburst from the rational Piggy with a corresponding reaction from Jack. Now in open mutiny, Jack aggressively disputes Ralph's authority and leads the boys onto the beach in a sort of tribal dance. Remaining on the platform, Piggy and Simon urge Ralph to summon everyone back to the platform but he resists, his confidence shaken. Suddenly, the three boys are startled by an unearthly wail as Percival wakes up to find himself alone in the dark.

Commentary

Chapter 3 addresses the issue of verbal communication and its place within a civilized society; this chapter implies that the primitive life leaves little mental energy for conceptual thought. Making his way to the platform, Ralph realizes "the wearisomeness of this life, where ... a considerable part of one's waking life was spent watching one's feet." With so much energy devoted to survival, little time is left to devote to the kind of conceptual thought or abstract reasoning available to those sheltered by the institutions found in civilizations.

The two boys who retain the most capacity for conceptual thought are Piggy and Simon. Note that Piggy does not participate in the physical endeavors of the other boys; his physical activities are limited by his poor physical condition. Simon makes the effort to be alone in his hidden spot, giving himself time to meditate in a place where he doesn't have to concern himself with hunting, building, or the needs of others. In the hidden spot, Simon develops his understanding of human nature as the true beast to be feared.

The silence of Simon's hideaway allows him to reflect on what he sees and feels. In contrast, silence is a threat to the other boys. Consider Jack's feeling oppressed by the jungle's silence while hunting in Chapter 3. During the assembly in this chapter, the boys respond almost aggressively to Percival's silence when asked his name: "Tormented by the silence and the refusal the assembly broke into a chant. 'What's your name? What's your name?'" Chanting is associated with primitive societies, not part of the order or domesticity from whence the boys came or that Ralph is trying to establish.

Ralph expends much energy on the needs of others as well as on the physical rigors of building huts, and he begins to feel the effects: He is gradually losing both confidence that they will be rescued and his feeling that they are involved in an exciting experiment without adults. As a boy who represents the civilized, English society, he is neither as savage as Jack nor as cerebral as Piggy. He provides an example of how the leader in a community must strive to utilize the intellectual resources available in solving communal problems. This chapter shows Ralph's skills of organization and governance starting to wane. He is struggling to implement his agenda for the meeting and finds he is unable to control the assembly, which degenerates into a mob of "noise and excitement, scramblings, screams and laughter." He finds himself lost "in a maze of thoughts that were rendered vague by his lack of words to express them." This lack of mental clarity recalls Jack's difficulty in expressing himself described in Chapter 3. Such a loss of verbal command bodes ill for Ralph and the community because his seat of authority is the platform, a symbol of the verbal communication and thoughtful debate. Ralph's mental acumen is subject to the same decay as his clothing, frayed as both are by the rigors of the primitive life.

Yet the crisis of the lost rescue opportunity spurs Ralph to grasp some new concepts, revelations following each other thick and fast as he makes his way to the platform and sits on the chief's log. His growth is evident in his musings as he ponders matters more conceptual than he ever has before. Realizing the difficulty of this lifestyle in contrast to its initial glamour, he "smiled jeeringly," as an adult might look back with cynicism on the ideals held as a youth. Ralph is losing his innocence quickly, but gaining an understanding of natural processes not available to him in the sheltered society he came from. "With a convulsion of the mind, Ralph discovered dirt and decay ... At that he began to trot" toward the platform and the civilization it represents, in a physical reaction to the abstract truth newly present within him.

Once on the platform, more revelations engulf Ralph. He considers the springy log that shifts during assemblies and throws off the boys sitting on it, and ponders how maintenance of the status quo has taken precedence over the simple solution of securing the log with a stone wedge. He notes that the light of late sunset makes the entire place look different, calling into question the reality of its usual appearance. Suddenly Ralph recognizes the value and talents of the intellectually gifted Piggy, a conscious appreciation foreshadowed by the allegiance formed in Chapter 4 when "Not even Ralph knew how a link between him and Jack had been snapped and fastened elsewhere." At the same time, Ralph realizes that "Piggy was no chief," understanding intuitively that a leader needs the popular support Piggy can't garner, hindered by his lack of charisma or popular appeal.

Up to this point, Ralph himself has been leading by instinct and charisma. Now he realizes that "if you were a chief, you had to think, you had to be wise ... thought was a valuable thing, that got results." Simultaneously, he realizes "I can't think. Not like Piggy." This sentiment echoes Piggy's question to the boys in Chapter 2, after they've accidentally caused the forest fire: "How can you expect to be rescued if you don't ... act proper?" In that scenario, Piggy links social conventions with results, in a logical relationship of cause and effect lost on the emotional crowd. Social conventions are not necessarily based in rational thought, but they do provide a framework for rational discussion and thought.

Ralph has clearly learned something about establishing a forum for discussion: "One had to sit, attracting all eyes to the conch, and drop words like heavy round stones among the little groups that crouched or squatted." Golding's word choices here evoke a distinct sense of primitivism, a savage lifestyle where words are stones and the chief presides over an electorate that crouches and squats to hear him speak. Just as Chapter 4 lays out a series of microcosms with the littluns' interactions, the diction here links the platform assemblies to both ends of the social or civil spectrum, from pre-verbal tribe gatherings to modern governmental institutions.

With hunting, Jack has a skill that is becoming increasingly more persuasive to the group in their present environment than does Ralph. Jack's appeal to the primitive, baser, instinctive nature of the community, coupled with his aggressive, self-assured combative personality, is now appealing more and more to the group. At the same time, Ralph's political and natural leadership abilities coupled with his visceral optimism and common sense are having diminishing impact on the affairs of the boys as their baser natures become increasingly prevalent.

In this chapter's assembly, Ralph's new appreciation for thought leads him to rely too heavily on logic. While he presents his agenda point by point, attempting a rational approach to the fear he knows they feel, night is falling and the boys are growing restless. "We've got to talk about this fear and decide there's nothing in it," he says, as if a phobia can be defused through discussion. As the brainy representative of civilization, Piggy continues along these utterly rational lines. "'Life,' said Piggy expansively, 'is scientific'" in his explanation that such an emotional concern can be addressed as a pathology with the twentieth-century invention of psychology. His assertion that soon humankind would by flying to Mars indicates his confidence in technology, which he holds out as a source of comfort.

Yet Jack provides the most comfort to the boys in this assembly because he portrays the object of their fear as an actual animal, one that can be tracked, and "[t]he whole assembly applauded him with relief" when he points out that he has never seen a frightening beast of any kind in the forest; his skills as a tracker are undeniable. Jack orders everyone to be frightened if they must—he acknowledges that even he feels that same fear at times—but not to fear an animal-beast. Jack pleases the crowd with his practical take on the beast and his definitive pronouncement that "you'll have to put up with [the fear] just like the rest of us."

Given the day's lost rescue opportunity, Ralph implements the additional precaution of using only the signal fire to cook rather than starting small wasteful fires on the beach—an idea that is solidly grounded in reality. Still counting on logic to carry his agenda, Ralph points out "You voted me for chief. Now you do what I say." Ralph thus raises the issue of the electorate's obligation to the rule. Winning of public opinion is both a reasoned and an emotionally based process. Every politician knows that popular opinion is easily swayed from one leader to another; the general public's perception of who is the best leader is frequently based not on which leader has benefited the group the most, but who has gained favour most recently. Already, Ralph's authority has lost ground, due to the concrete victory of a kill offered by Jack, the adventure and drama of the hunts, and the overall emotional nature of a crowd.

Ralph, Piggy, and Simon assume that adults could solve the problems they face on the island. After the assembly, the three boys detail the advantages adults bring, crediting adults with the greatest efficacy and civility: "Grownups know things They ain't afraid of the dark. They'd meet and have tea and discuss. Then things @'ud be all right." Ralph has been trying to uphold that model, using discussion as a means to set things right, but this chapter sees him lose faith in it. When the other boys have been once again led off by Jack, Ralph cannot bring himself to summon them back.

Although Piggy is an undoubted representative of logic and science, he is the first to address the idea that the fear could be based on a fear of self and each other, of something inherent in humanity. Piggy developed his shrewd understanding of human nature during the time spent bedridden by asthma—the equivalent for him of Simon's secret place in the jungle. For Piggy, the fear is less a concept rooted in knowledge of humanity's dark side than the practical fear of an outsider, a vulnerable boy disliked by the stronger, more aggressive boys.

Like Piggy, Simon is different from the others: He has fainting spells, sticks up for Piggy even if unobtrusively, and has the special hidden place in the forest; later chapters reveal him as a visionary. Because the other boys don't understand Simon, they fear him. When he reveals that it was he who inadvertently frightened one of the littluns by venturing into the jungle at night, he gives them a concrete reason to chastise him. Jack holds him up for ridicule; the "derisive laughter that rose had fear in it and condemnation"—two emotions that go hand in hand as the condemnation makes the group feel protected from the fear they've experienced.

Simon's death is foreshadowed in this chapter, as he is made scapegoat for the boys' unshakeable fear. His question to them, "What's the dirtiest thing there is?" demands an answer far too abstract for this crowd. Once again, Jack provides a concrete and non-threatening answer, an answer far simpler than the answer Simon seeks, which is evil. Simon can't express precisely what he understands because he lacks a sophisticated education or training in dealing with abstract concepts; he is, after all, a ten-year-old boy. Simon's inability to articulate what he sees as "mankind's essential illness" mirrors Jack's inability to effectively express "the compulsion to track down and kill that was swallowing him up." Both boys want to describe the same thing, but Simon has reached an abstract understanding of the animality that can produce evil effects while Jack is living it. Of course, Jack later stirs up the group into such a frenzy of animality that Simon is murdered.

This chapter expands upon the theme of humankind's latent depravity, resorting to the savagery of self-indulgence in the absence of social rules, mores, and control to the contrary. Such control is the basis of most social conventions and institutions, which are designed to promote self-control and civilized discourse. The symbol of such conventions and institutions is the platform. In this chapter the platform's protective powers break down when the assembly dissolves into "arguing, gesticulating shadows. To Ralph, seated, this seemed the breaking up of sanity." When Ralph sees the disorderly arguing breaking out and taking over the assembly, he perceives not only that he has lost control of the group but that the group is losing control of itself.

Glossary

- Lavatory [Chiefly Brit.] a flush toilet.
- Taken short informal phrase for having diarrhea.

- Jolly [Brit. Informal] very; altogether.
- Bogie an imaginary evil being or spirit; goblin.
- Mucking about [Slang, Chiefly Brit.] wasting time; puttering around.
- Sod you a vulgar British slang phrase showing extreme contempt.
- Nuts a slang exclamation of disgust, scorn, disappointment, refusal, etc.
- Bollocks a vulgar slang exclamation expressing anger, disbelief, etc.

Chapter 6

Summary

After the assembly, all the boys go to sleep. Above them an aerial battle is taking place. A casualty of the battle floats down to the island on his opened parachute. The wind drags the body to rest at the top of the mountain. The breeze inflates the parachute occasionally, making the body appear to sit up and then sink forward again. Samneric, tending the fire on the mountain, catch a glimpse of the body's movement and hear the parachute inflating. They flee to Ralph in a panic with a story exaggerated by their fear.

At dawn, Ralph calls an assembly, where they decide to investigate the only spot on the island left unexplored: the castle-like rock formation at one end. With Piggy and the littluns remaining behind on the beach, Ralph and the others go to the castle. Ralph goes first by himself, followed a few minutes later by Jack. After they establish that the beast is not there, the other boys join them in the castle and want to play there a while. They resist when Ralph announces that they need to all go check on the fire, but he forces the issue and Jack leads the way back up to the fire site.

Commentary

This chapter begins and ends ominously. The aerial battle that opens the chapter establishes that war continues to rage in the world where most of the boys long to return. Ralph,

Piggy, and Simon finished the previous chapter detailing the merits of adults and adult behaviour, how adults would remedy their unpleasant situation with ease and dignity. Yet that night, "a sign came down from the world of grownups" that is frightening and mysterious and changes the entire complexion of the group for the worse. When Samneric establish to everyone's satisfaction that an actual beast does exist, the boys shift automatically and instinctively into an aggressive mode based on fear: "the circle began to change. It faced out, rather than in, and the spears of sharpened wood were like a fence."

The main theme of this chapter is the effect of fear. For Samneric, their initial fright magnifies their involvement with the creature from merely seeing movement and hearing the parachute to being actively chased down the mountain as they flee. They report eyes, teeth, and claws that they couldn't possibly have seen. The other boys are so eager for a remedy to this fear that they feel the first unified urge for mutiny when Ralph forces them to leave the perceived safety of the fort-like castle rock to check on the fire.

Fear acts as a sort of litmus test for leadership. While Piggy and Jack both put forth unworkable plans of action—Piggy wanting to restrict their living area to the platform, Jack wanting to rush out and hunt the beast down—Ralph is able to proceed with sense and caution. Harkening back to his new appreciation for the power of thought, Ralph lays out his concerns about both plans and asserts, "So we've got to think." He points out that the beast obviously can't be hunted like the pigs because it leaves no tracks; otherwise, Jack would have already seen the tracks. Remaining all the time on the platform will not work due to lack of fire, food, and space. Ralph is able to keep the group's focus on the hope for rescue, despite Jack's attack on his authority.

Fear brings out the dictator in Jack. He attempts to take control of the group, claiming this situation is "a hunter's job" in which Ralph is not qualified to command. Showing yet again no mercy for the helpless or vulnerable, he advocates abandoning the littluns without a guardian while everyone else goes on the hunt. Like a dictator, he assigns a high value only to those he finds useful or agreeable to his views and looks to silence those who do not please him. Making a pitch for censorship, Jack declares, "We don't need the conch any more. We know who ought to say things. What good did Simon do speaking?"

Yet Simon is the only boy who has insight into the nature of the true beast, the abstraction that Jack feels watching him in the jungle. Pondering all the characteristics of this animal beast Samneric seem to have discovered, Simon sees that all the pieces don't add up: If this beast had claws and wings, why was it not fast or fierce enough to catch Samneric? When Simon tries to visualize what this beast might look like, "there arose before his inward sight the picture of a human at once heroic and sick" which is a depiction of Golding's vision of humanity as flawed by inherent evil. Golding gives this knowledge to Simon, an outsider, to reflect the place visionaries or mystics typically hold in society: on the fringes, little understood by the majority, and so often feared or disregarded. As a mystic, Simon is not fully present in the physical world, living so inside his head that he can't keep from banging it into a tree as they make their way to the castle rock. Simon was unable the night before to make the other boys see his outlook; even Ralph, with his new appreciation for thought and wisdom, dismisses Simon without considering that he may have valuable insight.

Ralph has more pressing concerns in light of this crisis. As the leader, he feels the obligation to lead the way into the unexplored territory at the castle rock, even though he is initially as frightened as everyone else. He even suggests that Jack go first, perhaps daring Jack to live up to his declaration that this is "a hunter's job." Yet Ralph is unable to overlook his own pressing sense of responsibility and takes the lead alone around the cliff. In a credit to the conditioning he received back home, politeness is his default even in this tense moment. As he is about to embark, Simon mumbles, perhaps in an attempt to comfort him, that he doesn't believe in the beast; Ralph "answered him politely, as if agreeing about the weather. 'No. I suppose not.'" British culture is famed for such civilized reserve in emotional times; by the standards of the society he's left behind, Ralph is a gentleman. The calmness of his reply is also a testament to his strong alliance with reason, further characterizing Ralph as person who values thought and logic.

When Ralph is actually on the path, he "realized with surprise that he did not really expect to meet any beast and didn't know what he would do about it if he did." This realization underscores Ralph's ability to remain calm and realistic in stressful situations. During the showdown with Jack during the morning's assembly, his clearheaded response helped him maintain his authority; the boys found his hope for rescue during this height of fear more appealing than Jack's desire to hunt. Jack self-indulgently seeks the glory of the hunt while Ralph seeks safety for the group, a fact not lost on the other boys at the time.

Inevitably, once Ralph has accepted the obligation that comes with leadership and has made his way alone toward the castle rock, Jack follows. "Couldn't let you do it on your own," he explains, motivated less by concern than by an inability to allow Ralph his full share of glory as a solo explorer. Immediately, Jack claims the area as ideal for a fort and identifies a loose boulder as a weapon. The other boys warm up to Jack's plan right away and prefer to remain there playing fort and feeling secure rather than follow Ralph's command that they all make the journey to the fire site to re-light the fire.

The group's favour swings back and forth from Ralph to Jack ever more rapidly. After the successful hunt led by the swaggering Jack, Ralph in contrast has begun to seem to the boys like the absurd, stodgy authority figures back home. Samneric mock his justifiable anger later when they are out of its reach. "Eric sniggered. 'Wasn't he waxy?' ... 'Remember old Waxy at school?'" Imitating the schoolmaster they had nicknamed Waxy for consistently waxing angry at his students' classroom antics, Samneric laugh at Ralph as well, despite the fact that their desertion of duty caused his anger and the loss of possible rescue. Perhaps they laugh to dispel their guilt or because their childish perspective has already allowed them to forget the loss they caused. Either way, Ralph's priorities are lost on them.

In this chapter, even Ralph begins to lose sight of his priorities. When he reminds Jack that they need to keep the signal going, he explains "That's all we've got." In the previous chapter, Ralph uses the same phrase about the rules when Jack challenges their usefulness. The rules represent a certain civility of domestic order, which Ralph was hard pressed to create or maintain prior to this current crisis. Now his focus narrows from civility to survival.

The smoke signal is truly all they have because he doubts they can kill or control a beast that can't be tracked; all he can hope for now is rescue. Once inside castle rock, however, the area that becomes Jack's domain, a "strange thing happened in his [Ralph's] head.

Something flittered there in front of his mind like a bat's wing, obscuring the idea"—the hope for a return to the ponies and tea time of which he dreams. The figure envisioned by Simon of "a human at once heroic and sick" could be a composite of Ralph and Jack. Now getting worn down by the hardships and incomprehensible fears of primitive life and out of reach of the conditioning of civilization, Ralph is gradually becoming infected by the savagery that is rapidly eating away at Jack's humanity.

Glossary

- Waxy [Brit. Informal] enraged.
- Polyp any of various cnidarians, as the sea anemone or hydra, having a mouth fringed with many small, slender tentacles bearing stinging cells at the top of a tubelike body.
- Plinth a course of brick or stone, often a projecting one, along the base of a wall.
- Embroil to draw into a conflict or fight; involve in trouble.
- Diffident lacking self-confidence; timid; shy.

Chapter 7

Summary

On their way back to the mountain, Ralph indulges in a fantasy of cleanliness and grooming. Disheartened by the group's dishevelment and dirt, he spends time staring out at the vastness of the sea and realizing how high the odds are against rescue. Simon joins him and, seemingly reading his mind, prophesies that Ralph will make it back home.

On the way to the mountain, Jack leads a pig hunt in which he gets slightly wounded. Ralph gets his first taste of hunting, striking a boar in the snout with his spear. After the boar gets away, the group begins a mock hunt that gets out of control and hurts the boy acting as the pig. Ralph urges the group back on their way, but the difficult path before them impedes their progress. Simon volunteers to cross the island alone to inform Piggy that the others won't be home until after dark.

By the time they reach the base of the mountain, darkness has fallen. Spurred on by Jack's bravado, Ralph, Jack, and Roger volunteer to continue the search for the beast while the other boys return to the platform. Once they reach the burnt patch, Ralph, tired of Jack's continual mocking, challenges Jack to go on by himself; Jack returns from the mountaintop terrified. Roger and Ralph investigate as well and are equally terrified by the image of the beast: the dead paratrooper appears to be a live ape-like creature that seems to look at them when the breeze catches his parachute. All three boys flee to the platform in the dark.

Commentary

Ralph undergoes significant emotional and psychological development in this chapter. Following his spontaneous participation in a pig hunt, he experiences the exhilarating mixture of emotions—"I hit him! The spear stuck in"—comparable to those that drive Jack and the other hunters and which underlie Jack's credibility with the group. He, then, "sunned himself in their new respect and felt that hunting was good after all." Heretofore, Ralph had failed to recognize this instinct to hunt and kill in himself. Now that he has experienced these emotions, he has gained an appreciation that Jack's perspectives and priorities are present, even if latent, within us all. This one experience communicates more to Ralph about hunting's attractions than all the bickering with Jack before. Ralph's humanity is deteriorating; his savage self has been touched and awakened.

Armed with this understanding, he is able to see Jack "infuriatingly, for the first time," recognizing that he could have potentially used Jack as a resource all this time rather than competing with him. Realizing that their current path is severely hindering their progress to the mountain, he now calls on Jack's knowledge of the island, garnered during his hunting activities, to identify an alternate path. As Jack continues to compete rather than cooperate with him, Ralph realizes that Jack becomes aggressive whenever he is no longer in charge.

As Ralph and Jack continue to compete rather than cooperate, the antipathy that each generates in the other becomes more evident. Jack becomes increasingly aggressive in situations involving Ralph and his leadership. At one point, Ralph calls on the knowledge passed on to him by Piggy and challenges Jack directly by asking him, "Why do you hate me?" He doesn't get an answer from Jack, but the reaction of the other boys is that "something indecent had been said." The boys recognize that Ralph is opening up the floodgates of aggression and dislike, which civilized conventions are intended to control. Nevertheless, as the situation slides increasingly toward confrontation, Ralph, the leader, the symbol of civility and hope, "turned away first."

Throughout this chapter, Ralph displays and surprises himself with his coolness under pressure—despite his participation in the crazed attack on Robert and in contrast to his grief-stricken, emotional loss of control in the last chapter. Again and again, he shows a realistic grasp of their situation only to be jeered at by Jack. Despite his pride in hitting the boar, he understands immediately that boys with "foolish wooden stick[s]" as spears are no match for the large powerful animal. "But he'd do us!" he protests when Jack orders the hunters to follow the boar's flight. Jack follows alone and is wounded for his lack of sense. Later Ralph is shocked to find himself accompanying Jack up the mountain in the dark to search for the beast, but his response does not betray him. The coolness of his reply renders invalid Jack's supremely taunting invitation. Such instinctual calm reflects again the same strength Ralph displayed in the previous chapter when he made sure to take the lead at castle rock. While Jack's aggressive resentment has no room for reason, Ralph is not afraid once they have set off to ask for another volunteer to accompany them or to point out that their journey up the mountain in the dark is foolish.

Despite his coolness, Ralph can't help competing with Jack, much to the bloodthirsty crowd's delight. Hearing Jack issue to Ralph the invitation to join him in the nighttime search for the beast, "the other boys ... turned back to sample this fresh rub of two spirits in the dark." The boys as a group display a certain lust for conflict, evident not only in their fascinated appraisal of the conflict of Jack and Ralph but also in their frenzied attack on Robert. The game innocently begun by Robert and Ralph is not so much boys at play as the beast at work.

Note that Golding uses the phrase "overmastering" to describe the urge to inflict pain, evoking the theme developed in Chapter 4 with the littlun Henry's experiments with mastery over the tide pool creatures and the hunters imposing their collective will on the slaughtered pig. Stimulated by this chapter's unsuccessful hunt and Robert's vulnerability at the hands of the crowd, the boys are mastered themselves by a larger force, impulses they can neither understand nor acknowledge. Even the victim, Robert, cannot address directly the forces that were driving the group. He alludes to his narrowly averted fate when he points out that to improve this so-called game that "You want a real pig ... because you've got to kill him." His initial response, however, is to downplay his justifiable fear and attempt to regain his place within the group by saying "Oh, my bum!" as if a sore bottom were the extent of the damage. Perhaps he realizes on an instinctive level that maintaining his status as one of the group is critical to survival: The next time the boys play this game, the outsider, Simon, dies.

Ralph attempts to defuse the frightening attack in which he has just participated by placing the beating within the context of their civilization's legitimate outlets for aggression. "'Just a game,' said Ralph uneasily. 'I got jolly badly hurt at rugger once.'" Maurice, on the other hand, looks to refine the process, suggesting that they add a drum and a fire to do the dance "properly," although he's not sure of why he feels they need these things. Maurice seems to be speaking out of some primeval urge to recreate the rituals of a tribal sacrifice. While both Robert and Roger point out that they'll need a pig to complete the game, realizing that this game properly ends in death, Jack looks for a human, someone who could dress up as a pig. He too must acknowledge on some level that this game will inevitably have fatal consequences and, like a true dictator, suggests using one of the littluns, the most vulnerable and, in his eyes, the least valuable of the group.

Given Simon's need to solitude, it's not surprising that he volunteers to take Ralph's message to Piggy by crossing the island alone. His loner tendencies make the other boys think he's odd, but, for the reader, Simon's credibility as a mystic is established in this chapter. As if he is reading Ralph's mind, Simon interrupts Ralph's strained, tense regard of the ocean's vastness by telling him, "You'll get back to where you came from." Ralph responds with the opinion all the boys hold of Simon: "You're batty." Simon knows he's right, however, and he repeats his prophecy with emphasis. Note that he uses "you" instead of "we," realizing, perhaps, on some level that he, himself, will not make it back. Consumed by his own concerns, Ralph doesn't question Simon's omission of himself but takes comfort in the express certainty of the other boy's prophecy.

Ralph seeks comfort throughout this chapter in images of home, indulging in a fantasy of bathing and grooming and a recollection of the peaceful life of ponies, cereal and cream, and children's books he had once known. Ralph's perspective on the island has changed drastically from the first day, when "A kind of glamour was spread over ... the scene." Now as he looks at the other boys and sees how thoroughly grimy they are, he finds their condition very different from "the spectacular dirt of boys who have fallen into mud," a temporary dirtying probably initiated by some good-natured horseplay and easily remedied by a warm bath. This dirtiness is an outer manifestation of the darkening of the soul—the emergence of the evil within.

Ralph now longs for the comfort of the familiar, but the home he wishes for is a glamorized ideal. He remembers his former life as a place where "Everything was all right; everything was good-humored and friendly." The reader, of course, is aware that back home—the world the boys have left—exactly the same sorts of human weaknesses which dominate the boys are playing out in the form of nuclear war. As Ralph looks out at the ocean and viscerally experiences its size and power, he considers how the other side of the island offers "the shield of the quiet lagoon" and midday mirages to protect them all from the truth of the ocean's vastness. Faced with the reality of the ocean, he feels as though hope for rescue, and by extension for civilization, has become a mirage.

The images of civilization are in his head as are its voices—the same voices that conditioned Roger's aim to miss Henry, for example, and Piggy's, chiding him for being childish and another voice scolding him for being foolish enough to allow Jack to goad him into seeking out a potentially dangerous animal in the dark with only two other boys and spears of wood. In counterpart to the voices of civilization in his head is Jack's voice, a disembodied voice in the dark like the figurative devil on his shoulder: "'If you don't want to go on,' said the voice sarcastically, 'I'll go up by myself.'" By not attributing this challenge directly to Jack, Golding not only indicates the supreme darkness in which the boys are working but also emphasizes the evil that Jack represents. He describes Jack as a "stain in the darkness;" when Jack leaves, "The stain vanished. Another took its place."

The other stain is Roger, the darkened figure who joined them when all the other boys fled to the safety of the beach. Roger has already established himself as mean-spirited, coldly following the littlun Henry to frighten him with stones that just miss. During Robert's beating, Roger was "fighting to get close," to take part in the hurting before it ended. Finally, it is symbolically significant that, in this second ascent up the mountain, Roger, who is evil and sadistic, has replaced Simon, who is spiritual and mystic, representing the devolution of the boys toward their primitive, savage nature. Later chapters reveal Roger as more sadistic even than Jack.

Confronted with the dead paratrooper, however, Roger is just as terrified as the other two boys. They fear the dead man because they believe him to be a live, predatory creature. He is merely a catalyst, however, for the savagery that will run amok on the island. Just as Ralph feels himself taken over by the bloodlust that infects the hunters, he gets a taste of hatred as a means of courage, forcing himself to approach the false beast by fusing "his fear and loathing into a hatred," a hatred that bolsters his will and drives him forward to investigate where his good sense tells him not to go. When this ape-like creature "lifted its head, holding toward them the ruin of a face," it is showing them the ruin of their humanity as their instinctive evil begins to take over when they are weakened by fear.

Glossary

- Dun dull grayish-brown.
- Coverts covered or protected places; shelters.
- Toilet the process of dressing or grooming oneself.
- Scurfy having a condition, as dandruff, in which the skin sheds little, dry scales.
- Brine water full of salt.
- Do us here, kill us.
- Bum [Brit. Slang] the buttocks.
- Rugger [Brit. Informal] rugby.
- Funk a cowering or flinching through fear; panic.
- Windy long-winded, pompous, boastful.

- Impervious not affected by something or not feeling the effects of something.

Chapter 8

Summary

Ralph angers Jack by telling Piggy that even Jack would hide if the beast attacked them. In retaliation, Jack attempts his most serious mutiny yet, trying to convince the other boys to impeach Ralph. When the boys refuse to openly vote against Ralph, Jack announces his defection and runs off into the forest.

Simon suggests they all go face whatever's on the mountain, but no one wants to go. Piggy, glad that Jack is gone, suggests they build a signal fire on the beach so that they won't have to go up the mountain. While everyone gathers wood, most of the biguns creep away to join Jack. Simon disappears as well, going to his hidden spot in the forest to rest after his unsuccessful address to the group. Piggy starts the fire with his glasses.

Meanwhile Jack leads another successful hunt, attacking and killing a nursing sow and then impaling her head on a stick as an offering to the beast, coincidentally in full view of the spot where Simon sits concealed. Simon hallucinates, thinking that the head is talking to him, until he loses consciousness. To get fire for a pig roast, Jack stages a theft of some burning branches from the beach fire and invites Ralph's group to the roast in an attempt to recruit them to join his tribe. Ralph tries to rally his group to his side but loses his train of thought when he tries to remember the importance of being rescued, causing them to doubt him briefly.

Commentary

Ralph speaks realistically when he tells Piggy that even Jack would hide if the beast attacked; after all, the night before Jack had been as terrified as the other two boys when he saw the dead paratrooper. Jack cannot accept this realistic view of himself. In defence, he offers to the group a rationale for impeaching Ralph—"He'd never have got us meat," as if hunting skills make for an effective leader. Noting that "He isn't a prefect and we don't know anything about him" opens up speculation about Ralph's qualifications as a leader.

Jack further condemns Ralph as one who talks rather than one who gets results, but Ralph himself has long ago lost patience with talk, finding it an ineffective and inappropriate tool for their situation. His position on the usefulness of rhetoric is clear in his response to Jack's assembly. "'Talk,' said Ralph bitterly, 'Talk, talk, talk.'"

Reluctant to vote openly against Ralph, the boys sneak off to join Jack and return only when masked by their new tribal war paint, which has a liberating effect. Jack so loses himself in this liberation that, symbolizing the casting off of all social and civil encumbrances, he abandons clothing altogether, wearing only his paint and his knife when he presents his invitation to Ralph's group. "He was safe from shame or self-consciousness behind the mask of his paint."

Jack strives to be a chief in some grand fashion seen in a book or a movie, evidenced by the bizarrely formal announcement and flourish he makes Maurice and Robert perform once he has spoken to Ralph's group. Little does he realise he himself is fulfilling the role of the beast. Wrapped up in the caveman-like activities of hunting, face-painting, and chest-beating disguised as addresses to the assembly, Jack doesn't feel the need for rescue and so distracts the other boys from keeping the fire lit. He tells the assembly "Yes. The beast is a hunter" without taking a moment to reflect that perhaps the hunter is the beast.

Having lost and been wounded by the powerful, aggressive boar in the previous chapter, Jack chooses now to attack a defenseless sow who is vulnerable while she nurses her piglets—an act of supreme cruelty. The sow's death and disfigurement marks the triumph of evil and the climax of the novel. Jack's selection of the vulnerable sow arises from his defeated attempt to depose Ralph and foreshadows his later actions. While he couldn't impeach Ralph openly and was wounded emotionally in the attempt, he can defeat him by killing the defenseless boys in his tribe, Piggy and Simon.

Voices can be a tool of evil as well. In the previous chapter, Jack's voice came unidentified out of the darkness like the devil's voice. While his choirboys-turned-hunters prepare unknowingly in this chapter to commit cruelty against their former friends and group members by joining Jack, Golding points out for contrast that "their voices had been the song of angels" back in civilization. Now they take part in slaughtering a mother pig and putting her head on a stake, offering it to the supposed beast while "The silence accepted the gift."

Note that when the sow's head speaks to Simon, it takes on a male voice, becoming the Lord of the Flies. Interestingly, Piggy and the Lord of the Flies both give the same answer to the same question, although they each phrase it slightly differently. Ralph asks Piggy "what makes things break up like they do?" and receives the reply "I dunno. I expect it's him ... Jack." Meanwhile Simon hears the staked head tell him, "You knew, didn't you? ... I'm the reason why it's no go? Why things are what they are?" The Lord of the Flies, a literal translation of the Greek word Beelzebub, symbolizes evil, and Jack is evil personified. Piggy's assessment of the problem is actually much tamer in intent, based not on a consideration of evil but what he terms a lack of common sense (reason).

True to Piggy's assertion that "It's them that haven't no common sense that make trouble on this island," Jack doesn't seem to have much common sense. He dictates to his hunters that they forget the beast and stop having nightmares, as if either mental process could be controlled on command. Piggy has a more rational solution to their situation, one that actually requires more courage on the boys' part than Jack's foolishly unrealistic demands. "We just got to go on, that's all. That's what grownups would do." Ralph wishes he could think more like a grownup, impressed with Piggy's astuteness in noting that Samneric need to take separate shifts in tending the fire rather than taking their turn together. Piggy and Ralph rely on adult behaviour as a model because they still maintain the image of grownups as eminently capable and reasonable. They equate adulthood with knowledge and higher understanding.

In a way, Simon shares the same perception but sees the

darker side of knowledge. He sees the sow's eyes as "dim with the infinite cynicism of adult life" and later hears the head speak with a schoolmaster's voice, telling him to accept the presence of evil on the island. This view of adults is not defined by the civilized politeness and capability the boys imagined just two nights before, after the assembly. Cynicism results from gaining experience while losing optimism; having witnessed the pig's slaughter and defacement has given Simon experience in death and brutality and caused him to lose hope. Yet he soldiers on in his quest to discover the identity of the beast on the mountain top, the beast he knows is false because he has just had a conversation with the true beast.

Just as Piggy and Simon seem to share an idea about the cause of the island society's disintegration, Simon and Jack have similar revelations as well. During the first successful hunt in Chapter 4, Jack is excited by "the knowledge that had come to them when they closed in on the struggling pig." In this chapter, Simon's "gaze was held by that ancient, inescapable recognition" as he looks upon the Lord of the Flies. Both boys are connecting with the savagery that begets evil, but Jack revels in it while Simon is undone by it, trapped by his vision of the Lord of the Flies in his hidden spot until he passes out.

Another concept related to this knowledge of savagery is a twist on the idea of fun. From the beginning, Ralph's goal for the group was for everyone to have fun. Such a goal did not seem farfetched given that the boys were on a pristine tropical island, the type featured in the adventure stories they all had read. Once Jack defects and lures his hunters away, he also promises fun, the kind that comes with dressing up like savages and having adventurous hunts. Although Jack may not realise the fun he is promising will turn into deadly cruelty, Simon knows that Jack holding a position of power can have only ill effects for the more vulnerable boys like Piggy, the littluns, and himself. Simon hears the Lord of the Flies say, "We're going to have fun on this island! So don't try it on ... or else." Now the offer to have fun is a threat, with the Lord of the Flies warning Simon not to try stopping the consequences of Jack's new regime but to accept the savagery that will overtake the island. Ralph responds to the defection of the hunters with increasing despair. Wishing he could think more like an adult, he turns to Piggy for advice and insight. Piggy keeps alive the fire when he has the "intellectual daring" to suggest maintaining a fire on the beach instead of on the mountain. During the small assembly held after rebuilding the fire, Piggy prompts Ralph when he forgets what he was going to say. By reminding him of rescue and thinking to move the fire, Piggy is fighting for his survival with his intellect just as Jack looks to conquer with physicality.

In the end, Ralph will have to combine both physical abilities and brains to outrun Jack's tribe. For now, Ralph relies on Piggy for hope and for answers. Earlier, Simon asked the boys a question so fundamental that they couldn't answer it: "What else is there to do?" In a way, the boys spend the rest of the book responding to this question but never in the way Simon wants them to. He sees the need to face their fears, to approach the beast on the mountain in daylight in order to understand its true identity and get on with the business of facing the beast within themselves. Instead, the others respond with various avoidance methods: Jack offering a libation, a head on a stake, Ralph moving the fire to the beach, Piggy advocating a pragmatic perseverance. Their responses are indicative of each boy's character: Jack focuses on the concrete action of a primitive offering, Ralph wants to keep the home fire burning, and Piggy remains devoted to logic and realism.

Glossary

- Prefect in some private schools, esp. in England, an older student with disciplinary authority.
- Rebuke to blame or scold in a sharp way; reprimand.
- Cracked [Informal] mentally unbalanced; crazy.

Chapter 9

Summary

As a storm builds over the island, Simon awakens from

his faint and makes his way to the beast sighting on the mountain. He finds the paratrooper's body, inspects it, and realizes its true identity. From his vantage point, he can see that most of the boys are at the fire at Jack's camp, so he heads there to give everyone the news. He is so weakened by the day's experiences that he can barely walk.

Ralph and Piggy realise even the biguns loyal to Ralph have gone to Jack's party. They go as well, out of curiosity and hunger. Jack allows them to eat but, when everyone is finished eating, calls for all the boys to indicate whether they'd like to join his group or remain with Ralph's. Ralph makes a pitch for the boys to stay with him, reminding them of the first day's election. Jack has a strong hold on them, however, playing up the role of tribal chief.

The storm breaks over the party. Jack orders a dance in response to the downpour. Ralph and Piggy join in the outer fringes of the dance as well. Suddenly, Simon crawls out of the forest and into the centre of the dance circle. He tries to tell them about the true identity of the beast sighted on the mountain but can barely make himself heard over the storm and the boys' now frenzied chanting. Overcome by its own momentum, the group turns on Simon as if he were the beast and kills him. The rain increases and the boys back off, leaving Simon's body on the beach. That night, the tide carries his body away. The storm's wind fills the dead soldier's parachute and lifts him up and over the island and out to sea. This sight terrifies the boys, and they scatter, screaming.

Commentary

This chapter focuses on Simon and the fulfillment of his role as a visionary mystic. Awakening from his faint, he asks again out loud the question he put to the assembly in the previous chapter: "What else is there to do?" He must face whatever is on the mountain. That confrontation seems to have aged him: he walks with the difficulty of an old man, as if bowed down by "the infinite cynicism of adult life" that he saw in the pig's eyes.

Simon doesn't seem to fear the beast sighted on the

mountain. Given the doubts he had in Chapter 6 about this supposed beast and having had a visitation from the true beast, the Lord of the Flies, Simon has moved past fear into another arena of emotion. Approaching the frightful figure on the mountain, he sees it sit up and look at him; in response "He hid his face" as if in shame over the boys' misconceptions about its menace. Then he frees the lines of the soldier's parachute from the rocks, enabling the dead soldier to fly off during the storm, which it does upon Simon's death.

In a way, the soldier is actually working as an agent of the true beast, bringing out the worst in the boys. They do not band together to overcome this fearful situation but allow their own worst impulses to surface and dominate, fragmenting into opposing groups and killing one of their own in a frenzy of fear and savagery. Considering that his arrival on the island was brought about by a battle of the ongoing war, the soldier truly was an emissary of the beast, the savagery that lurks in humanity.

Of the boys, only Simon took the presence of an unidentified creature on the mountain as a sign to be explored or a symbol to be considered, rather than as an indication of an animal-beast's presence. By courageously seeking out the figure on the mountain, Simon fulfills his destiny of revelation. Having confronted both the Lord of the Flies (the sow's head on a stick) and the so-called beast (the soldier's corpse), Simon understands the nature of the evil on the island. He doesn't get to share his revelation with the other boys because they are not ready to accept or understand it. They are living out the true beast's actions while they think of themselves as playacting the roles of painted savages, which is Jack's idea of fun—and the true beast's as well.

When the tide carries off Simon's body, covered in the jellyfish-like phosphorescent creatures that come in with the tide, Golding shifts the focus from Simon's body's movements to the much larger progressions of the sun, moon, and earth because Simon represents a knowledge as fundamental as the elements. Golding uses the weather to symbolize a kind of universal assessment of the actions that have taken place in the novel and as a way to underscore the tension between and extreme reactions of the boys. He opens the chapter with an ominous description of the odd weather over the island: "the air was ready to explode ... a brassy glare had taken the place of clear daylight." Then the downpour starts in earnest immediately after Simon's death, as though the weather were responding to the boys' actions. The use of the weather as a dramatic technique is an ancient and effective tool.

The desire for drama underlies the other boys' desertion, Ralph tells Piggy. He assesses accurately their basic motivation not as a wish to do evil but for the drama and game of Jack's primal theater. They are also drawn in by the enticement of meat and the protection that Jack seems to provide as a fearless, aggressive hunter. Jack certainly is taken with the drama of it, forcing the other boys to perform the bizarrely formal rituals. This role is no game for him though; by the time Ralph and Piggy reach the party, Jack has clearly gone power-mad. Evoking images of Kurtz from Joseph Conrad's Heart of Darkness, Jack sits on a large log, "painted and garlanded ... like an idol." Around him are arranged piles of food and drink as though they are offerings to him.

Just as Jack and the dead soldier seemed to have in common a desire to keep the fire from being lit, they now have in common a link with apes. Ralph saw the dead soldier as "something like a great ape" hunched over—a connection between the animality of the apes from which humans are descended and the animality still present in humankind today. Now as Jack sits in front of his tribe and considers the new arrivals, Ralph and Piggy, "Power ... chattered in his ear like an ape." The devil on his shoulder is his own animality, looking to master other creatures.

He already has achieved mastery of those of his tribe: When he commands that someone bring him a drink, someone does. They also address him as "Chief," a formality not demanded by Ralph. Jack expects subservience from his tribe, which they accept as though he can protect them through strength of personality alone. Ralph is unable to enforce his rules or his authority because he lacks Jack's punitive nature and relies instead on the boys' sense of honour in following through on their promises. When the rain starts, Jack orders the boys to dance in the rain, playing out the same mock hunt in which Robert was hurt. The dance gives order to the boys' panicked energy during the downpour and acts as a defiance of the elements, a sort of rain dance in reverse. Even Ralph and Piggy decide not to run immediately for the shelters but instead join in on the fringes. In this situation, they find themselves seeking a more abstract kind of shelter instead in "this demented but partly secure society" wherein "the brown backs of the fence ... hemmed in the terror and made it governable."

The sense of protection in the repetitive chanting and the circular movements of the dance provides the boys with another strong motivation for staying with Jack, a motivation Ralph hadn't considered when he commented to Piggy that the biguns joined Jack to play like savages with the hunting and face paint. Jack has tapped into the power of repetitive rituals, where the person performing the ritual feels "as though repetition would achieve safety of itself" despite the circumstances. Repetitive rituals are present in nearly every cohesive group, from churchgoers performing the same prayers and rites every Sunday to political parties chanting their slogans to military personnel following their prescribed daily routines. Repetition provides comfort for the group because all the individual members know what is expected of them within the context of the ritual and, by extension, within the group.

Being part of Jack's tribe, with its attendant rituals and subservience, allows the boys to feel as though they are relieved of all responsibility for what happens during their ritual dance. While some of the boys, such as Ralph, felt uneasy with the beating Robert received in Chapter 7, other boys simply enjoyed the "game" and thought of ways to refine it, such as Maurice suggesting they add drums. Yet they all participated, drawn in by their animal selves. In this chapter, the same effect is aggravated by the intensity of the thunder and the darkness.

Golding describes the mob murder scene: "There were no words, and no movements but the tearing of teeth and claws." Again savagery is connected with a lack of verbal communication; language is, of course, one of humankind's greatest inventions and that which separates humanity most dramatically from the lower forms of creatures. Further, Golding uses the phrase "teeth and claws" (representing the primitive use of physical attributes or features as weapons) instead of spears (the use of tools as weapons). The phrase also recalls Samneric's fanciful description of the beast as having teeth and claws (although they neither felt nor saw them in reality). In this instance, the true beast—evil —acts through the frenzied mob; those imagined teeth and claws bare themselves for real. Once the frenzy dies down, however, the boys back off their prey and are astonished to see "how small a beast it was." The truth of what they have done begins filtering in. Their responses to the act they have committed are explored in Chapter 10.

Glossary

- Derision contempt or ridicule.
- Phosphorescence a continuing luminescence without noticeable heat

Chapter 10

Summary

The next morning, Ralph finds that only Piggy, Samneric, and some littluns remain in his camp. Brooding over the previous night's events, he points out to Piggy that they murdered Simon. Piggy objects to the use of the term "murder" and doesn't want Samneric to know that he and Ralph were at least somewhat involved in the deadly dance. Samneric don't want to admit their own involvement, either.

Jack begins acting ever more like a cruel dictator to his own tribe members, having one of the boys tied up and beaten for angering him. He plans a raid on Ralph's camp to get fire for another pig roast and tries to convince his uneasy followers that they had beaten but not killed the beast the previous night. The beast had come to them in disguise, he asserts, in utter denial that they had killed one of their former group.

Back at Ralph's camp, the boys decide to let the fire die for the night rather than collect more wood in the dark. Because Jack and his raiders can't steal burning branches, they attack Ralph's group and steal Piggy's glasses.

Commentary

This chapter reveals the boys' responses to their actions of the night before, when they beat Simon to death in a tribal frenzy. Ralph is the only character who names the deed as murder and has a realistic, unvarnished view of his participation. Back at the platform, he takes a seat in front of the chief's log rather than on it and contemplates the horror of what they've done. He feels both loathing and excitement over the kill he witnessed, as Jack experienced the first time he killed a pig. He shudders at Piggy's touch on his shoulder; humanity has let him down. Putting the pieces together, he recalls the parachuted figure drifting off the night before and Simon's shouting about a dead man on the mountain, musing that the life-like figure they saw on the mountaintop might have been the dead paratrooper rather than an actual animal-beast. Getting to the heart of the matter, he says, "I'm frightened. Of us."

Although he initially owns up to his active role in the fatal dance, as a defence mechanism, Ralph willingly takes the opportunity Piggy gives him to deny full participation, entering into a sort of functional denial. When Piggy reminds Ralph that he himself remained on the outside of the circle, Ralph tries to amend his position as well, now claiming that he, too, was on the outside of the circle and so could not have done as much damage as the boys in the inner ring.

Piggy is in full-fledged denial of anyone's responsibility, unable to process the death without blaming Simon for his seemingly odd behaviour. Ever the pragmatist, Piggy complains, "What good're you doing talking like that?" when Ralph brings up the highly charged issue of Simon's death at their hands. True, his involvement is somewhat limited; as Ralph mentions, Piggy stayed on the outside of the circle. Golding doesn't provide a reason as to why Piggy remained on the outside, whether his position was due to his physical inability to make his way into the inner circle or whether he simply wasn't able to tap into the animality of the more physically abled boys or both. Golding, however, does include Piggy in the damning description of the boys as they sit on the platform that morning, with the sun shining on their "befouled bodies."

Piggy tries to keep life scientific and intellectual, despite the previous night's emotionally charged incident, "searching for a formula" to explain the death. He asserts that the assault on Simon was justifiable because Simon asked for it by inexplicably crawling out of the forest into the ring. Piggy, of course, is unaware that Simon had to crawl because his visionary confrontation with the true beast had so weakened him. In responding to the death, Jack takes an entirely different direction from logic or common sense, in direct conflict with the actual events they had all witnessed. Perhaps acting out of some guilt he is unable to acknowledge, Jack becomes paranoid, posting guards at the entrance to the castle rock area in case any of Ralph's tribe tries to enter. One of the boys questions this concern and Jack replies, "They'll try to spoil things we do." Ironically, he is also taking the part of the true beast, the Lord of the Flies, who told Simon not to try and stop the "fun" that was going to take place on the island.

The entrance guards serve another purpose as well—to protect the tribe from the beast. Jack tells his tribe that they did not, in fact, kill the beast, just beat it as it came in disguise. Therefore, they still need to appease it and be on the alert. He prescribes their reality now as he had dictated their dreams and emotions in the previous chapter.

This technique for truth control is standard in tyrannical regimes. Because none of the boys want to admit their participation in the "obscene" dance, they allow Jack to dictate their reality. They find comfort in his overbearing authority, as if he can protect them from their indefinable fears through strength of his personality alone. More concretely, Jack offers them the protection of weaponry and an instinct for warfare. When Roger sees the boulder that stands ready to crush interlopers at the entrance to Castle Rock, he deems Jack "a proper chief" because he's got weaponry, the makings of war.

For a sadist like Roger, joining the tribe offers him the chance to unleash his cruelty amidst Jack's reign of "irresponsible authority." All his life, Roger has been conditioned to leash or mask his impulses, as evidenced by his inability to actually hit Henry with the stones in Chapter 4. Hearing that Jack has had Wilfred arbitrarily bound and left to wait hours for punishment strikes a responsive chord in Roger. By the end of the next chapter, he carves out a distinct niche in the tribe as the hangman, the torturer who plays a key role in all dictatorships.

Jack doesn't consider himself "a chief ... in truth" until he accomplishes the theft of Piggy's glasses. In this way, Jack symbolizes a twisted Prometheus, stealing fire from the humans to profit the savages as opposed to stealing from the gods to benefit humans. Note that originally he and his group of choirboys were to play the role of Prometheus in maintaining the fire, maintaining a visual plea to civilization for rescue and quick return home.

Ralph's connection with his civilized self fades even more rapidly now, although he fights to maintain it and is baffled by the "curtain" that seems to fall when he tries to stress the importance of the fire. When the twins question the value of keeping the fire lit, Ralph "tried indignantly to remember. There was something good about a fire." Piggy, of course, instantly knows what this good is, as his connection to civilization remains very strong because it offers him protection that is lacking on the island.

Piggy is so intent on preserving some remnant of civilization on the island that he not only remains loyal to Ralph but to the concept of civilized discourse represented by the conch. He assumes, improbably enough, that Jack's raiders have attacked them to get the conch. Just as he takes for granted that Ralph has not lost his focus on rescue and home, he figures that Jack still places a value on what the conch represents when obviously Jack has abandoned all that, preferring the life of savagery. Jack's leadership is based on fear; he has abandoned the conch for the dance.

The loss of his glasses to the savages literally renders Piggy more helpless and ineffectual and symbolically deprives Ralph of his intellectual counselor. The alert reader understands that Piggy will be the next victim.

Glossary

- Gesticulate to make or use gestures, esp. with the hands and arms, as in adding nuances or force to one's speech, or as a substitute for speech.
- Torrid so hot as to be parching or oppressive; scorching.
- Reds [Slang] Communists.
- Lamp standard lamppost.
- Barmy [Brit. Slang] crazy.
- Round the bend [Brit. Informal] crazy; insane.
- Bomb happy [Slang, Chiefly Brit.] crazy; insane.
- Crackers [Slang, Chiefly Brit.] crazy; insane.
- Pills [Vulgar Brit Slang] the testicles.
- Bowstave here, slightly curved arc like that of a bow.

Chapter 11

Summary

Ralph calls an assembly at Piggy's urging, wherein they decide the four remaining biguns will ask Jack's tribe for the glasses back, reminding them of a signal fire's importance. Samneric express a real fear of approaching the other boys who have now become complete savages.

Jack's tribe is hostile to Ralph's little group; Roger throws stones at the twins to scare them. Jack emerges from the forest where he had been hunting and tells Ralph to go back to his end of the island. When Ralph calls him a thief for stealing Piggy's glasses, they fence briefly with their spears before Piggy reminds Ralph to focus on their agenda.

The savages laugh derisively at Ralph's impassioned speech about the necessity of a signal fire. Then Jack orders his tribe to grab Samneric and tie them up, prompting a fistfight between himself and Ralph. Again, Piggy interrupts and, holding the conch, attempts a speech as well. While Piggy admonishes the boys for becoming savages, Roger releases a huge boulder in Piggy's direction, knocking him off the cliff to his death on the rocks below. A large wave quickly carries off his body.

Jack screams in victory at Ralph and then throws his spear at him. The spear wounds Ralph but bounces off, and Ralph flees for his life. Samneric remain tied up in the hands of the savages, menaced by Jack and soon to be tortured by Roger.

Commentary

As the last three biguns remaining with Ralph, they have a great stake in quickly developing some solutions to Piggy's virtual blindness and the loss of a signal fire, as well as protecting themselves from Jack's deadly tribe. Piggy insists that Ralph call an assembly to discuss the matter. Although blowing the conch to summon only themselves seems rather ridiculous, Piggy asserts that "It's the only thing we got." Assemblies regulated by the conch still bring him comfort despite their lack of effectiveness.

In fact, the conch is the only tool of authority or action left to them, but it's an ineffectual one, given the savages' loss of regard for it. When Ralph blows the conch at Castle Rock, for example, the savages greet him with silence and a stone thrown at Sam by Roger. The conch symbolizes not only the power to speak during assembly but also the power of speech itself, an ability that separates humans from animals. In a way, the savages cause Ralph to lose his power of speech, when he gives up his address on the importance of rescue because he is "defeated by the silence and the painted anonymity." With the exceptions of Jack's commands, the savages' reactions to Ralph's and Piggy's speeches are all non-verbal: jeering, laughing, booing, and a general "clamor." Following Roger's impulsive assassination of Piggy, "the silence was complete" as Piggy provided the last bastion of human intellect and reason on the island. Even up to the moment of his death, Piggy's perspective doesn't shift in response to the reality of their situation. At their little assembly, he demands action, still relying on Ralph to get things done despite the obvious disregard for his authority shown by all of Jack's tribe. Piggy cannot think as the others think or value what they value. Because his eminently sensible approach to life is modeled on the attitudes and rules of the authoritative adult world, he thinks everyone should share his values and attitudes as a matter of course.

Speaking of the deaths of Simon and the littlun with the birthmark who had first brought up the beast as a concern, he asks "What's grownups goin' to think?" as if he is not so much mourning the boys' deaths as he is mourning the loss of values, ethics, discipline, and decorum that caused those deaths. Claiming that Jack has "got to" return his glasses because "what's right's right," he reveals that he holds a certain code of ethics to be universal and non-negotiable, as fundamental as fire. In reality ethics originate from a particular society's values and expectations; Jack's subculture has radically different ethics from Ralph's.

Samneric fully appreciate this difference; their change in perspective is evident at the assembly. In Chapter 6, they speak mockingly of a schoolmaster nicknamed Old Waxy as if his waxing anger was nothing to fear. Now they fear for their lives, saying that if Jack "gets waxy we've had it." Even more devastating to their morale is Ralph's oddly timed outburst of "smoke! We've got to have smoke." From his delivery, they realise Ralph can't remember why they need smoke but is just mouthing the words as a sort of desperate plea for clarity. Piggy, too, grasps that Ralph has forgotten the purpose of smoke; his reminder of smoke's purpose makes Ralph defensive. Ralph's denial of his fallibility causes them to view him as fallible. They look at him as though "seeing him for the first time": a boy trying to accomplish what an adult would have difficulty achieving in these circumstances—reasoning with a pack of killers.

Roger, the sadist, relishes the role of a killer. In Chapter 4, Roger is restrained from throwing stones directly at other boys by the social discipline internalized during his former life. When he makes Sam nearly lose his footing with a well-placed stone throw, Roger experiences viscerally the mastery he can now wield over others, and the reader recognizes a dramatic change. Like Samneric, Roger's perspective has changed with the power shift on the island. From his point of view on top of Castle Rock, "Ralph was a shock of hair and Piggy a bag of fat"; they are not humans or other boys to him. Mentally dehumanizing those not in his group frees Roger from the restraints of decency, an effect he feels as "a sense of delirious abandonment" when he releases the rock that kills Piggy.

Perceiving other humans as less than human is the basis of an infinite number of prejudices and bigotry as well as the moral underpinning of genocide. Jack's boys enthusiastically bind Samneric because they sense Samneric's "otherness"; that otherness allows the savages to justify their cruelty against their own kind. Such a mental adjustment is also necessary for soldiers to make in order to justify killing their enemies who are part of the family of humanity, an adjustment made even by the very civil and polite naval officer who ultimately rescues the boys. All the boys made that adjustment themselves when they chose to perceive Simon as the beast rather than as one of their own.

Although all the boys were guilty in Simon's death, the other savages perceive Roger differently after Piggy's death. Because he calmly and single-handedly kills someone, he is marked as a hangman, one who "wields a nameless authority." Just as Ralph has an instinct for diplomacy and leadership, Roger has an instinct for torture. Without the "protection of parents and school and policeman and the law" which surrounded Henry in Chapter 4 and forced Roger to miss when he threw stones, Roger is free within Jack's primitive subculture to make deadly contact.

Ralph seeks to remind the savages of those very constraints, to summon the conditioning voices of civilization that always warned them to play nice and share with others. At the assembly, he suggests that his group present an image of their former, civilized selves when approaching the savages. He wants to differentiate his group from Jack's tribe, as if to remind them of what they've lost or tantalize them with what they could have if rescue is achieved. In contrast, Samneric want to put on paint, hoping for mercy through assimilation. They fear that reminding Jack of the constraints he's now free of will only aggravate his abuse of power. "They'll be painted! You know how it is." Sadly, the twins turn out to be correct about the antagonizing effect of "otherness." When Jack orders his boys to bind the twins, Samneric "protested out of the heart of civilization" with language that marks them as outsiders in this group, which has left behind such civilized verbal niceties as "Oh, I say!"

Seeing the twins bound, Ralph's language gets to the heart of the matter quickly. He shouts at Jack, calling him "a beast and a swine and a bloody, bloody thief!" This emotional accusation is in fact truthful. Jack is living out the beast's urges, the beast that spoke to Simon in the guise of a swine head. Jack stole not only Piggy's glasses, but also hope, rescue, Simon's life, Ralph's authority, and the vestiges of civilization from their small island culture. Ralph's use of "bloody" works not only as an expletive but also as an accurate adjective, considering the deaths Jack has caused by fostering an environment of enmity coupled with ferocity.

Initially, Jack and Ralph feel some reluctance to engage fully in combat. When Ralph calls him a thief, Jack rushes at Ralph threateningly with his spear, but they each wield their spears more like sabers, unwilling to use the "the lethal points." They verbally square off, daring each other to come fight but remaining out of each other's reach. Up to this point, none of the boys have fought to the death one on one. Simon's death occurred in the midst of a group frenzy. Even Roger does not engage in hand-to-hand combat but acts more as a physically removed assassin. Until Jack acts after Piggy's death and flings his spear dead-on at Ralph, he is no doubt at some level reluctant to kill another boy for the same reason he couldn't kill the first piglet he encountered in Chapter 1: "because of the enormity of the knife descending and cutting into living flesh."

In addition, Ralph and Jack are connected through a love/ hate relationship that neither one of them understands, a link Ralph thinks of as "an indefinable connection" in Chapter 12. They began on the first day with the glamour of a new friendship; "They were lifted up: were friends." Golding's use of the phrase "lifted up" to describe their friendship implies that a partnership between the humane and the bestial components of humanity can result in great things.

Yet the two forces must remain in balance to produce positive effects. The conflict on this island begins with Jack attempting to dominate the group rather than work with Ralph to benefit it. For his part, Ralph remains so focused on promoting a sense of order that he overlooks the boys' desire for food more substantial than fruit. Because Ralph so strongly identifies with the civilized part of himself, he cannot understand how Jack can live so far within his animal side. Once Jack makes an attempt on Ralph's life, however, appreciation for each other's perspectives is rendered moot as Ralph becomes re-classified as prey rather than as another human being.

Evil has triumphed: Spirituality, creativity, and religion went with the demise of Simon; intellect and reason die with Piggy; and rules, authority, and tradition are destroyed with the conch.

Glossary

- Myopia nearsightedness.
- Propititate win or regain the good will of; appease or conciliate.
- Pinnacles pointed formations; peaks, as at the tops of mountains.
- Pinch [Slang] to steal.
- Truculent fierce; cruel; savage; ferocious.
- Talisman anything thought to have magic power; a charm.

Chapter 12

Summary

While the tribe feasts inside Castle Rock, Ralph makes his way back to the platform. Once there, he is reluctant to spend the night alone in the shelter and decides to return to Jack's end of the island to try reasoning with them again. On the way, he encounters the pig's skull that had spoken to Simon. Finding it eerily life-like and knowing, he knocks it to the ground and takes the stake as a weapon.

Back at Castle Rock, he sees that Samneric are on watch, having been forced to join the tribe. He approaches them cautiously, hoping to win back their loyalty. They tell him of the manhunt planned for the next day and give him some meat. Someone from the tribe hears them talking to Ralph and punishes them.

Ralph finds a place to sleep for the night. The next morning, his hiding place, a dense thicket, is betrayed by Samneric. The tribe is unsuccessful at reaching him in the thicket, so they flush him out by rolling boulders into it and setting it on fire. Once Ralph is on the run, the tribe follows him, communicating with each other with an ululating cry.

Ralph finds another impenetrable thicket to hide in but is discovered there as well. Now the fire has spread across the island so that he has to outrun the savages and the fire. He makes it to the beach and falls at the feet of a newly arrived British naval officer, whose ship had been attracted by the smoke from the huge fire. The officer confirms that his ship will take them off the island. Ralph breaks into sobs, weeping for all he has lost.

Commentary

Watching the savages retreat, Ralph tries to identify them as individuals and guesses one to be Bill. Then he realizes that, in fact, "this was not Bill" and he's right: Once divorced from his previously civilized self in appearance, behaviour, and values, the individual who was Bill is gone. In the previous chapter, after Jack throws a spear with deadly intention at

Ralph, Golding stops using Jack's name and refers to him as "the chief." The boy named Jack has been totally replaced with a primal entity, the personification of the beast's lust for power and the rejection of the civilizing forces represented by Ralph.

Even after the attack, Ralph so craves human companionship—the devil he knows—that he returns to Castle Rock to reason with Jack's tribe again on the next day, relying on their "daylight sanity." "Daylight sanity" is another term for common sense; Piggy tells Ralph in Chapter 8 that lack of common sense is the source of all the trouble on the island. At the time, Piggy referred to practicality, or a sound judgement of the actions they would need to take to attract a rescue ship and co-exist with some amount of civility.

Common sense could also be understood, however, as communal sentiment, a shared sensibility of what's important and what's allowed. Ralph "knew he was an outcast. 'Cos I had some sense,'" he tells himself—not just common sense but a sense of his identity as a civilized person, a sense of the particular morality that had governed the boys' culture back home. When Jack threw the spear at Ralph, Jack made him an outcast, disallowing his easy assimilation into the group even if he had wanted to forsake rescue in favour of hunting. When Ralph tries to reason with the newly tribal twins and gain an understanding of Jack's hatred of him, Eric says "Never mind what's sense. That's gone." Jack's tribe lacks sense in terms of logically justifiable attitudes and behaviors.

In response to his desperate situation, bereft of any companion and the conch as well, Ralph reverts to a childish state. He "whimpered and yawned like a littlun" when facing the coming night with its attendant fears. Later, as he is hunted, he reverts back not in time but in character to his primal self, squatting in a thicket, baring his teeth, and snarling. Becoming the prey brings out the animal survival instincts coupled with innate human intellect in him: He seeks a "lair" in which to spend the night and thinks ahead to his hiding place the next day. He prepares himself to poke whoever discovers him with his spear so that the manhunter "would be stuck, squealing like a pig." Acting purely out of the fundamental drive for survival, he attacks two savages who stand between him and escape, and wounds a third from his hiding place. The members of Jack's tribe have ceased to be human for him; he thinks of them as "those striped and inimical creatures." Hunting has become their identity rather than their activity. In contrast, Ralph still thinks sensibly even when on the run: when the forest fire burns the fruit trees, he curses the tribe for failing to think ahead when they set the fire: "Fools! ... what would they eat tomorrow?"

During his flight, Ralph longs for Piggy's counsel, wishing for the solemnity of the assemblies made dignified by the conch rather than having to make life or death decisions while on the run for his life. "If only one had time to think!" he laments. Civilization makes for plenty of time to think, providing institutions like universities where the scholars can devote themselves to mental activities. Such protection allows the abstract arts such as philosophy and theoretical work in the arts and sciences to flourish; in such a protected environment, a fragile boy like Simon could have learned to express fully and accurately his intuitive understanding of humanity's dark side. Note that Simon's prophecy comes back to Ralph in a flash during the hunt. In a moment of great desperation, cornered in his hiding place by a savage and having just realized the purpose of a stick sharpened at both ends, the phrase "You'll get back" surfaces, as if Simon's spirit haunts the island.

If Simon's ghost is present, it is there to comfort Ralph and reach out to him with its knowledge, unlike the Lord of the Flies. When Ralph encounters the Lord of the Flies, he finds a "skull that gleamed as white as ever the conch had done." This description symbolizes the universal and infinite struggle between good and evil. The skull is vested with the knowledge that was revealed to Simon: Evil is present in us all, and we must struggle not to allow it to dominate us.

Knocking the skull to the ground and breaking it into pieces is a small victory over the beast for Ralph. More to the point, he takes the stake on which the head rested so that he has his own stick sharpened at both ends. Like a blade that cuts both ways, he'll use the savage's stick to defend himself from them. Preoccupied with keeping on the move, he doesn't realise until late in the hunt that he is himself carrying a stick sharpened on both ends. At this point he realizes that his head is meant to become the ultimate offering to the beast, the beast's greatest victory yet on the island.

The officer of the gunboat that Ralph encounters simultaneously represents Ralph's original moral naiveté and Jack's propensity toward evil and destruction. As Ralph encounters the officer, he sees not a face but all the markings of the officer's "tribe": the cap with the crown, anchor and gold leaves, the uniform with epaulettes and buttons, and the revolver. The decorative elements of his uniform symbolize his civilized war paint. From the officer's point of view, Ralph is hardly the prey of a deadly tribe but a boy who "needed a bath, a haircut, a nose-wipe, and a good deal of ointment." When he sees Jack's tribe wearing war paint and carrying spears, he assesses the situation as "Fun and games." Although he doesn't recognize it or understand his complicity in his own "fun and games," the naval officer has correctly identified the hunt: It's the sort of fun the Lord of the Flies assured Simon would take place on the island; the type of fun that, even at the time of the boys' rescue, is taking place on a larger scale with the war.

The officer echoes a sentiment expressed by Jack in Chapter 2 ("we're not savages. We're English ... So we've got to do the right things"). Learning of the two deaths, the officer comments "I should have thought that a pack of British boys ... would have ... put up a better show than that." Both Jack and the officer are equally ignorant of the truth of the matter: Like all of humanity, these boys have and act on impulses that are at best uncivil and at worst deadly. In the novel, Golding uses events and mores associated with the British (his own culture), but his theme is universal. Although one could limit the interpretation to British imperialism (bestial aspects of British colonialism contrast sharply with the supremely polite British identity, for example), to do so would be to deny the larger truth: That all people—and therefore all societies—

possess and display, to varying degrees, these deadly impulses.

Glossary

- Pax peace, here meant as a call for a truce.
- Acrid sharp, bitter, stinging, or irritating to the taste or smell.
- Inimical hostile; unfriendly.
- Gibber to speak or utter rapidly and incoherently; chatter unintelligibly.
- Essay to try; attempt.
- antiphonal sung or chanted in alternation.
- Ululate to howl, hoot, or wail.
- Cordon a line or circle, as of soldiers or ships, stationed around an area to guard it.
- Diddle [Informal] to move back and forth jerkily or rapidly; juggle.
- Mold here, loose, soft, easily worked soil.
- White drill a coarse linen or cotton cloth with a diagonal weave, used for work clothes, uniforms, etc.
- Epaulette shoulder ornament as for military uniforms.
- Cutter a boat carried, esp. formerly, aboard large ships to transport personnel or supplies.
- Rating an enlisted man in the Navy.
- Stern sheets the space at the stern of an open boat

Critical Essays

The Very Unhappy Ending of Lord of the Flies

William Golding's Lord of the Flies indeed has a happy ending in the literal sense. The boys are rescued as their foolish cruelty reaches its apex by the loving, caring, and matured outside world. On the other hand, by whom and what are the boys rescued? Symbolically, the "happy ending" is exactly the opposite. Far from sacrificing artistic excellence, Golding's ending confirms the author's powerful symbolism.

Readers know ample about the boys society and where it heads long before the "rescue." Ralph will be killed and to remain a perpetual gift to the "beastie." The boys' xenophobic view of the beastie is ironically unfounded because the beastie emerges from within the boys: they themselves are the dangerous and scary monsters for all to fear, and they kill the first person to suggest so (Simon). Although the parachutist may symbolize civilization's archetypical fall, he is only a "beastie" insofar as civilization is to be feared. (The boys' fear of the beastie may, then, be well-founded, but only symbolically). As action progresses, readers see no signs of a veer from the boys' self-destructive course. Shortly before the boys' "rescue," they expect the boys to perish either from the fire (which actually ends up saving Ralph), a tragedy of the commons, or internal war. Golding could either have extended the book to its predicted bloody end, or he could have changed course. The surprise course of action becomes Golding's central theme.

Golding's theme is not just the obvious evils of the boys' society; it includes the notion that the boys are a microcosm of society. While readers may be able to ascertain his theme immediately prior to the ending, the connection to the real world is weak and underdeveloped. Critics who claim that something was sacrificed for the sake of a "happy ending" fail to understand Golding's thesis: the boys are allegorical of society as a whole, yet are "rescued" by that very society which they symbolize. In a sense, the boys swap one war for another. Instead of being at war with other children, they re-join a society which is at war lead by adults who are supposedly more mature than the boys. Like the island, the world is an isolated entity, but no one can rescue the world. Golding's boys are symbolic of the world, but he cannot juxtapose the world and the boys without the rescue.

Moreover, the "rescue" provides the logical continuation of Golding's loss of innocence theme by cementing the parallels between the boys and society. The boys' killing of a mother sow was, at least, shocking, but similar events occurred in Golding's time: Hitler's Holocaust and blitz of Austria, Czechoslovakia, and Poland; the Japanese Rape of Nanjing and "Hidden Holocaust;" and Britain's brutal imperialistic exploits.

The loss of innocence represented by the sow's murder leads to brutal killings, much like Hitler's anti-Semitism lead to the brutal killing of nations. The military "rescue" brings the symbolism full circle by fusing the symbolism. The boys may be rescued, but no one can rescue the earth should savagery go out of control as on the island.

Another parallel is rather inverse. The boys are on a paradise island, but they dirty themselves as they become more vicious. The officer who rescues the boys, however, has a clean white uniform complete with medals and epaulets. As the boys become dirty, they become savage, but as adults become savage, they are awarded cleaner uniforms. Golding again asserts that adult society is little more than a clean, orderly-appearing version of the boys' savage island.

Golding's ending, then, is not an escape, but the capstone of his allegory. He welds the boys' symbolism to that of the outside world. He presents an ironic ending which beseeches readers to recognize their own helpless quagmire of 'clean' savagery. Golding does not have a "happy ending" for the sake of either happiness or an ending, but for the purposes of powerful symbolism.

Golding's conclusion serves a final purpose. Golding creates dramatic irony with the officer's blunt ignorance of the boys' savagery. Perhaps he is at a loss for words, but the officer treats the boys as if they were playing a backyard game. "Jolly good show, like Coral Island," he remarks, followed by the inquiry, "You're all British, aren't you?". The officer thinks that the boys have formed an enlightened, orderly society like in the novel Coral Island, but he fails to realise that even the British, "the best at everything," can fall into the trap of brutish war. The officer shreds readers' stereotypes of themselves as superior to war because he shows that war is a virus which can infect everyone.

In short, Golding's ending is as symbolic as it is unhappy. The ironic rescue transcends the remote island to affect readers, especially the British, to recognize their potential for evil. The naval officer points to how far the boys have fallen and why their "rescue" wasn't really so happy.

True Portrayal of Children in Lord of the Flies

In the novel The Lord of the Flies, by William Golding, one can see how children react to certain situations. Children, when given the opportunity, would choose to play and have fun rather than to do boring, hard work. Also, when children have no other adults to look up to they turn to other children for leadership. Finally, children stray towards savagery when they are without adult authority.

Therefore, Golding succeeds in effectively portraying the interests and attitudes of young children in this novel. When children are given the opportunity, they would rather envelop themselves in pleasure and play than in the stresses of work. The boys show enmity towards building the shelters, even though this work is important, to engage in trivial activities. Af ter one of the shelters collapses while only Simon and Ralph are building it, Ralph clamours, "All day I've been working with Simon. No one else. They're off bathing or eating, or playing.". Ralph and Simon, though only children, are more mature a nd adult like and stray to work on the shelters, while the other children aimlessly run off and play. The other boys avidly choose to play, eat, etc. than to continue to work with Ralph which is very boring and uninteresting. The boys act typically of m ost children their age by being more interested in having fun than working. Secondly, all the boys leave Ralph's hard-working group to join Jack's group who just want to have fun.

The day after the death of Simon when Piggy ! and Ralph are bathing, Piggy points beyond the platform and says, "That's where they're gone. Jack's party. Just for some meat. And for hunting and for pretending to be a tribe and putting on war-paint.". Piggy realizes exactly why the boys have gone to Jack's, which would be for fun and excitement. The need to play and have fun in Jack's group, even though the boys risk the tribe's brutality and the chance of not being rescued, outweighs doing work with Ralph's group which increase their chance s of being rescued. Young children need to satisfy their amusement by playing games instead of doing work. In conclusion, children are more interested in playing and having fun than doing unexciting labour. When children are without adults to look to for leadership, they look for an adult-like person for leadership. At the beginning of the novel, when the boys first realise they are all alone, they turn to Ralph for leadership. After Ralph calls the first meeting, Golding writes, "There was a stillness about Ralph as he sat that marked him out: there was his size, and attractive appearance, and most obscurely, yet most powerfully, there was the conch. The being that had sat waiting for them.". The b oys are drawn to Ralph because of his physical characteristics and because he had blown the conch. The fact that there are no adults has caused the boys to be attracted to Ralph as a leader.

The physical characteristics of Ralph remind the boys of their parents or other adult authority figures they may have had in their old lives back home. There is also the conch that Ralph holds which may remind the boys of a school bell or a teacher's whistle. Finally, at the end of the novel, the boys turn to Jack to satisfy their need for some much-needed leadership. When the boys are feasting on the .neat of a freshly killed sow, the narrator says: Jack spoke 'Give me a drink.' Henry brought him a shell and he drank.

Power lay in the blown swell of his forearms; authority sat on his shoulder and chattered in his ear like an ape. 'All sit down.' The boys ranged themselves in rows on the grass before him. Jack now has full authority over the other boys. The boys look to Jack for his daunting leadership which intimidates them. Jack is very forceful and his ways most likely remind the boys of authoritative figures in their pastwho may have strapped, beaten or used other forms of violence when disciplining the children. Therefore, the children when left without adult authority figures turn to others who can replace that adult authority figure.

In addition to seeking adult-like authority figures, children lose their innocence and stray towards savagery when not around adult authority. When the boys have been on the island for a short time, they start to show more violence, but when they realiz e what they have done they become contrite, embarrassed by their actions. After Maurice destroys Percival's sandcastle and some sand gets in Percival's eye, the narrator writes: Percival began to whimper with an eyeful of sand and Maurice hurried away. In his other life Maurice had received chastisement for filling a younger eye with sand. Now, though there was no parent to let fall a heavy hand, Maurice still felt unease of wrongdoing.

Maurice has hurt Percival but feels bad about it because in his past life he would have been punished for it. Without adults, Maurice is turning towards barbarianism but has not been away from the order and discipline of his previous life to be considere d a savage. Children misbehave when not around adults because there is no one to discipline or punish them. Yet, for a brief time after the children have been away from adults, the children will feel remorseful. Also, after the boys have been absent fr om structured discipline, they become blatant savages and retain absolutely no innocence. When Piggy and Ralph visit Castle Rock to get back Piggy's glasses, Golding says: Roger, with a sense of delirious abandonment, leaned all his weight on the lever. The rock struck Piggy.

Piggy fell forty feet and landed on his back across that square across that square red rock in the sea. His head opened and stuff came out and turned red. Without apprehension, Roger performs the horrible and violent act of killing Piggy. Roger has now been without adults to discipline him for quite a long time and his actions have become more intensely brutal. The boys have been unpunished for so long that t they continually become more and more violent and thus, have made the final step to becoming all out savages.

Typically, children are reprimanded for their misbehavior and as they mature, what is right and what is wrong becomes embedded in their brains to the point where they almost never stray towards uncivilized behaviour. Clearly children can quickly forget what is right and what is wrong, especially when being away from adults for an extended period of time, often resulting in a loss of innocence. Lastly, at the end of the novel when around the naval officer arrives, the boys return to their old ways of being orderly and civilized. When Ralph is chased onto the beach by Jack's tribe and finds the naval officer, the narrator says, "A semi-circle of little boys, their bodies streaked with coloured clay, sharp sticks in their hands, were standing on the beach making no noise at all.".

The previously wild savages are now quiet little boys in an orderly semi-circle. With the arrival of an adult authority figure from the outside world, the boys are beginning to return to the decorum of their innocent, more childlike past. The boys are in a semi-circle instead of in a pack of savages, they are coloured with clay instead of gaudy war-paint, they are holding sticks instead of spears and they are absolutely as quiet as they would have been around adults in their previous lives. Children are usually more ordered, disciplined and civilized under adult supervision just a s the boys are the instant they see the naval officer. To summarize, when not around adult order, discipline and punishment, children become very much like savages and lose most of their innocence. In conclusion, in the novel The Lord of the Flies, Golding succeeds in showing the actions, decisions and thinking of young children.

Children would choose to play and have fun rather than work. When children need to look for leadership and there are no adults around to provide this, children look for another child who has adult-like qualities for leadership. Children are disobedient, violent and lose their innocence when there are no adults to supervise them. A child's life is a long and winding road in which they can be sidetracked quite easily.

Cruelty in The Lord of the Flies and Of Mice and Men

"Man's inhumanity to man makes countless thousands mourn."Man's inhumanity to man is clearly demonstrated in William Golding's work, The Lord of the Flies, as well as John Steinbeck's novel, Of Mice and Men.

In the novel Of Mice and Men by John Steinbeck there are many events in the plot of the story that occur that prove that when man is cruel to man, some peoples lives are negatively affected. One instance in where this is proven true is when the men on the ranch and Curley's wife are cruel and discriminative against Crooks causing him to be the one to mourn. An example of how the men are discriminative towards Crooks is that he is forced to live in a shack away from the bunkhouse and also Crooks says that "They play cards in there, but I can't play because I'm black. They say I stink" and "I ain't wanted in the bunkhouse."

An example of when Curley's Wife is critical towards Crooks is when she looks into his room to see what Lennie and Crooks are doing and then she states, shaking her head, that they left the weak ones behind. Also, she threatens to have Crooks hung because a black man should never talk to a white woman the way he just had. As a result of all of these discriminatory acts against him, Crooks feels unwanted and lonely because of his colour and placement on the farm. Also those examples are part of the theme of the novel, people need to accept and understand those different from themselves, which also helps to prove the interpretation of the quote. Another example in this novel that proves that when man is cruel to man, the lives of people are negatively affected is when Curley picks on and tries to hurt Lennie.

Curley chooses to fight Lennie because he thinks he won't fight back but because George gets angry and tells Lennie to fight back, he does. George being angry is not the only negative effect that Curley's teasing had on man, but also now Lennie is angry and in danger of getting in trouble and Curley himself gets hurt. The last example in the novel Of Mice and Men that proves this quote is when the men talk Candy into letting them kill his dog. They feel that the dog is old now and that they will only be helping the dog and themselves. This act contradicts the quote a little in that it is a humane act for the dog but it does leave Candy lonely and without a companion, causing him to mourn.

The other novel that helps to prove the interpretation of Robert Burn's quote to be correct is Lord of the Flies. In this novel there are many times when the characters are inhumane. Also the characterization of these characters helps to show the amount of cruelty in the story. One example in this story as to how the characters are inhumane and how this inhumanity to other humans causes people to mourn is when the boys are mean to Piggy and kill him. Throughout the story, Jack is the meanest of the boys to Piggy, whether it is not giving him food from the feast, just plain teasing him or stealing and breaking his glasses, he is being cruel and Piggy suffers because of this. And not only does Piggy suffer from this but some of the other boys do as well. For instance, Simon suffers because when Jack won't give Piggy his share of the meat, Simon feels obliged to give Simon some of his share, causing him not to have as much as he deserved. Also when Jack teases him, Ralph begins to feel bad for Piggy and guilty for teasing him in the beginning as well. And lastly, when Jack steals Piggy's glasses or causes them to break, the other boys are negatively affected because now they have nothing to use to light a fire. When the boys kill Piggy during the end of the novel, this is very inhumane, killing Piggy when all he was trying to do was being back order and rule to the island. And not only is Piggy affected but so is Ralph because now he has lost his best and one of his few friends. Another example in this novel that proves that a man's inhumanity to man causes many men to mourn is when the boys kill Simon. This act is inhumane because they make Simon suffer until his death and this causes many negative effects on other people. One of these effects is that now Simon is dead and he was the only one who knew the truth about the "beast" and how to try to conquer the beast. The second negative effect is that now there is no priest-like figure on the island and Ralph, Piggy and Samneric are feeling guilty and upset about being involved in the death of Simon.

The last example in this novel that helps to prove the interpretation of the quote to be true is when Jack and his followers' torture Samneric. This is not humane because they are physically hurting Samneric and causing them to betray Ralph. This inhumane act not only affects Samneric but it also affects Ralph and the entire island. Because of Samneric giving up Ralph's hiding place during the torturing, the boys light the island on fire to drive Ralph (who is now in danger) out of his hiding place. Ralph is being affected because the other boys are hunting him and the entire island is affected because the fire is killing all the plant and animal life on the island. Although in the end Ralph is saved so he is no longer in danger, him and the rest of the island and boys, in many other ways, were still negatively affected through inhumane acts.

As seen through the two novels, Robert Burn's quote is proven mostly correct. Where the quote states that "countless thousands mourn", I feel that this should really be replaced by the statement that "many people are negatively affected". This is because man's inhumanity to man sometimes cause people to mourn, but more often the people are just hurt by the inhumanity and not necessarily mourning. So, in conclusion, the inhumanity of one man to another causes a negative effect on themselves and on the lives of many other people as well.

Inherent Evil of Man Exposed in Lord of the Flies

The novel Lord of the Flies by William Golding used a group of British boys beached on a deserted island to illustrate the malicious nature in mankind. Lord of the Flies dealt with the changes the boys underwent as they gradually adapted to the freedom from their society. William Golding's basic philosophy that man was inherently evil was expressed in such instances as the death of Simon, the beast within the boys, and the way Ralph was fervently hunted.

Through the story Simon acted as the Christ Figure. The death of Simon symbolized the loss of religious reasoning. As the boys killed Simon they had let out their savage urges and acted in a cannibalistic manor. Even after the death of Simon Jack and his tribe did not feel any penitence to what they had done, killing to them had become second nature.The circle became a horseshoe. A thing was crawling out of the forest. It came darkly, uncertainly. The shrill screaming that rose before the beast was like a pain. The beast stumbled into the horseshoe."Kill the beast! Cut his throat! Spill his blood!".In this quote a figure had crawled out of the forest and the ring had opened to let it inside. Mistaken as the beast by the Jack's tribe, Simon was beaten to death. After the group disbanded for shelter from the storm. The storm subsided and the tides moved in and out, Simon's body was washed to sea. Here because of the storm, the darkness and fear the boys became hysterical. They acted savagely not knowing what they were doing. The boys did not take a second look to what their actions were. They had let their malicious urges control them. He cam-disguised. He may come again even though we gave him the head of our kill to eat. So watch; and be careful. Here Jack is warning his tribe about the beast. Not caring or taking any notice to what had taken place with Simon. Jack or his tribe does not feel any remorse for the murder they had committed, whether they realized that or not. To Jack and his tribe what they had done was a pretentious accomplishment. A death could go by their eyes blindly.

One example in the book referring to William Goldong's view to society was the beast. The beast which lied within the boys, represented the evil which dwelled inside humanity. William Golding believed that savagery was always in mankind, but need the proper situation tocome out and cause a transformation of even the most innocent of us. For the boys the fear of the unknown on the island caused the terror of the beast. That fear was allowed to grow because they could not fully accept the notion of a beast, nor could they let go of it. Their attempts to resolve their fears were too feeble to convince themselves. Soon the boys had whipped themselves into hysteria. He raised his arm in the air. There came a pause, a hatitus, the pig continued to scream and the creepers to jerk, and the blade continued to flash at the end of a bony arm. The pause was only enough for them to understand what an enormity the downward stroke would be. Then the piglet tore loose of the creepers and scurried into the undergrowth. They were left looking at each other and the place of terror. In this quote Jack was hesitant to kill the pig, and what other boy would not have been? This showed how when the boys had just landed on the island they could not let go of the rules society had taught them. "Look! We've killed a pig-we stole up on them -we got in a circle". Once the island's surroundings had taken it's toll on the boys Jack and the others before long had bloodlust. They had killed a pig and were proud of that. Jack and the other boys shortly carved the challenging hunt. The freedom of the island had allowed them to further develop the darker side of their personalities which had always been within them. Once the boys were accustomed to the hunt of pigs, they began craving a more challenging hunt. "Viciously, with full intention, he hurdled his spear at Ralph. The point tore the skin and flesh over Ralph's ribs, then sheared off and fell in the water". This signifies the transformation from civilized British boys to savages. The lose of civilization let them kill with no grief. Their emotions and feelings of remorse had been lost, but the island had other effects on the boys as well. The hunting of Ralph also symbolized the loss or religion.

"Roger sharpened a stick at both ends". The mysterious words of Samneric could be heard. For the newly formed savage tribe Ralph was a thrill to hunt. He had brains, wits, and cunning much more challenging than a pig. At the beginning of this new merciless tribe, Jack and the other boys had killed a sow. They had cut it's head of and stuck it on a stick. A stick sharpened at both ends. To the boys this was a scarifies to the beast. If the boys did not feel and believe they had to please the beast they would not have any reason to kill Ralph, for he was not a threat to them.

The islands surrounding had caused them not only to lose reasoning but religious beliefs as well. Now the boys hunted for Ralph. He was next scarifies to their new found god figure. Lord of the Flies was an exciting adventure into the nether region of the mind. Simon's demise, the beast within the boys, and the way Ralph was fervently hunted were all examples of William Golding's philosophy, that society was inherently evil. A well thought novel that depicted the evils of human nature. Lord of the Flies showed that the evil residing within everyone could be unleashed. It proved the dark side of human nature could be as vicious and as terrifying as the unknown it itself, and even the most innocent of us are vulnerable to it.

The Lord of the Flies: Biblical Allegory or Anti-Religious Critique?

One of the major points of debate between critics who have studied Lord of the Flies is the significance of the substantial number of allusions to Judeo-Christian mythology.

While many scholars have argued that these references qualify the novel as biblical allegory, others have suggested that the novel's allusions to the Old and New Testaments turn out to be ironic and thus criticize religion. A careful reading of Lord of the Flies should take into account not only the abundance of biblical images and themes in the text, but also the ways in which religion and religious themes are used.

In particular, the biblical account of good and evil is invoked-but the account in the novel is not quite the same. Take, for instance, the narrative of Eden. The early chapters of the novel, the island itself resembles the Garden of Eden from Genesis, with its picturesque scenery, abundant fruit, and idyllic weather. Accordingly, the boys are symbolically linked to Adam and Eve before the fall. Ralph's first act after the plane crash is to remove his clothes and bathe in the water, a gesture that recalls the nudity of the innocent Adam and Eve and the act of baptism, a Christian rite which, by some accounts, renews in the sinner a state of grace.

Naming also becomes important in Genesis, reflected in the novel as the boys give their names. Golding extends the Edenic allusion when he presents the contentment of island life as soon corrupted by fear, a moment that is first signified by reports of a creature the boys refer to as "snake-thing." The "snake-thing" recalls the presence of Satan in the Garden of Eden, who disguised himself as a serpent. But unlike Adam and Eve, the boys are mistaken about the creature, which is not a force external (like Satan) but a projection of the evil impulses that are innate within themselves and the human psyche. Still, it is the boys' failure to recognize the danger of the evil within themselves that propels them deeply into a state of savagery and violence.

They continue to externalize it as a beast (again "Lord of the Flies" and "the Beast" are used in religion to refer to Satan), but they become more and more irrational in their perception of it, and they end up developing alternative religious ideas about the Beast and what it wants and does. Although Satan in the Genesis account also has been read as a reflection of evil within human nature, readers usually consider Satan an external force. Original sin enters human nature because of Satan. Without a real Satan in the novel, however, Golding stresses the ways that this Eden is already fallen; for these boys, evil already is within them waiting to be discovered.

On the positive side, Simon's story is that of a prophet or of Jesus Christ. Simon is deeply spiritual, compassionate, non-violent, and in harmony with the natural world. Like many biblical prophets and like Jesus, he is ostracized and ridiculed as an "outsider" for what the others perceive as his "queer" or unorthodox behaviour. Critics also have noted that Simon's confrontation with The Lord of the Flies resembles Christ's conversation with the devil during his forty days in the wilderness as described in the New Testament gospels, and critics have noted parallels between Simon's murder and Christ's sacrifice on the cross. But Simon's revelation is more of a debunking and a turn to the secular, rather than a prophetic condemnation of evil or a call to the higher things. His revelation is that the beast does not exist but is just a dead human.

Two Faces of Man

William Golding was inspired by his experiences in the Royal Navy during World War II when he wrote Lord of the Flies. Golding has said this about his book

The theme is an attempt to trace the defeats of society back to the defects of human nature. The moral is that the shape of society must depend on the ethical nature of the individual and not on any political system however apparently logical or respectable. The whole book is symbolic in nature except the rescue in the end where adult life appears, dignified and capable, but in reality enmeshed in the same evil as the symbolic life of the children on the island.

In the novel he displays the two different personalities that mankind possesses, one civilized, the other primitive. Golding uses the setting, characters, and symbolism in Lord of the Flies to give the reader a detailed description of these two faces of man.

The story's setting is essential for the evolution of both

sides of man. When an airplane carrying a bunch of school boys crashes on an island, only the children survive. The island the children find themselves on is roughly boat-shaped. It is ironic that the children are stuck on an island shaped like the thing that could save them (a boat). Despite this irony, they are trapped. They are surrounded by ocean and no one knows where they are. The boys, isolated from society, must now create their own.

The children soon realise that there are, "No grownups!" This means that the boys must fend for themselves until they are rescued. There are no parents or adults to give the boys rules or punish them if they do wrong, so they must learn how to control and govern themselves. Their first attempt mimics the society that they have grown up with, that of a civilized democracy. A conch shell is used to call assemblies and decisions are voted on. The fire that they try to keep going on the top of the mountain is a symbol of their civilized society because it represents their hopes for rescue and a return to their ordinary lives.

Unfortunately, the children soon grow tired of this civilized life. They want to have fun and quickly lose interest in whatever job they are doing. Ralph states the problem when he says to the group of children, " ŒWe have lots of assemblies. Everybody enjoys speaking and being together. We decide things. But they don't get done. We were going to have water brought from the stream and left in those coconut shells under fresh leaves. So it was for a few days. Now there's no water. The shells are dry. People drink from the river.' " All of their resolutions soon degrade and fall apart. The society gives into its more primitive side and now only concerns itself with having fun. Hunting, which originally was only a practice of getting food so that they could survive until they were rescued becomes all important. All of the children's fears become condensed into a monster that they fear and awe. They make sacrifices to "the beast" to appease it and keep themselves safe. In the end, their grand society becomes no better than a bunch of savages in this lush island setting.

The island is abundant in resources, with lots of fresh

water and plentiful fruit ripe for the picking. "He walked with an accustomed tread through the acres of fruit trees, where the least energetic could find an easy if unsatisfying meal." Although rich with nature's splendor, the children are sorely lacking in the technology with which they have become accustomed to. They do not even have matches. If not for Piggy's "specs", they would not be able to create fire. This lack of technology both hinders their attempts to be civilized and hastens their progression towards savagery.

The story's characters serve as archetypes that display the struggle between man's quest for civilization and his urges to become primitive. The most important characters in the story are Ralph, Piggy, Simon, and Jack. Roger, Sam, and Eric, although not as important as the others, also serve to add colour to the story and lend to its progression towards savagery. Ralph is the story's protagonist. He is a natural leader because of his superior height, strength, and good looks. He is also the democratic man, the keeper of the civilized ways. He was chosen chief by a vote from his peers and strives to maintain order, to "rule through persuasion, with the consent of the governed." Ralph is "every man" and his body serves as the battle ground between reason and instinct.

Ralph loses this battle and eventually starts to regress to a primitive state. This is shown near the end of the story when he has trouble reasoning things through. "Then, at the moment of greatest passion and conviction, that curtain flapped in his head and he forgot what he had been driving at." Ralph's regression continues until he is no more than an animal, who uses its most basic instincts to escape the fire which threatens to burn the island down and the rest of the tribe who want to hunt him down . "He [Ralph] shot forward, burst the thicket, was in the open, screaming, snarling, bloody."

Piggy is fat, nearly blind, and asthmatic. He also embodies reason and intelligence. Piggy represents rationality, logic, science, and the ways of thinking that a civilized society depends on. He has a strong urge to distinguish and to order until reduced to a manageable system. He insists on collecting the names of all the stranded children, using the conch to call assemblies, and having meetings Piggy is the brains behind Ralph's leadership. Piggy is the first one who suggests using the conch Ralph found to assemble the others. He is the one who brings Ralph back to the topic at hand near the end of the novel when Ralph's reasoning starts to deteriorate under the constant pressure of trying to remain civilized. He assumes that civilized society is all powerful because it seems more reasonable for people to co-exist with rules and mutual respect, rather than obedience and terror. " ŒWhich is better- to have rules and agree, or to hunt and kill?' "

Simon is the Christ figure of the book and the voice of revelation. He consistently reveals a kindness that no one else seems to possess whether it be through his comforting of Ralph, .offering of food to Piggy, or getting fruits for the younger children. He is the most self-conscious of the boys, and prefers to withdraw into solitude for lonely mediations. He is the first to suggest that there is no beast, that, " Œ... maybe it's only us.' ". Simon seeks to confront his fears and comes to accept the evil that exists both in him and in everyone. He does this by speaking to a pig head that was put on a stick and climbing the mountain to find that the "beast" is really just a dead pilot. Simon is mistaken for the "beast" when he comes back to explain to the rest of the children what he found and is ironically killed by those he wished to save.

Jack is the novel's antagonist. He is the opposite of Ralph, distinguished by his ugliness and red hair. He loses both elections when voting on who will become the leader of the group and is obsessed with power. This is why he is so intent on hunting, it is a way of imposing his will upon a living thing.

Jack's rise to power first begins when the younger children's fears start to distort their surroundings: twigs become creepers, shadows become demons, etc.. Jack uses this fear to become the younger children's protector. If they do what he says, the "beast" cannot get them. Jack soon decides to form his own society. It becomes based on this kind of ceremonial obeisance to himself and is shown by those sacrifices by which the tribe creates its beast, thereby sanctifying the fear and irrationality that govern the children's actions. Roger is Jack's henchman. He has a sadistic soul and delights in tormenting others. An example of this is when he throws stones at a younger child when nobody is watching. As the children's society degrades, Roger slowly loses the inhibitions that society has imposed upon him. Where once he was afraid to hit a child with a stone when no one was around, he soon becomes a deadly enforcer. He kills Piggy by pushing a bolder on him while in plain sight of everyone and also tortures Sam and Eric until they tell him where Ralph is hiding. Roger gladly enacts the evil deeds that help the story progress in its downward spiral towards savagery.

Sam and Eric are identical twins in this novel. In the beginning, they are two separate beings, but as time goes on they merge into one being, "Samneric". They represent the average man of good who will stick to his principles for as long as possible, but will eventually join the majority when it becomes too hard to stand alone on his own ground. This is shown by their fierce loyalty to Ralph, even when almost all of the other kids have abandoned Ralph's group for Jack's fun tribe. Only after being tortured do they agree to become part of Jack's tribe.

The symbolism in the story lends a deeper meaning to the chain of events that eventually unfurl. Most of these symbols can be divided into two groups: symbols that represent civilization and order, and symbols that represent chaos and savagery.

The conch used to regulate the assemblies is the symbol of democracy and free speech. Although adequate when used to gather the boys together, it holds little power when confronted with violence and tyranny. This is shown to us when Roger destroys the conch with the same bolder that kills Piggy, effectively destroying the last remnants of Ralph's civilized society.

The signal fire, and Piggy's glasses (which are used to light the fires), are also symbols of civilization. The signal fire represents rescue, but it is also a distant end that will only be reached at the price of an everyday effort. Like most things in our society, culture and education to name a few, it is a duty that must be done for no immediate end. Piggy's glasses serve as a marker for their society's progression into darkness. As Piggy loses his sight, so too, do the boys lose sight of their original goal: rescue. One of the lenses of Piggy's glasses breaks after a fight with Jack. The fight started when Jack let the signal fire die out while a ship was passing, thereby costing them a chance at being rescued.

Golding names the pig head that Jack puts on a stick as a sacrifice for the beast, "Lord of the Flies" It symbolizes the anarchic, amoral, driving force of Jack's tribe. Only Simon knows that the reason why the beast cannot be found outside is because the beast lives inside all of us. We all have a little of the Lord of the Flies in us.

The "beast" becomes a sign of the children's unrest It goes from being a nightmare in some little boy's dreams in the beginning of the novel to something very real that requires sacrifice if one is to be safe. The beast represents the children's superstitious fears which become so overpowering that it eventually takes control of the situation

The mask that Jack wears takes away his self-consciousness by striping him of his individuality. When the rest of the group begins to wear masks, they cease being individuals and become a mob. By destroying their personal identity they lose their personal responsibility "He had even glimpsed one of them, striped brown, black, and red, and had judged that it was Bill. But really, thought Ralph, this was not Bill. This was a savage whose image refused to blend with that ancient picture of a boy in shorts and shirt." Even to Ralph, who once knew him, Bill has become something completely different once he dons the mask and makeup.

The sequence of killing can be used to track the children's turning from innocence to savagery. First, the boy with the birth mark accidentally dies in a fire. Then, Simon dies in a violent act committed by a group of people. Piggy is killed by an individual (Roger) quite deliberately. Finally the change is complete and the children have become complete savages. They choose to hunt Ralph down near the end of the novel, knowing full well that the hunt will end in murder and sacrifice William Golding uses Lord of the Flies to teach us that the most dangerous enemy is not the evil found without, but the evil found within each of us. At the end of the novel, Ralph and the other boys realise the horror of their actions

The tears began to flow and sobs shook him. He [Ralph] gave himself up to them for the first time on the island; great shuddering spasms of grief that seemed to wrench his whole body. His voice rose under the black smoke before the burning wreckage of the island; and infected by that emotion, the other little boys began to shake and sob too. And in the middle of them, with filthy body, matted hair, and unwiped nose, Ralph wept for the end of innocence....

Unfortunately, the naval officer who rescues them has yet to learn the lesson these boys have. He will take them back to the "civilized" world, which happens to be engulfed in war at the moment. Ironically, the children have survived one primitive and infantile morality system only to be thrown back into a bigger one, World War II. Evil will always be a part of man's nature. Golding's novel was meant to show us that this evil must be accepted, not ignored, or grave will the consequences be.

Symbolism In Lord of The Flies

Piggy, Jack, Simon, and Ralph can all be seen as symbolic characters in William Golding's novel Lord of the Flies. Golding uses symbolism to display his belief of the nature of mankind. He believes that the change from good to evil, from civilization to primitivism is unavoidable if there is not any direct authority over people. Piggy, an overweight asthmatic boy about 8 years in age, who cannot see without his glasses represents physical weakness and mental strength. His poor vision and obesity immediately establish to the reader his traits of physical infirmity and incompetence. The glasses, however, help illustrate his intellectual strength, his ability to think situations over logically and use reason, rather than emotions to decide upon important dilemmas. Piggy does not let his emotions guide him. Through the course of the novel, we observe how the allegorical society on this uninhabited tropical island in the Pacific Ocean makes the transition from carefully organized democratic reasoning to feeling-driven anarchy.

The climax of this transition is marked by the death of Piggy and the destruction of the conch shell, which has very similar symbolism to Piggy. The gradual shift is also measured by various incidents that hinder Piggy's mental reasoning, such as the breaking of his spectacles, and the loss of the boys' faith in him. Piggy's character is used by William Golding to show how even the best solution to a problem can easily be overlooked because of the lack of respect, pre-established prejudices, and the lack of mature thinking processes.

Jack's role in " Lord of the Flies" is to show the transition from the opposite perspective. Jack Merridew first appears in the novel leading his choir in a strictly organized fashion. He is the epitome of discipline. Then, for some reason, he becomes gradually obsessed with the killing of pigs, stealing from the other boys, and fighting the 'beast'. The most substantial point in this transformation is the first time he kills a pig. Shortly after the boys have accidentally landed on the island, Jack is reluctant to kill the pig. He is frighıened to draw blood from a living thing. A quotation from Jack himself describes this perfectly: "I was going to [stick the pig].

I was choosing a place. Next time—!" Jack was not only afraid of the enormity of his knife cutting into living flesh, but he was also greatly concerned of what the other boys thought of him. Then, for some reason, Jack overcomes his fear and is able to slaughter the pig fiercely and brutally. This is a result of his changed identity due his painted face, and the fact that he has adapted to the island. Jack further evolves into a relentless dictator who gains followers by promising to fulfill the children's desire for a reversion to primitivism.

His character unfolds even beyond this point into the killing of people, when his 'gang' kills Piggy and when he gives orders to his followers to track down Ralph and to kill him. Jack transforms from good to evil simultaneously as Piggy changes from power to death. Simon is the most mature of the boys because he does not fear the imaginary beast and he realizes that it is only in the boys' minds. His symbol is that of a Christ-like figure who sees the truth, but is killed because of ignorance. He has the solution for surviving on the island, but is unable to pass it on to the boys when he is killed in a mob-like fashion. His role is similar to Piggy's in this manner. This just shows how again, the emotions of the boys prevail in a life threatening situation, even if the 'life threatener' is only imagined. Simon's hallucinations symbolize messages from God, to be passed on to the people.

Ralph is the best leader of the boys, even though they cannot see it. He runs a democratic government, is totally fair, has the right priorities. The change from good to evil is shown in Lord of the Flies by the shift from Ralph to Jack as the boys' choice of leaders. The boys start off by choosing Ralph as the leader, but over time all the boys except Piggy decide to follow Jack. Ralph is the evenhanded, honest, thoughtful leader, while Jack is the exact opposite, an unjust, callous dictator. When Ralph is being hunted, it symbolizes a total revert to primitivism and evil. In "Lord of the Flies", William Golding uses the four main characters to symbolize different aspects of the inevitable change from civilization and happiness to primitivism and instinct that occurs when people are placed in an environment without direct authority.

Chapter 10

Study Questions

Q. Discuss the theme of Lord of the Flies by William Golding?

Or

Q Discuss the concept of freedom in Lord of the flies?

In his first novel, William Golding used a group of boys stranded on a tropical island to illustrate the malicious nature of mankind. Lord of the Flies dealt with changes that the boys underwent as they gradually adapted to the isolated freedom from society. Three main characters depicted different effects on certain individuals under those circumstances. Jack Merridew began as the arrogant and self-righteous leader of a choir. The freedom of the island allowed him to further develop the darker side of his personality as the Chief of a savage tribe. Ralph started as a self-assured boy whose confidence in himself came from the acceptance of his peers. He had a fair nature as he was willing to listen to Piggy. He became increasingly dependent on Piggy's wisdom and became lost in the confusion around him. Towards the end of the story his rejection from their society of savage boys forced him to fend for himself.

Piggy was an educated boy who had grown up as an outcast. Due to his academic childhood, he was more mature than the others and retained his civilized behaviour. But his experiences on the island gave him a more realistic understanding of the cruelty possessed by some people.

The ordeals of the three boys on the island made them more aware of the evil inside themselves and in some cases, made the false politeness that had clothed them dissipate.

However, the changes experienced by one boy differed from those endured by another. This is attributable to the physical and mental dissimilarities between them.

Jack was first described with an ugly sense of cruelty that made him naturally unlikeable. As leader of the choir and one of the tallest boys on the island, Jack's physical height and authority matched his arrogant personality. His desire to be Chief was clearly evident in his first appearance. When the idea of having a Chief was mentioned Jack spoke out immediately. "I ought to be chief," said Jack with simple arrogance, "because I'm chapter chorister and head boy." He led his choir by administering much discipline resulting in forced obedience from the cloaked boys. His ill-nature was well expressed through his impoliteness of saying, "Shut up, Fatty." at Piggy. However, despite his unpleasant personality, his lack of courage and his conscience prevented him from killing the first pig they encountered. "They knew very well why he hadn't: because of the enormity of the knife descending and cutting into living flesh; because of the unbearable blood." Even at the meetings, Jack was able to contain himself under the leadership of Ralph.

He had even suggested the implementation of rules to regulate themselves. This was a Jack who was proud to be British, and who was shaped and still bound by the laws of a civilized society. The freedom offered to him by the island allowed Jack to express the darker sides of his personality that he hid from the ideals of his past environment. Without adults as a superior and responsible authority, he began to lose his fear of being punished for improper actions and behaviours.

This freedom coupled with his malicious and arrogant personality made it possible for him to quickly degenerate into a savage. He put on paint, first to camouflage himself from the pigs. But he discovered that the paint allowed him to hide the forbidden thoughts in his mind that his facial expressions would otherwise betray. "The mask was a thing on its own behind which Jack hid, liberated from shame and self-consciousness." Through hunting, Jack lost his fear of blood and of killing living animals. He reached a point where he actually enjoyed the sensation of hunting a prey afraid of his spear and knife. His natural desire for blood and violence was brought out by his hunting of pigs. As Ralph became lost in his own confusion, Jack began to assert himself as chief. The boys realizing that Jack was a stronger and more self-assured leader gave in easily to the freedom of Jack's savagery. Placed in a position of power and with his followers sharing his crazed hunger for violence, Jack gained encouragement to commit the vile acts of thievery and murder.

Freed from the conditions of a regulated society, Jack gradually became more violent and the rules and proper behaviour by which he was brought up were forgotten. The freedom given to him unveiled his true self under the clothing worn by civilized people to hide his darker characteristics.

Ralph was introduced as a fair and likeable boy whose self-assured mad him feel secure even on the island without any adults. His interaction with Piggy demonstrated his pleasant nature as he did not call him names with hateful intent as Jack had. His good physique allowed him to be well accepted among his peers, and this gave him enough confidence to speak out readily in public. His handsome features and the conch as a symbol of power and order pointed him out from the crowd of boys and proclaimed him Chief. "There was a stillness about Ralph as he sat that marked him out: there was his size, and attractive appearance; and most obscurely, yet most powerful, there was the conch." From the quick decisions he made as Chief near the beginning of the novel, it could be seen that Ralph was well-organized. But even so, Ralph began repeatedly to long and daydream of his civilized and regular past. Gradually, Ralph became confused and began to lose clarity in his thoughts and speeches. "Ralph was puzzled by the shutter that flickered in his brain.

There was something he wanted to say; then the shutter had come down." He started to feel lost in their new environment as the boys, with the exception of Piggy began to change and adapt to their freedom. As he did not lose his sense of responsibility, his viewpoints and priorities began to differ from the savages'. He was more influenced by Piggy than by Jack, who in a way could be viewed as a source of evil. Even though the significance of the fire as a rescue signal was slowly dismissed, Ralph continued to stress the importance of the fire at the mountaintop. He also tried to reestablish the organization that had helped to keep the island clean and free of potential fire hazards.

This difference made most of the boys less convinced of the integrity of Ralph. As his supporters became fewer and Jack's insistence on being chief grew, his strength as a leader diminished. But even though Ralph had retained much of his past social conditioning, he too was not spared from the evil released by the freedom from rules and adults. During the play-fight after their unsuccessful hunt in the course of their search for the beast, Ralph for the first time, had an opportunity to join the hunters and share their desire for violence. "Ralph too was fighting to get near, to get a handful of that brown, vulnerable flesh. The desire to squeeze and hurt was over-mastering." Without rules to limit them, they were free to make their game as real as they wanted. Ralph did not understand the hatred Jack had for him, nor did he fully comprehend why their small and simple society deteriorated.

This confusion removed his self-confidence and made him more dependent on Piggy's judgement, until Piggy began prompting him on what needed to be said and done. Towards the end of the novel, Ralph was forced into independence when he lost all his followers to Jack's savagery, and when Piggy and the conch were smashed by Roger's boulder. He was forced to determine how to avoid Jack's savage hunters alone. Ralph's more responsible behaviour set him apart from the other savage boys and made it difficult for him to accept and realise the changes they were undergoing. Becoming lost in his exposure to their inherent evil, Ralph's confusion brought about the deterioration of his initial self-assurance and ordered temperament, allowing him to experience brief outbursts of his beastly self.

Piggy was an educated boy rejected by the kids of his age group on account of his being overweight. It was his academic background and his isolation from the savage boys that had allowed him to remain mostly unchanged from his primitive experiences on the island. His unattractive attributes segregated him from the other boys on the island. He was not welcomed on their first exploratory trip of the island. "We don't want you," Jack had said to Piggy. Piggy was like an observer learning from the actions of others.

His status in their society allowed him to look at the boys from an outsider's perspective. He could learn of the hatred being brought out of the boys without having to experience the thirst for blood that Ralph was exposed to. Although he was easily intimidated by the other boys, especially by Jack, he did not lack the self-confidence to protest or speak out against the indignities from the boys as the shy former choirboy Simon did. This self-confidence differed from that of Ralph's as it did not come from his acceptance by their peers nor did it come from the authority and power Jack had grown accustomed to. It came from the pride in having accumulated the wisdom that was obviously greater than that of most of the other kids at his age. Piggy not only knew what the rules were, as all the other boys did, but he also had the patience to at least wonder why the rules existed.

This intuition made Piggy not only more aware of why the rules were imposed, thereby ensuring that he would abide by them even when they were not enforced. When the boys flocked to the mountaintop to build their fire, Piggy shouted after them, "Acting like a crowd of kids!" Piggy was a very liable person who could look ahead and plan carefully of the future. He shouted at the boys' immature recklessness, "The first thing we ought to have made was shelters down there by the beach... Then when you get here you build a bonfire that isn't no use. Now you been and set the whole island on fire." Like Ralph, his sense of responsibility set him apart from the other boys. The author used the image of long hair to illustrate Piggy's sustenance of his civilized behaviour. "He was the only boy on the island whose hair never seemed to grow." The author's description of his baldness also presented an image of old age and made Piggy seem to lack the strength of youth. The increasing injustice Piggy endured towards the end of the novel was far greater than any that he had encountered previously. In his fit of anger, Piggy cried out, "I don't ask for my glasses back, not as a favour.

I don't ask you to be a sport, I'll say, not because you're strong, but because what's right's right." This new standard of harshness brought tears out of him as the suffering became intolerable. For a brief moment, Piggy's anger at the unfairness and his helplessness robbed him of his usual logical reasoning, which returned when he was confronted with his fear of the savages. Piggy was an intelligent boy with a good understanding of their situation on the island. He was able to think clearly and plan ahead with caution so that even in the freedom of their unregulated world, his wisdom and his isolation from the savage boys kept him from giving into the evil that had so easily consumed Jack and his followers. The resulting cruelty Jack inflicted upon him taught Piggy how much more pain there was in the world.

Lord of the flies used changes experienced by boys on an uninhabited island to show the evil nature of man. By using different characters the author was able to portray various types of people found in our society. Their true selves were revealed in the freedom from the laws and punishment of a world with adults. Under the power and regulations of their former society, Jack's inner evil was suppressed. But when the rules no longer existed, he was free to do what malice he desired. Ralph had grown so used to the regularity of a civilized world, that the changes they underwent were difficult for him to comprehend. He became confused and less capable of thinking clearly and independently. Although he too had experienced the urge for violence that had driven Jack and the hunters to momentary peaks of madness, his more sensitive personality and his sense of obligation saved him from complete savagery.

These two traits also helped to keep Piggy from becoming primitive in behaviour. He was made an outcast by his undesirable physique and his superior intelligence. This isolation and wisdom also helped Piggy to retain his civilized behaviour. As well, he was made painfully more aware of the great amount of injustice in the world. From these three characters, it could be seen that under the same circumstances, different individuals can develop in different ways depending on the factors within themselves and how they interacted with each other. Their personalities and what they knew can determine how they would interpret and adapt to a new environment such as the tropical island. Not everyone has so much malevolence hidden inside themselves as to become complete savages when released from the boundaries of our society. Some people will, because of the ways they were conditioned, remember and abide by the rules they had depended on for social organization and security.

Q. Analyse William Golding's Lord of the Flies.

or

Q. Critically summarise the Lord of the flies

The island is very dense covered in shrubbery and plantations including tropical pines. This is generally recognised when the ground is described as "steamy". The island itself is very hard and rocky this is shown by piggy's quote "no plane could've landed here with wheels anyway". There were a beautiful lagoon not too far in from the reef that went out from see-it was (the coast) surrounded with palm trees. There was a coral reef and beyond that, dark blue leading out to the ocean. The island was also quite large "to Ralph's left the perspectives of palm and beach and water drew to a point of infinity". The island was not perfect landscaped either, large pink granite rocks which also become a source in the novel. In general, the island was not a flat surface with hills; it was one with rockiness, weeds, vines, terrible fruit in which the children get diarrhoea, jungle (shade) and sand. But perhaps Golding sums it up the best when he explains "It was roughly boat-shaped: humped near this end with behind them the jumbled descent of the shore." The ship is an old symbol of human society.

- As soon as Ralph gets back to the meeting after exploring the island and seeing a Ginny pig on the way, he begins to set-up rules along with his partner in command (at the time) Jack.

The rules include "A sense of working together". Ralph says "We need hunters to go and get us meat". He also quotes, "We need to look after ourselves because there are no grown-ups". No talking at once (a democracy) Ralph-"it needs to be like school" The first rule to be broken was straight away by Jack, as he climbed up the mountain, with the crowed of littluns following him. Meanwhile Ralph and Piggy are left stranded-Ralph still with the CONCH in his grasp.

Another key rule which is broken following this was on top of the fire mountain in which Piggy's specs were used.

This was mainly due to Piggy's appearance (hence the name!) and intellectual ability. His glasses represent the power of science and intellectual endeavourin society. They end up taking his glasses with force. Thus, when later on Jack's hunters raid Ralph's camp and steal the glasses, the savages have taken the power to make fire, and Ralph's civilization is left helpless.

But more importantly Piggy should've had the right to say something, after all he did have the conch-but they didn't care. Rules end up failing towards the end of the novel and the obvious culprit is Jack. He is the one who leads them into savagery.

He is arrogant and does not let the others have a fair say-He wants people to say what he wants to hear. This is clearly demonstrated when Jack looses his temper and shouts to Piggy "You, Shut-up!" Roger is like Jack's sidekick-he represents evil, whilst Simon is the first one to realise the Lord of the Flies is coming into the island and therefore represents goodness. (In a more generalised term)

- The dead fire symbolises the hope of rescue and for the boys' connection to civilization. As long as the fire is well maintained, the boys exhibit a desire to return to society, but when the fire burns low or goes out, the boys lose sight of their desire to be rescued, having accepted their savage lives on the island.

Ironically, at the end of the novel, it is a fire that finally summons a ship to the island, but not the signal fire: it is the fire of savagery-the forest fire Jack starts as part of his quest to hunt and kill Ralph.

Ralph therefore feels like the boys do not have the same incentive to get rescued as he does and becomes naturally cross at the boys.

Dossier: Piggy

Name: Piggy

Age: 12 approximately

Physical Description: Wears big thick glasses, is in quite poor health (his as-mar), very fat and round, fine brown hair, freckles and with a "piggish" type face.

Personality: He likes intellectuals who discuss matters of interest and have concern for one another. He dislikes people who are rude and do not listen to others (JACK-"Piggy was so full of delight on Jacks departure, so full of pride on his contribution to the good of society, which he helped to fetch wood.") Beliefs: A democratic society in general.

Other: He is always left to baby sit the littluns when the boys go off on adventures, told by Ralph that he "isn't good for this sort of thing." Obviously made fun of in school, he often feels left out and isolated early on in the story although increasingly as Jack and Ralph drift apart, Piggy's voice of reason and insight come to fill the gap, and he and Ralph become good friends.

Dossier: Ralph

Name: Ralph

Age: 12 approx.

Physical Description: attractive young boy, thinly built, his mouth and eyes reflected his skin and represented no evil. His skin is dark, tanned with fine brown hair-A boy whom looks like a leader-Golding-His body described as 'golden'.

Personality: Establishes a mock-democratic government for the group in order for them to be rescued, and to maintain peace and order. Also likes intellects (Piggy) and jobs being completed for the good of society. Dislikes include: Jack, arrogance and not following orders atoll.

Other: Ralph is the one boy at the close of the novel who is not a hunter. Having been pursued ruthlessly by Jack and his tribe, Ralph begins weeping on the beach before his grown-up rescuers. The naval officer shows disapproval at the destructive state of things on the island, which Ralph laments that he had done everything he could do to be a good leader.

Dossier: Simon

Name: Simon

Age: 13-15

Physical Attributes: He is a small skinny boy along with a small chin "and eyes so bright they had been deceived as wicked". A long mop of black hair concealed most of his forehead and ears. His feet were bare and his skin colour was dark which glistened by his sweat.

Personality: When he is given orders he does what is needed (shown when Ralph and Simon build shelters for everyone). He was very quiet and yet there was something about him as though he was always suggesting something. He is also kind and thoughtful in thinking.

Beliefs: Represents natural human goodness.

Dossier: Jack

Name: Jack Merridew

Age: 15-16

Physical Description: Tall, thin, and bony...his hair was red beneath the black cap. His face was...freckled, and ugly without silliness' (Chapter 1 pg. 19). His eyes were bright blue and turned to anger if necessary.

Personality: Likes; being in charge (power), being important, telling others what to do, build up a colt??? Dislikes; People telling him what to do, people saying he's wrong, people like Piggy (intellectuals).

Beliefs: Only when Simon faints does he show sympathy, to create his own number of hunters. Other: It is Jack who leads the boys' turn to savagery, or at least gives it a certain order. The Conch Shell-The conch shell is the first important discovery Piggy and Ralph make on the island, and they use it to summon the boys together after they are separated by the crash. As a result, the conch shell becomes a powerful symbol of civilization and order. It is used to govern the boys'

Meetings: the boy who holds the shell is given the right to speak, making the shell more than a symbol; it is an actual vessel of political legitimacy and democratic power. As the island civilization erodes and savagery begins to dominate the boys, the conch shell loses its power and influence among them. Ralph clutches it desperately when he talks about his role in murdering Simon. Later, he is taunted and pelted with stones when he attempts to blow it in

Jack's camp at Castle Rock. When Roger kills Piggy with the boulder, the conch shell is crushed, signifying the complete demise of the civilized instinct among almost all the boys on the island.

Piggy's Glasses-Piggy is the most intelligent, rational boy in the group, and his glasses represent the power of science and intellectual endeavour in society. This is most clearly demonstrated when Piggy's glasses are used to make fire by intensifying sunlight with their lenses. Thus, when Jack's hunters raid Ralph's camp and steal the glasses, the savages have taken the power to make fire, and Ralph's civilization is left helpless.

The Signal Fire-The signal fire burns on the mountain, and later on the beach, to attract the notice of passing ships that might be able to rescue the boys. As a result, the signal fire becomes a symbol for the boys' connection to civilization. As long as the fire is well maintained, the boys exhibit a desire to return to society, but when the fire burns low or goes out, the boys lose sight of their desire to be rescued, having accepted their savage lives on the island. The signal fire thus functions as a kind of measuring stick by which the strength of the civilized instinct on the island can be judged. Ironically, at the end of the novel, it is a fire that finally summons a ship to the island, but not the signal fire: it is the fire of savagery-the forest fire Jack starts as part of his quest to hunt and kill Ralph.

The hunters lose their Identity primarily when "play was good and life so full that hope was not necessary and therefore forgotten." They start to get caught up in this 'frenzy' of hunting and as they kill more and more. There desires take over-for killing and even sexual desires "right up her ass!" This soon leads to power corrupting and eventually wanting more control over the island itself.

- Lord of the Flies: This is the name given to the inner

beast, to which only Simon ever actually speaks. As Simon's waits for the beast's arrival near the bloody sow's head on the stake (buzzing with flies), The Lord of the Flies speaks to him, warning him not to get in its way or else he shall be killed by the boys. The Lord of the Flies name comes from the sow's head and the countless flies buzzing about it, which soon move from the sow's head to swarm around the head of Simon as the Lord of the Flies tells him, "I'm a part of you." It is quite ironic that in biblical terms the term means a demon of Hell and cohort of Satan.

- The Lord of the Flies came into being by civilization and savagery. One is devoted to values that promote ordered society and the other is devoted to values that threaten ordered society. When 'evil' comes onto the island the Lord of the Flies has now come down on the boys and society has changed.
- Simon conversers with the pig head because he is the one who understands what the pig head is coming to. He realises it is evil after the head says "Aren't you just a silly little boy?" Simon clearly tries to ignore the interrogation speaking to him and says virtually nothing. From that point on Simon realises that the beast is in all of them and collapses rolling into the pig's head.
- The conversation to Simon is I believe about changing his ways and turning into evil if possible "I'm warning you. I'm going to get waxy. D'you see? You're not wanted. Understand?" The pigs head knows that Simon is its only threat in wanting to turn good into society and says "Where going to have fun" "Don't you mess it up" If Simon does not change into the evilness that most of the boys are getting possessed by-he will end up dead, which is exactly what happens.
- The weather was dark and there was a sense of dullness in the air. It reflects what is happening to

Simon when he makes his way to the feast, he starts acting less secure and starts to question what is actually happening on the island. The weather has a dramatic affect on the boys, they want to go home and further more it is the turning point into savagery as Jack breaks up and society is heading to its downfall. "Power lay in the brown swell of his forearms: authority sat on his shoulder and chattered in his ear like an ape".

Ralph Diary Entry 1

I arrived on this island with my fellow friend 'Piggy' and what was to seem quite a good place to have a functional society with no grown-ups to tell us anything of the sort. I blew this thing called a conch explained to me by the cockney 'Piggy'. It had a great low frequency sound which ended up calling boys from all over the island; they and I were greatly pleased for performing an act of leadership.

Soon afterwards a group of choir boys dressed in black clothes appeared up on the beach where we held a meeting, one of them was the obvious leader named Jack. Jack and I sort out a vote on who should become chief of this new island paradise and I was elected naturally with the exception of Jack's choir boys.

Out of the corner of my eye I saw that Jack had taken this matter quite disapprovingly, so as a good Englishmen would do I gave him the choir group to be governed by him. They would become hunters that would supply us with food. After the matter of voting who would be chief was sorted out we decided to do some exploring, Piggy wanted to come to but was not wanted so Jack and I made him stay back to look after the littluns (children).

The island was very dense with all kinds of plantations growing everywhere it was also hard and rocky. The beach was surrounded by sea which then lead to dark blue and not a single grown man or woman in sight. I returned with many thoughts and issues in my head. We needed to be rescued and to be rescued we needed a plan. I quickly realised that the boy called Piggy was also a determined intellect that had thoughts in his head. He raised the issue to me that a smoke signal was need on top of a big mountain. So all of the biguns (adults) went up the mountain enthusiastically to create a great smoke signal, in which was for us to become rescued.

Ralph Diary Entry 2

They have become savages. Jacks lot have gone mad. I do not know what to do and Piggy, Samneric and I all need help though there is none in sight. Civilization has become ruined and Simon is dead and word of this beast is spreading. I know we cannot fix this situation. Jack has become brutal and has taken power through force and ignorance. They have set up camp at castle rock. Piggy and I have arranged that we will travel there tonight in search of answers, though I am aware that it is a faint possibility.

There is an evil force on this island, and yet there is quietness. We need help, if only adults were hereâ€¦ they'd understand. Tis no good, it looks like we must become savages or die here.

Jack Diary Entry 1

I am disappointed on my involvement on the island. I clearly should've been chief, but this Ralph person doesn't seem to be too bad. My group of hunters have been unfortunate with no kills yet, but we'll get them. I think Ralph doesn't know how to run the place that well. He's like Piggy, however I don't wanna talk to dem-they might get upset and do something. Not enough gets done here. The littluns just play all day in the beach and throw sand at each other. We need a chief like me a hard one, that doesn't allow this sort of behaviour.

They should be told to do there jobs and shut-up, otherwise they do nothing and just want to live off our hard work. I don't like some of the boys here, especially that Piggy. That fat ogre I'd like to give him some stick O'well I got get back to do some hunting, using war paints so I can get the bastards.

Jack Diary Entry 2

At last things have been put to good uses. We have formed our own camp outside of Ralph's-serves him right for standing up to Piggy and not being a proper leader. Tonight we will toast my victory and the goodness of the tribe. Finally thing's are lookin up and I don't wanna see Ralph and dem lot Eva again unless they join us or else they'll cop one. Me and Roger have plans for this island and where gonna hunt with spears and hold ceremonies and dances.

The island finally seems to have got order and it's gonna stay dat way forever. The Most powerful character in the novel I believe is Roger. Although he does not say a great deal and character is not mentioned that much, he still has a vital impact on the novel and outlines the key allegorically. Once again, The overriding theme of the novel is the conflict between two competing impulses that exist within all human beings: the instinct to live by rules, act peacefully, follow moral commands, and value the good of the group on the one hand; and the instinct to gratify one's immediate desires, act violently to obtain supremacy over others, and enforce one's will on the other. These two instincts may be called "the instinct of civilization" and "the instinct of savagery," as one is devoted to values that promote ordered society and the other is devoted to values that threaten ordered society.

The conflict might also be expressed as order vs. chaos, reason vs. impulse, law vs. anarchy, or in any number of other ways, including the more generalized good vs. evil. Throughout the novel, the instinct of civilization is associated with goodness, while the instinct of savagery is associated with evil-In this case Roger represents evil. Roger is a character almost like the Lord of the Flies-He represents all evil in human being's whether it may be power or corruption. Roger has outlined the significance in the way human being's react and their focus towards the way in which human being's lose there moral principals. Indications from Golding have lead to the conclusion that Roger represents brutality and bloodlust at their most extreme. Golding, however, writes that the children all have innate evil and savagery within themselves.

Civilisation, in other words, can mitigate but never wipe out the innate evil that exists within all human being's.

Q. Discuss the Symbolism used in the Lord of the Flies?

Or

Q. Discuss author's view of savagery and reason in Lord of the flies?

William Golding's, Lord of the Flies, shows the movement from order to chaos through the use of symbolism. The symbolism used in the novel supports Golding's view of human nature. He believes that "people are inherently evil...[and] corrupt". The author also believes that "law and order control evil, but savagery is more powerful than reason". Golding's view of human nature is exhibited by three main symbols that foreshadow the events to occur on the island. It is appropriate for Piggy to be the owner of the specs that are used as a symbol of intelligence because the author creates the character's image as an adult-like figure. The slow deterioration of the glasses foreshadows the events of the plot. In contrast to the glasses, Jack's knife symbolizes the boys' infinite savagery and the growing antagonism among the inhabitants of the island. In Ralph's possession is the "creamy [conch which] lay among the ferny weeds". The conch symbolizes the rules and boundaries that bind society to modern civilization with the democracy, order and respect which it entails. Therefore, throughout Lord of the Flies, Golding, uses inanimate objects, (the glasses, knife and the conch), as symbols to reveal his belief that "[l]aw and order control evil, but savagery is more powerful than reason [and that] people are inherently evil".

Golding uses the specs as a symbol of intelligence, rationality and common sense-all qualities possessed by a civilized human being who functions in a society bound by rules, laws and taboos. The glasses symbolize many ideals on the island and within the boys. The glasses evidently show "intelligence [that is] traceable to Piggy" because of his adult-like appearance and his ability to rationalize and assess the conflicts on the island very thoroughly. Because of the reason and rationality symbolized by the specs, they portray the wearer as an adult; one who is intelligent, rational and sensible. The glasses are one of two man-made objects on the island, which demonstrates a symbol of intelligence through the technology needed to create such an object. Although, because the boys continuously ignore and exclude Piggy from daily activities, they are also removing the rational thought to which they are accustomed to: "everyone but Piggy [is] busy". Throughout the novel, the specs become soiled with dirt, or the sins and extremities of the boys.

When he speaks in front of the assembly, Piggy often finds himself "tak[ing] off his glasses and wip[ing]" them in attempt to remove the blur of sins from the falling society. Evidently, the specs are frequently used for the wrong purpose. The boys "use them as burning glasses") to start the fire on top of Castle Rock. Ironically, the item which symbolizes intelligence and reason is the object which starts the decent into savagery during the spreading of the fire; this proves Golding's theory that "savagery is more powerful than reason". The savage boys are beginning an inescapable decent into anarchy and evil by the slow deterioration of the glasses.

After Jack slaps Piggy, the glasses "[fly] off and [tinkle] on the rockso]ne sides broken"; the lens is demolished. As Piggy`s vision begins to diminish and he becomes literally blind, the boys are metaphorically blinded to reason, common sense, and rationality. At the beginning of the novel, the rules made by Ralph slowly diminish, along with a civilization. This is shown by the crime committed by the savages upon another human being: the death of Simon. One night, Jack and his savages "c[o]me for somethingPiggy's broken glasses"). They steal Piggy's specs for the use of lighting the fire; the initial event which begins the boys decent to savagery. The stealing of Piggy's glasses symbolizes the loss of intellectualism to a savage. The final stage of the glasses occurs when Roger bluntly murders Piggy. When "Piggy [falls] forty feet and land[s] on his back" the "island of adventure" has now surrendered into savagery. A total deterioration of society, intellectualism and rational thought has occurred. Therefore, the specs are used throughout the novel to foreshadow events and as a symbol of intelligence, rationality and common sense. The entire purpose of the specs is destroyed by savages, proving Golding`s belief that "savagery is more powerful then evil".

The "creamy [conch which] lay among the ferny weeds") is a symbol of democracy, order, respect and authority, and as the novel progresses, it illustrates its relationship to Golding's view of human nature. Golding shows the conch as a symbol of democracy and order through the rules made by the boys. "We'll have rules", ones which must be continuously followed, even though they will continue having fun. The rules are made in the form of laws, therefore, the conch is used as a symbol of authority because in a structured and orderly civilization rules and laws are respected and enforced by authority. The conch also allows the boys to make democratic decisions by "having a vote"(for a leader.

Golding shows throughout the novel that the respect for the conch is deteriorating. The respect for the conch is exhibited by the laws and rules fabricated by the boys. Whenever one boy wants to speak at an assembly, "he won't be interrupted" when holding the conch. Although, as the boys begin their decent into savagery respect for the conch and its authority is abolished. The loss of respect for the conch shows the movement from order to chaos; as order dissipates.

But as "Ralph lift[s] the conch" the boys fall to silence, as if the symbol of authority is respected as is a teacher or other authority figure. The symbol of authority is further defined by Ralph when he "finishe[s] blowing the conch [and] the platform is crowded". This occurrence symbolizes the boys attraction civilized society, in relation to a bell from school of a buzzer in parliament. The respect for the sound (that the conch produces), attracts the boys to a civilization dominated by authority and respect.

In comparison, after most of the boys on the island join Jack's band of savages, Ralph "calls an assembly" and "(s)ilence" falls upon the boys. The symbol of respect and authority is still an influence upon the boys. They continue to have respect for an authority figure that is democratic, not a dictator (as their society appears to be evolving to with Jack as a leader). Even as Jack orders the savages to "(g)rab them(and)no one moved" the respect for a democratic society is still fondling within their once innocent souls.

The final act of the conch strongly emphasizes the desire for democracy and order, which is expressed by Piggy. Jack decides "they don't need the conch anymore". All democracy, order and authority is lost to a society of dictatorship and savagery, as Golding's view imposes (that all man is inherently evil). The savages have no respect for authority, and order has been lost. This is shown by Jack's statement that "[w]e know who ought to say things".

When the "conch explodes into a thousand white fragments and ceases to exist" the significance of the conch is destroyed. The shattered conch symbolizes the end of reason and a once known civilization with all of its structure and ideals pertaining to it. In correlation to the view of the author, after authority is destroyed on the island, the boys succumb to savagery. The savages' "images refuse to blend with the ancient picture of a boy in shorts and shirt".

The boys have turned away all known civilization, which entailed authority and order. Therefore, the conch is a symbol of authority, order, democracy and respect. The symbols are depicted to support and portray Golding's view of human nature by the shattering of the conch and the boys succumbing to savagery. Yet again, "savagery is more powerful than reason" and is shown by the conch as authority and respect diminish towards authority figures.

The knife symbolizes the boys' infinite savagery and growing antagonism. In relation to Golding's view of human nature, the knife is a symbol of evil, intimidation, control, violence and power; all qualities of a savage society. The symbolism of the knife is demonstrated by the actions of Jack, the chief of the savages. As Jack and the others begin to accept the dominating savagery, the knife is used as a weapon to show an endless source of power, control and intimidation through the negative connotation which the knife provokes. The knife is one of two man-made objects on the island, it also relates to Golding's view of human nature because only an internally corrupt society could create such an object used for a weapon. As the boys first venture through the island, Jack, Simon and Ralph come upon a pig.

As "Jack [draws] his knife with a flourish [and] pause[s] long enough for them to understand the enormity of the downward strokeportrays the boys initial movement from structured civilization to savagery. As well, the context emphasizes the powerful intimidation that the knife possesses and imposes upon the other boys; it is a symbol of destruction and death. As the novel proceeds, the violence on the island increases as well. Jack "snatches his knife out of the sheath and slam[s] it into a tree trunk) creates the powerful imagery of intimidation through the context. Jack attempts to enforce intimidating pressure upon the other boys by exhibiting his brutal strength. As Jack begins a hunt, he wears nothing but "shorts held up by his knife belt).

This symbolizes (and supports Golding's belief) that an inherently evil savage needs no more then to slaughter the unsuspecting prey of the hunters. With the "bloodied knife in his hand"(and a painted face, Jack realizes the "fierce exhilaration) of killing, being violent, ultimately, being a savage. As the boys accept their savage chief, Jack, a metaphorical symbol appears. The knife has violently sliced their once innocent souls by intimidating them with power and control. Violence is symbolized by the knife when Jack "stab[s] downward with his knife)and the boys discover that they enjoy killing an innocent beast, yet they are not powerful enough to realise the beast plaguing the tribe.

The final use of the knife in the novel summarizes the symbolic nature it possesses. After Jack finishes sharpening the spear, he "ram[s] one end into the earth as if violently slaughtering an animal and attempting to kill the small traces of the forgotten world (civilization). As he "jam[s] the soft throat onto the spear, it "pierce[s] through its mouth"), symbolizing Jack's developed savage and violent nature. Although their failing society is "demented but partly secure", the knife is used as a negative symbol to support Golding's belief that "humans are inherently evil and corrupt". Jack's knife is a symbol of power, violence, intimidation and control. But most of all, it is a symbol of the boys` overruling savagery. The actions of Jack with the knife relates to Golding's view of human nature by Jack's savage behaviour and desire to destroy his civilized past.

Throughout Lord of the Flies, William Golding exhibits his belief that "human nature corrupts all society"(Themes) and "people are inherently evil. This belief is illustrated by the use of three symbols: the glasses, conch and the knife. The glasses are used as a symbol of intelligence. However, as they slowly deteriorate, so does the social structure of a civilized society with a movement from structure to savagery.

Likewise, the conch symbolizes the rules and boundaries which bind society to civilization through democracy, order, respect and authority. Although, when the conch is destroyed, the symbol of the loss of intellectualism is illustrated. The knife, which enables a group of English schoolboys to develop into corrupt savages, symbolizes growing antagonism, violence and savagery among the group. These three symbols support Golding's view that "Human nature is corrupt and law and order control evil, but savagery is more powerful then evil" in the novel Lord of the Flies.

Q. Discuss the Significance of Leadership in Lord of the Flies.

Or

Q. How can you say that Ralph possess better leadership qualities than Jack

There are always people who, in a group, come out with better qualities to be a leader than others. The strongest people however, become the greater influences which the others decide to follow. However, sometimes the strongest person is not the best choice. Authors often show how humans select this stronger person to give an understanding of the different powers that people can posses over others.

In William Golding's novel, Lord of the Flies Ralph though not the stronger person, demonstrates a better understanding of people than Jack which gives him better leadership qualities.

Ralph displays these useful human qualities as a leader by working towards the betterment of the boys' society. He knows the boys need stability and order if they are to survive on the island. He creates rules and a simple form of government to achieve this order. Jack does not treat the boys with dignity as Ralph does.

Ralph understands that the boys, particularly Piggy, have to be given respect and must be treated as equals. This makes Ralph a better leader as he is able to acknowledge that he was not superior to any of the other boys. Ralph's wisdom and ability to look to the future also make him a superior leader. Ralph has the sense to keep his focus on getting off the island. He insists on keeping the fire burning as a distress signal. Ralph's leadership provides peace and order to the island while Jack's leadership makes chaos.

Under Jack's rule, the boys become uncivilized savages. They have no discipline. Ralph, however, keeps the boys under order through the meetings which he holds. At these meetings a sense of order is instilled because the boys have to wait until they hold the conch to speak. When Ralph says, "I'll give the conch to the next person to speak. He can hold it when he's speaking.") he enforces his role of leader by making rules and gives the boys the stability of an authority figure, mainly himself. By doing this he wins the boys respect and confidence in his leadership abilities. Ralph uses his authority to try to improve the boys' society.

By building shelters he demonstrates his knowledge of the boys' needs. When he says to Jack, "They talk and scream. The littluns. Even some of the others." he is referring to why the boys need shelters. They are afraid. Ralph understands that by building the shelters, the boys will feel more secure. This illustrates his superior knowledge of people, which makes him a better leader than Jack. Jack fails to realise the boys need security, stability and order in their society.

Ralph's treatment of the boys also demonstrates his knowledge of human nature. While Jack considers the boys inferior to himself, Ralph treats the boys as equals. Ralph's superior leadership qualities are reflected in his constant defence of Piggy. Piggy is the weakest of the group and is therefore treated unfairly much of the time. When Jack hits Piggy and breaks his glasses, Ralph calls it "A dirty trickThis shows Jack's disregard for other humans; while at the same time demonstrates Ralph's compassion and ability to empathize with others thus illustrating his understanding of people. Ralph's "government" is a form of democracy which gives each boy equal rights and an ability to express themselves. Jack treats the boys, especially Piggy, as inferiors. When Jack gets meat from hunting, he gives everyone some except for Piggy.

When Piggy asks for some, Jack says, "You didn't hunt.") Ralph and many of the littluns did not hunt, yet only this treatment is directed at Piggy. Jack's contempt for Piggy shows his inability to understand people, as a good leader would take care of all of his followers. Ralph possesses this knowledge and is therefore a better leader because of it.

Ralph's common sense and ability to recognize what is best for the group as a whole further demonstrates his superior leadership skills. His main focus throughout the book is getting rescued and he puts much emphasis on this. He instructs the boys to make a fire and to keep it burning as a distress signal. When the boys do not share his enthusiasm for getting rescued, he becomes exasperated. "The fire is the most important thing on the island. How can we ever be rescued except by luck, if we don't keep the fire going?" Ralph's determination to get rescued is not for purely selfish reasons, but rather, it is in the best interest of the group. When the boys join Jack's tribe; Jack only satisfies their short term wants and needs, such as the desire for meat.

A good leader however, should look to the future and plan accordingly such as Ralph does. Although these choices may not always be popular, the better leader will carry out long term plans. When Piggy says "Which is better-to be a pack of painted niggers like you are, or to be sensible like Ralph is?" he demonstrates how the boys; by not following Ralph, have been lead astray by Jack. Ralph's main priority, which is getting off the island, is a wiser choice than for the boys to follow Jack. Unfortunately, the boys take the easier choice, which is to hunt and play games rather than keep the fire burning. Had they listened to the better leader, the novel may not have ended as tragically.

Q. "What makes things break up like they do?" Alternative Explanations For the Societal Breakdown in William Golding's Lord of the Flies?

Or

Q. Discuss the Societal Breakdown in Lord of the Flies.

Or

Q. Signify the meaning of this phrase in William Golding's Lord of the Flies, ""[W]hat makes things break up like they do?"

In William Golding's Lord of the Flies, Ralph asks Piggy, "[W]hat makes things break up like they do?". It is a question that has given rise to much speculation in critical circles. What causes the societal breakdown on the island in Lord of the Flies? Golding himself has said the cause is nothing more than the inherent evil of man; no matter how well-intentioned he is, and no matter how reasonable a government he erects, man will never be able to permanently contain the beast within. But other critics have offered alternative explanations, most of which are based on the assumption that the beast can, in fact, be contained.

Bernard F. Dick argues that the suppression of this natural, bestial side of man results in its unhealthy eruption and the consequent societal breakdown. John F. Fitzgerald and John R. Kayser suggest that, in addition to original sin, society's failure to reconcile reason with mystery causes the breakdown. Finally, Kathleen Woodward contends that when the beast is not suppressed strictly enough, when law and order is lax, evil erupts. Although we need not automatically accept Golding's explanation of his own text, when alternative views fail to provide an appropriate rationale, it is not unreasonable to assume the author's viewpoint. The three aforementioned critical views can be refuted, and Golding's simple summary can explain what these more complex theories do not.

Golding's own explanation for the breakdown of

civilization in Lord of the Flies was delivered in a lecture given in 1962 at the University of California at Los Angeles. He describes the breakdown as resulting from nothing more complex than the inherent evil of man: "So the boys try to construct a civilization on the island; but it breaks down in blood and terror because the boys are suffering from the terrible disease of being human". For Golding, the structure of a society is not responsible for the evil that erupts, or, at least, it is responsible only insofar as the society reflects the nature of the fallen man. The shape of the society the boys create is "conditioned by their diseased, their fallen nature". Indeed, Golding claims to have intentionally avoided inserting some things into the novel that might have led readers to conclude that the society itself, rather than the fallen man, is responsible for the breakdown

The boys were below the age of overt sex. They did not have to fight for survival, for I did not want a Marxist exegesis. If disaster came, it was not to come through the exploitation of one class by another. It was to rise, simply and solely out of the nature of the brute. Many critics, in spending time explaining the breakdown, talk about what the children did (or failed to do) to make the breakdown occur. The implicit assumption behind all of these explanations is that if the children had simply done something different, the breakdown might not have occurred; in other words, the beast within man can be contained under certain circumstances. But Golding's explanation provides no such hope. Disaster arises "simply and solely out of the nature of the brute."

Of course, we need not accept Golding's explanation for the breakdown in Lord of the Flies simply because he is the author. New Critics, for instance, will argue that meaning is inherent in the text itself, and Reader-Response critics will tell us that it is the reader who creates meaning. Whatever an author's intention may be, his work may end up communicating something quite different. As even Golding himself admits, at a certain point, the author loses authority over his text: "I no longer believe that the author has a sort of patria potestas over his brainchildren. Once they are printed they have reached their majority and the author has no more authority over them, knows no more about them, perhaps knows less about them than the critic who comes fresh to them, and sees them not as the author hoped they would be, but as what they are". Other views than the author's may certainly be entertained, but they must provide an adequate explanation for the breakdown as it is depicted in the text itself before we can accept them.

One such alternative view is Bernard F. Dick's argument that the societal breakdown is caused by the suppression of the Dionysian, or "brute" side of man. Dick agrees with Golding that "evil is indigenous to the species" Indeed, he seems to believe that his own explanation for the breakdown is perfectly consistent with Golding's view.

Yet, implicit in Dick's argument is the assumption that the brute side of man can, in fact, be contained under other circumstances, a possibility that Golding's view, as presented in his 1962 lecture, does not supply. Dick argues that, in moderation, this brute side of man can actually be "beneficial to society".

This is an optimism that Golding does not seem to share when he says, "Man is a fallen being. He is gripped by original sin. His nature is sinful and his state perilous". Furthermore, Dick argues that Ralph's "class consciousness" causes him to "think in terms of excess" which leads to his suppression of Jack's bestial side and its consequent eruption. Golding, as has already been mentioned, believes that the breakdown "was not to come through the exploitation of one class by another".

We can not, of course, rule out Bernard F. Dick's view simply because it differs from Golding's. We must at least give a hearing to his arguments and see if they are consistent with the text and if they manage to adequately explain the breakdown in Lord of the Flies. Dick bases his explanation on the obvious similarities between Lord of the Flies and Euripede's Bacchae. In the Bacchae, the god Dionysus represents the brute side of man while Apollo (who is associated with Pentheus in the Bacchae) represents his rational side. Dionysus, like Jack, "can be gentle when he is propitiated, but when he is rejected, he exacts a terrible vengeance".

The Apollonian Pentheus, who is "rooted in a frigid intellectualism," refuses "to acknowledge the new religion" of Dionysus just as Ralph refuses to acknowledge Jack's counter society . And, just as Simon is mistaken for the beast and killed, Pentheus is mistaken for a lion, hunted down, and dismembered. According to Dick, "[b]oth Lord of the Flies and the Bacchae portray a bipolar society in which the Apollonian refuses or is unable to assimilate the Dionysian". This refusal, this "immoderate Apollonianism," proves "fatal," and the society breaks down.

Jack has many Apollonian characteristics. Apollo is associated with music. It is Jack, and not Ralph, who is head of the choir, who can "sing C sharp". Apollo is associated with rationalism. But it is Jack, and not Ralph, who realizes that Piggy's glasses can be used to start the fire. Dick points out that Ralph insists not just on rules, "but more rules," and he argues that this is evidence of Ralph thinking in "terms of excess". Yet Dick ignores the fact that it is Jack, and not Ralph, who is the first to leap to his feet and cry excitedly: "We'll have rules... Lots of rules!". And even when Ralph does say they need more rules, Jack readily agrees

Just as the Apollonian is clearly present in Jack's character, so too is the Dionysian evident in Ralph's. When Ralph summons the first meeting by blowing on the conch, "His face [is] dark with the violent pleasure of making this stupendous noise" Ralph participates in the ritual reenactment of a pig killing, and as he does, his Dionysian instincts are described in more detail than Jack's: "Ralph too was fighting to get near, to get a handful of that brown, vulnerable flesh. The desire to squeeze and hurt was over-mastering". This scene, as John F. Fitzgerald and John R. Kayser point out, "conspires against the Bacchae interpretation... for the authors of that interpretation concluded that Ralph was Pentheus who tried to repress irrationality causing his downfall. He demonstrates that he too can be carried away by mad frenzy". And even "more damning is [Ralph's] participation in yet another pig killing ritual: the murder of Simon" (.rather lamely dismisses these events by saying, "There are also moments when some of the Dionysian rubs off on the Apollonian".

As we have seen, neither Ralph nor Jack are Apollonian or Dionysian extremes. Therefore it makes little sense to argue that extreme rationalism (represented by Ralph), when imposed upon man's primal urges (represented by Jack), causes the breakdown. But this is just what Dick argues. Dick's point is also argued by James Baker, who writes that the boys "attempt to impose a rational order or pattern upon the vital chaos of their own nature, and so they commit the error and 'sin' of Pentheus... The penalties... are bloodshed, guilt, utter defeat of reason" But in fact, the Pentheus representative, Ralph, is never particularly oppressive of the Dionysian representative, Jack. At the very beginning of the novel, Ralph attempts to appease Jack. When Jack insists that he ought to be chief, Roger calls for a vote. Everyone shouts out Ralph's name, but Ralph raises the conch for silence and gives Jack a chance: "Alright," he says, "Who wants Jack for chief?"). When Jack loses the election, "Ralph look[s] at him, eager to offer something," and he puts Jack in charge of the choir It is true that Ralph does not fully appreciate Jack as a hunter, and belittles him when the fire burns out. But he never actually takes any action to prevent Jack from hunting, so it can not accurately be said that he suppresses the Dionysian element in Jack's personality. And, since he joins in the pig killing ritual, it can not even be said that Ralph suppresses the Dionysian element in his own personality.

Dick's argument can not adequately explain the presence of the Dionysian and Apollonian in both boys, but Golding's view can and does. For Golding, evil is inherent in every man; thus it is not surprising to find so many elements of the Dionysian even in Ralph. And, if Golding is trying to show that the breakdown arises from the nature of the brute itself, and not any political system, then it is not surprising to find Jack and Ralph sharing so many Apollonian characteristics. Were they really opposite extremes, the breakdown would not have been so tragic. But because both are "men of goodwill... searching for some hope, some power for good, some commonsense," the divide which arises between them is truly lamentable.

Dick argues that Lord of the Flies depicts "a clash not so much of wills as of extremes". This does not appear to be true. Jack and Ralph clash at the second meeting, when the Apollonian-Dionysian distinction is by no means clear. They argue over the issue of the beast, although both agree that there is no beast. Jack says, "Ralph's right of course. There isn't a snake-thing. But if there was a snake, we'd hunt it and kill it," and Ralph loudly responds, "But there isn't a beast!"). Since the two boys do not yet represent extremes (if they can ever be said to), this clash can not be explained in terms of the Dionysian-Apollonian dichotomy.

However, all of the clashes can be explained in Golding's view; they are the result of the beast inherent in both boys. The clash that arises from the discussion of the beast does not result from Ralph's extreme rationalism, but rather from the murmurings of the beast within him: "Something he had not known was there rose in him and compelled him to make the point, loudly and again". Motivated by that inherent evil, that original sin of pride, both boys assert their power.

Later, Ralph agrees to look for the beast, and "[s]omething deep" within him speaks for him when he says, "I'm chief. I'll go. Don't argue". When the boys begin to clash yet again, Ralph senses "the rising antagonism, understanding that this was how Jack felt as soon as he ceased to lead". Although Ralph may end up agitating for reason and Jack for sensation, the two begin in the same place. Both are a mixture of the Dionysian-Apollonian. They are rational, well-intentioned, and desire law and order, but the beast within both leads them to an inevitable and horrifying clash. "Things are breaking up," Ralph says, "I don't understand why. We began well; we were happy. And then—". And then the beast drew them apart.

Having realized that Dick's Dionysian-Apollonian dichotomy is unsustainable, John F. Fitzgerald and John R. Kayser draw a different mythical parallel in their article "Golding's Lord of the Flies: Pride as Original Sin." They compare the novel to the Egyptian myth of Osiris and Set-

Typhon, which "accounts for the emergence of discord and... thereby demonstrates the precariousness of civilization". In the myth, Osiris's brother Set-Typhon seeks to usurp his throne.

Typhon drowns Osiris, but Osiris's wife recovers the body. Then Typhon discovers the body while hunting for pig, and he mutilates it. Typhon, who Fitzgerald and Kayser argue is represented by Jack, symbolizes the harmful and destructive aspect of human nature. They argue that Osiris, who may be identified "with both the reasonable and creative elements of the soul" is represented by Piggy and Simon respectively. Fitzgerald's and Kayser's mythical parallel avoids some of the inconsistencies of Dick's. Because they do not compare Ralph to Osiris, as Dick compares him to Pentheus, their argument is not weakened by the same textual evidence that assaults Dick's. Ralph is not killed as Pentheus is killed; but Piggy and Simon are killed as Osiris is killed.

Ralph is not as severely intellectual as Pentheus. "What intelligence had been shown was traceable to Piggy"). Piggy is the one who knows how they got on the island, what the conch is, and how to use it; and it is Piggy, rather than Ralph, who suggests calling an assembly. Piggy, therefore, can easily be defended as representative of the "reasonable" side of Osiris. Finally, because Ralph represents, in Fitzgerald's and Kayser's view, nothing more than the "better than average humanity," and not Pentheus's frigid intellectualism, they do not need to explain why he is carried away by Dionysian impulses.

Although the mythological parallel to Osiris and Set-Typhon is superior to the parallel to Pentheus and Dionysus, it still fails to explain one aspect of the text: the reasonable and magnanimous side of Jack. Typhon, these critics tells us, "represents 'the element of soul which is passionate... without reason, and brutish'". But Jack is not without reason. When the boys land on the island, he is very practical; he immediately explores to see if there is "water all around," to determine if they are, indeed, on an island. He suggests hunting pigs for meat, which is wise, since the fruit is causing diarrhea. And he thinks of using Piggy's spectacles to start a fire. Neither is Jack always brutish. When he first approaches a pig, he can not bring himself to kill it, "because of the enormity of the knife descending and cutting into living flesh; because of the unbearable blood". He wants "to do the right things". And even when he does finally kill a pig, Jack seeks, "charitable in his happiness, to include [Ralph] in the thing that had happened".

Fitzgerald and Kayser, as one of their explanations for the societal breakdown, give Golding's own answer. They say it is caused by original sin, by the natural depravity of man. But their addition of this mythological parallel, although interesting, unnecessarily complicates the explanation, because Typhon is without reason, whereas Jack is not. Golding's simpler explanation poses no such problem. Even if Jack is reasonable, he can still have the beast within, because it is inherent to the race. And, as I have mentioned before, the very fact that Jack is reasonable makes his deterioration all the more horrific. Were Jack as obviously demonic as Set-Typhon, then the exposure of "the darkness" of his heart might not have left Ralph weeping "for the end of innocence".

Although Fitzgerald and Kayser agree with Golding that the ultimate cause of the societal breakdown in Lord of the Flies is the evil (or sin) inherent in man, they suggest that there may also be a political reason. The cause of the breakdown is "[t]he separation of rational and revelatory knowledge". Golding himself, they say, has seen this separation as "both the essence and the illness of the West". Golding may very well believe that this separation has "'begotten that lame giant we call civilization'". But in his 1962 lecture, he does not use this separation as an explanation for the societal breakdown in Lord of the Flies. This separation may have begotten western civilization, but the question Lord of the Flies is seeking to explain is not what creates civilizations, but rather what destroys them.

As an explanation for the breakdown of society in Lord of the Flies, the separation of reason and intuition proves insufficient. Presumably, the breakdown could have been avoided had the two been reconciled: "Until Simon and Piggy together comprise an Osiris, Western civilization cannot... cure... its essential illness". Perhaps the greatest flaw in this theory is that Fitzgerald and Kayser offer no proof for their assumption that a reconciliation of reason and intuition would actually bring man closer to curing his essential illness. In fact, the very myth upon which this argument is based suggests otherwise. Osiris reconciled reason and intuition within himself, but he was nonetheless drowned and mutilated by his demonic brother Set-Typhon.

Kathleen Woodward, like Fitzgerald and Kayser, also opposes Dick's interpretation, but not by introducing a third mythological parallel. Rather, her argument directly contradicts Dick's, despite the fact that she applauds him for "[a]ptly" describing Lord of the Flies "as an anthropological passion play". For whereas Dick argues that the suppression of the beast within leads to its eruption, Woodward argues that the indulgence of it does. In her article, "The Case for Strict Law and Order," Woodward contends that Lord of the Flies actually presents a convincing argument for the imposition of strict law and order to suppress violent behaviour. Dick claims that Ralph excessively insists on more rules, while Woodward asserts that "the problem is that there are not enough rules: a system of rules is necessary for when the rules are broken".

Woodward begins her argument by declaring that "Golding presents us with a completely unrealistic model of the origins of human politics". She claims that Golding does not show us how a rational society breaks down, but "how the conceivably pleasant condition of anarchy disintegrates under the pressure of aggression". Ignoring for the moment the seeming oxymoron of a disintegrating anarchy, we can see that Woodward is still addressing basically the same question as the other critics. Why does the trouble arise in Lord of the Flies? Woodward's answer contradicts her premise that Golding is showing how anarchy disintegrates. She argues that the problem is the lack of strict law and order. But if strict law and order is imposed, then anarchy ceases to exist. The imposition of strict law and order can not stop the disintegration of anarchy; if it could stop anything, it would be the disintegration of society. So let us assume, for the moment, that what Kathleen Woodward is really addressing here (despite her reflections on anarchy) is the reason for the disintegration of society.

Golding, Woodward says, "has misread the moral of his own fiction". He does not show that violence arises "'simply and solely out of the nature of the brute'," but rather "how a society... can degenerate into lawlessness when there seems to be no apparent... ties binding people together". Lord of the Flies is not so much a "resigned plea" that the shape of a society depends on the ethical nature of the individual as it is "an argument for strict law and order within the democratic system".

Jack causes the break up of the society; had he been contained, had "the sweet persuasions of democracy [been] sharpened by force," the problem would not have occurred. Jack must be fought, for "aggression requires aggression". Basically, Woodward argues that the only way the beast can be contained, the only way that society can endure, is if Ralph were to "smash Jack's political machine, which involves us in an unpleasant contradiction that Golding does not face (England was forced to go to war against Hitler)"

Golding does not fail to face the issue of World War II. In fact, the issue is very much at the heart of his novel. And if he declines to confront Woodward's "unpleasant contradiction," then that is because it does not exist, at least not in Lord of the Flies. The novel presents the war of the "grownup" world not as an "unpleasant contradiction," but as a tragedy, a breakdown of society not unlike the one that is occurring on the island. If Roger's sadism is temporarily restrained by the taboos that were once imposed through strict law and order, then let us not forget that this restraint is "conditioned by a civilization that knew nothing of him and was in ruins". If the civilization is in ruins, then obviously strict law and order did not work there.

Piggy remarks that "Grownups know things... They'd meet and have tea and discuss. Then things 'ud be all right—

". And Woodward believes that this is "possible. Realism and maturity might help one to see clearly, diplomacy might work". But Piggy's assertion is clearly meant to be perceived as naive. There are only two "grownups" in the story. The first is the dead parachuter whose corpse is the result of a horrible war and who is associated with the beast. The second is the officer who comes to rescue the boys. As Golding has been quoted as saying, here "'adult life appears, dignified and capable, but in reality enmeshed in the same evil as the symbolic life of the children on the island. The officer, having interrupted a man-hunt, prepares to take the children off the island in a cruiser which will presently be hunting its enemy in the same implacable way'".

The officer's white drill, epaulets, and revolver are not all that far removed from Jack's stick, sharpened at both ends. The officer's "row of gilt buttons down the front of a uniform" is something like the paint that frees the savages from the shame of killing.

The officer asks Ralph cheerfully, "What have you been doing? Having a war or something?". And he also says, "I should have thought a pack of British boys... would have been able to put up a better show than that". But since the officer is himself involved in a war, there seems no logical reason why he should have expected better of the boys. And, since the officer is himself a part of a democracy that employs strict law and order, there is no reason Kathleen Woodward should think that Lord of the Flies makes a case for its success.

Not only does Lord of the Flies not make a case for strict law and order, it shows how horrifying it can be. Woodward argues that democracy is clearly preferable to tyranny. Yet Jack's tyranny supplies most of the things she says are lacking in Ralph's democracy (the want of which causes the society to fall). Woodward bemoans the fact that "[t]here are no kinship structures whatsoever, no bonds... among these boys". But Jack draws the boys together in a tight bond through the ritual reenactment of the pig killing. She complains that the society "has no objective". But Jack certainly gives the boys an objective: to hunt and kill pig in order to eat and later to hunt and kill Ralph in order to eliminate the last nonconformist. Woodward says that in Ralph's democracy there "is no apparent need to work with each other". But in Jack's society, the boys must work together to hunt and kill and defend their fortress.

In the weak democracy, says Woodward, there are no rules for when the rules are broken. But in Jack's society, there are direct consequences—conform or die. Jack's tyrannical society seems to supply all the things that Woodward argues are lacking in Ralph's weak democracy, including a strict law and order.

Yet nowhere in Lord of the Flies is this strict law and order portrayed in a positive light. In fact, rather than being a means of containing the beast, it is presented as a symptom of the emergence of the beast. Sam and Eric tell Ralph

"You don't know Roger, he's a terror."

"And the chief—they're both—"

"—terrors—".

When Roger approaches Sam and Eric to punish them for breaking the society's rules by not conforming, he "advance[s] upon them as one wielding a nameless authority". And when Jack sharpens his sweet persuasions with force, he is portrayed as arbitrary and ruthless

"He's going to beat Wilfred."

"What for?"

"I don't know. He didn't say. He got angry and made us tie Wilfred up... "

"But didn't the chief say why?"

"I never heard him."

Sitting on the tremendous rock in the torrid sun, Roger received this news as an illumination. He... sat still, assimilating the possibilities of irresponsible authority.

Presumably, Woodward's democracy of strict law and order would have been more responsible. After all, "the electorate, uniformed as it is, makes the best choice". But, as Woodward herself asks (without fully explaining her reason for asking it) what if, instead of Ralph, "Roger had been elected chief? Or Jack?". Would their democracy have been anymore responsible than their tyranny? And, ultimately, is their man-hunt that far flung from the man-hunt of the democratic officer who rescues them?

Woodward's view can not explain the terrible light in which Jack's strict rule of law and order is depicted; neither can it illuminate the comparison that the text draws between the children and the grownups. But once again, Golding's simple view can and does. If evil is inherent in man, then Jack's tyranny is but an outgrowth of the beast within, and thus we can be horrified by it. And if the beast is inherent in all men, then we can expect to find similarities between Jack's head-hunt and the officer's man-hunt. Finally, if all societies are inherently flawed because man is inherently flawed, then we can expect to see Ralph's society, however well intentioned, fail. E.L. Epstein calls Golding's explanation "merely a casual summing-up on Mr. Golding's part of his extremely complex and beautifully woven symbolic web".

Yet it is this "casual summing-up" that ultimately provides the most consistent explanation of the breakdown in Lord of the Flies. Of course, the four views examined in this paper are not the only possible explanations for the breakdown, and literary criticism may yet find a theory that explains the breakdown as well as or better than Golding's own simple summary. Neither does the fact that these other theories inadequately explain the breakdown in Lord of the Flies necessarily mean that they inadequately explain the breakdown of societies in the real world. Lord of the Flies is, after all, a fiction, and one may object to its premise.

Q. Explain the Conflicting Societies in Lord of the Flies

Or

Q. Is Conflicting Societies one of the major themes of the William Golding's Lord of the Flies?

Or

Q. Discuss the conflict between the group of boys in Lord of the Flies by William Golding?

Throughout the novel Lord of the Flies by William Golding, many different conflicting societies develop. These groups of young English schoolboys have conflicts between them for many different reasons. Some of them are so spread apart in age that their beliefs and actions are very different. Other groups are conflicting because they have different opinions about who the leader of the entire group should be. The groups also argue about what their priorities should be while trapped on the island. These conflicts continue to grow until the very end, when one group finally gains supremacy.

From the very beginning it can be seen that the boys have already begun to divide into two groups. When Ralph calls the first meeting the boys have together by summoning them with a conch shell, he decides they should vote on a leader. A boy named Jack Merridew thinks that he should be the chief because he is "chapter chorister and head boy." Another boy nominates Ralph for leader, because he is the one that called for the meeting. When it comes time to vote, the choir members vote for Jack, while all the other boys vote for Ralph. After he is elected leader, Ralph tells Jack that he is in charge of his choir. Jack tells Ralph that they will be the hunters, and Ralph agrees. This causes the boys to be divided into one group led by Ralph, and the hunting group made up of the choir members, led by Jack Merridew.

Being organized and civilized is very important to Ralph. He decides that the group will have regular assemblies to discuss important issues. He also decides that the person holding the conch shell, and this person alone, will be the only one aloud to talk. At first, Ralph's ideas help the group to be more organized. Another decision that Ralph makes is to build a fire. This fire will be built at the top of the mountain, so that ships passing by will be able to see it. Ralph assures the rest of the boys that his plan will work, and that they are sure to be discovered. Shortly after the boys arrive on the island, there is a big storm. Ralph decides that the boys need to make shelters, so they will be safe and warm at night. He tells everyone that this is very important to their safety on the island, and that they all need to help build them. However, everyone does not help build the shelters. Ralph and Simon end up being the only ones working on them, while everyone else is off hunting or playing.

Jack, as opposed to Ralph, seems to be more interested in the boys' present lives being fun and exciting. He thinks more about hunting pigs for sport and food, rather than building fires and shelters for warmth and safety. In fact, while Ralph and Simon are hard at work building shelters for everyone, Jack and his hunters are off in the jungle trying to kill a pig. They spend all day doing this, and are unsuccessful. This causes Ralph to get upset, because he previously told the group that their priority should be building shelters before they went off hunting. When Ralph tells Jack this, he doesn't seem to understand. This is not the only case in which Jack's hunting causes conflict between Ralph and Jack. Shortly after the shelter incident, Jack and his hunter's decide to go hunting again. This time, similar to the last, they leave an important job previously assigned to them to do so. Ralph has assigned some of the hunters to make sure the signal fire stays burning, which means they must closely watch it at all times. However, they decide to leave their job to participate in the excitement of the hunt. While they are busy hunting, Ralph discovers a ship sailing by in the distance. He looks up to the mountain to see if the fire is burning so the ship will see it, and discovers that it is not. He is furious that Jack would let his hunters be so careless. When Jack and the other hunters return from the hunt, they bring with them the pig which they successfully killed. They are so thrilled that they were finally successful, that the news of the ship hardly seems to faze them. Because of these events, the conflict between the two groups is greatly increased.

During the time in which these events take place, another group of boys begins to be distinguished from the rest. This group comes to be known as the "littluns." The littluns' average age is about six. The lives that the littluns lead is "quite distinct, and at the same time intense.") They eat for the majority of the day, and sleep and play for the remainder of it. They are "very brown, and filthily dirty." Because they are so young, the littluns don't understand many of the actions that the older boys make. When Ralph tells them they should help make shelters, they don't understand why it is such an important job. For this reason, most of the littluns aren't much of a help with the shelters, fire, or much of anything else. One day, a littlun with a mulberry-colored birthmark spoke out at an assembly.

He told the rest of the boys that he had discovered a "beastie". He claimed that it looked like a "snake-thing", and that he saw it in the woods. This news creates great tension among the boys. The littluns are all scared by the frightening discovery, and the "biguns" (as the older boys are called), do not believe him. When Jack tells the young boy that if there is a beastie he and his hunters will kill it, it makes Ralph angry. Ralph does not believe that the beast exists, so when Jack plays along with it, he is upset with him. This causes the tension between Ralph and Jack to grow even more.

As time goes by, Jack and his hunters become more and more savage. They seem to be possessed by the danger and excitement that the hunt creates. They paint their faces in order to look more daring. They no longer have any order or civilization in their lives, and do not pay attention to the commands made by Ralph. Many of the boys who used to be considered part of "Ralph's group" have now become part of Jack's hunters. They no longer think about how to be rescued, but instead want to participate in the thrill of the hunt. Many of the older boys have also started to believe in the beast since the time when the littlun claimed to see it. Some of them even claimed to have seen it themselves. This gives the boys another reason to become more savage. They want to find the beast and kill it. Even Ralph and Piggy start to become more interested in hunting than being rescued. They have all been trapped on the island for so long, that hope of being rescued is beginning to fade away. The cruel ways of Jack and his hunters gains supremacy over all other groups.

The boys have become so savage and enchanted by killing, that they go so far as to kill one of their own kind. One night at a feast, they start to dance and chant, "Kill the beast! Cut his throat! Spill his blood!") When Simon approaches the group, looking quite torn apart, the boys believe he is the beast. They run at him, and begin to bite and tear at him until he is dead. However, some of the boys, even though they participated in this feast, are still not completely transformed into savages. They remain separate from Jack's tribe, with Ralph as their leader. Jack's tribe raids Ralph's group, and steals their fire and Piggy's glasses. When they go to confront Jack about this, Jack's tribe murders once again. A boy named Roger rolls a giant boulder onto Piggy, and crushes him. The only boys left with Ralph are forced to become part of Jack's tribe, so Ralph is the only one left. Even Ralph is now beginning to forget about the civilized world, and being orderly. All hope is gone. Jack and his tribe have managed to turn a once educated group of English schoolboys into a pack of animal-like beasts. To rid of the one boy who has not become a beast, Jack's tribe decides to have a man hunt. They all get together and try to murder Ralph. They start a great fire which takes over the whole island, trying to burn Ralph to death. The only reason that Ralph is not killed is because a Navy ship spots the fire, and rescues the boys.

The novel Lord of the Flies shows how one group, when put under certain circumstances, can be completely transformed. The group starts out as a group of schoolboys who try to work together in order to survive. They try to use the skills they have been taught as civilized human beings to do whatever they can to be rescued. However, things fall apart very quickly. They lose sight of what they are trying to accomplish, and lose hope of being rescued. The evil nature within the boys comes through, taking over their minds. All they can think about now is hunting and killing. Even the most responsible ones are transformed into savages, or they are murdered.

Q. The Metamorphosis of Characters in Lord Of The Flies.

Or

Q. Discuss William Golding's Usage of Significant Character Development in the Lord of the Flies.

In his novel, Lord Of The Flies, William Golding used a group of boys stranded on a tropical island to illustrate the malicious nature of mankind. Lord of the Flies dealt with changes that the boys underwent as they gradually adapted to the isolated freedom from society. Three main characters depicted different effects on certain individuals under those circumstances. Jack Merridew began as the arrogant and self-righteous leader of a choir. The freedom of the island allowed him to further develop the darker side of his personality as the Chief of a savage tribe.

Ralph started as a self-assured boy whose confidence in himself came from the acceptance of his peers. He had a fair nature as he was willing to listen to Piggy. He became increasingly dependent on Piggy's wisdom and became lost in the confusion around him. Towards the end of the story his rejection from their society of savage boys forced him to fend for himself. Piggy was an educated boy who had grown up as an outcast. Due to his academic childhood, he was more mature than the others and retained his civilized behaviour. But his experiences on the island gave him a more realistic understanding of the cruelty possessed by some people. The ordeals of the three boys on the island made them more aware of the evil inside themselves and in some cases, made the false politeness that had clothed them dissipate. However, the changes experienced by one boy differed from those endured by another. This is attributable to the physical and mental dissimilarities between them.

Jack was first described with an ugly sense of cruelty that made him naturally unlikeable. As leader of the choir and one of the tallest boys on the island, Jack's physical height and authority matched his arrogant personality. His desire to be Chief was clearly evident in his first appearance. When the idea of having a Chief was mentioned Jack spoke out immediately. "I ought to be chief," said Jack with simple arrogance, "because I'm chapter chorister and head boy." He led his choir by administering much discipline resulting in forced obedience from the cloaked boys. His ill-nature was well expressed through his impoliteness of saying, "Shut up, Fatty." at Piggy. However, despite his unpleasant personality, his lack of courage and his conscience prevented him from killing the first pig they encountered.

"They knew very well why he hadn't: because of the

enormity of the knife descending and cutting into living flesh; because of the unbearable blood". Even at the meetings, Jack was able to contain himself under the leadership of Ralph. He had even suggested the implementation of rules to regulate themselves. This was a Jack who was proud to be British, and who was shaped and still bound by the laws of a civilized society. The freedom offered to him by the island allowed Jack to express the darker sides of his personality that he hid from the ideals of his past environment.

Without adults as a superior and responsible authority, he began to lose his fear of being punished for improper actions and behaviors. This freedom coupled with his malicious and arrogant personality made it possible for him to quickly degenerate into a savage. He put on paint, first to camouflage himself from the pigs. But he discovered that the paint allowed him to hide the forbidden thoughts in his mind that his facial expressions would otherwise betray. "The mask was a thing on its own behind which Jack hid, liberated from shame and self-consciousness". Through hunting, Jack lost his fear of blood and of killing living animals.

He reached a point where he actually enjoyed the sensation of hunting a prey afraid of his spear and knife. His natural desire for blood and violence was brought out by his hunting of pigs. As Ralph became lost in his own confusion, Jack began to assert himself as chief. The boys realizing that Jack was a stronger and more self-assured leader gave in easily to the freedom of Jack's savagery. Placed in a position of power and with his followers sharing his crazed hunger for violence, Jack gained encouragement to commit the vile acts of thievery and murder. Freed from the conditions of a regulated society, Jack gradually became more violent and the rules and proper behaviour by which he was brought up were forgotten. The freedom given to him unveiled his true self under the clothing worn by civilized people to hide his darker characteristics.

Ralph was introduced as a fair and likeable boy whose self-assurance made him feel secure even on the island without any adults. His interaction with Piggy demonstrated his pleasant nature as he did not call him names with hateful intent as Jack had. His good physique allowed him to be well accepted among his peers, and this gave him enough confidence to speak out readily in public.

His handsome features and the conch as a symbol of power and order pointed him out from the crowd of boys and proclaimed him Chief. "There was a stillness about Ralph as he sat that marked him out: there was his size, and attractive appearance; and most obscurely, yet most powerful, there was the conch". From the quick decisions he made as Chief near the beginning of the novel, it could be seen that Ralph was well-organized. But even so, Ralph began repeatedly to long and daydream of his civilized and normal past. Gradually, Ralph became confused and began to lose clarity in his thoughts and speeches. "Ralph was puzzled by the shutter that flickered in his brain. There was something he wanted to say; then the shutter had come down". He started to feel lost in their new environment as the boys, with the exception of Piggy began to change and adapt to their freedom. As he did not lose his sense of responsibility, his viewpoints and priorities began to differ from the savages'.

He was more influenced by Piggy than by Jack, who in a way could be viewed as a source of evil. Even though the significance of the fire as a rescue signal was slowly dismissed, Ralph continued to stress the importance of the fire at the mountaintop. He also tried to reestablish the organization that had helped to keep the island clean and free of potential fire hazards. This difference made most of the boys less convinced of the integrity of Ralph. As his supporters became fewer and Jack's insistence on being chief grew, his strength as a leader diminished. But even though Ralph had retained much of his past social conditioning, he too was not spared from the evil released by the freedom from rules and adults. During the play-fight after their unsuccessful hunt in the course of their search for the beast, Ralph for the first time, had an opportunity to join the hunters and share their desire for violence.

"Ralph too was fighting to get near, to get a handful of that brown, vulnerable flesh. The desire to squeeze and hurt was over-mastering". Without rules to limit them, they were free to make their game as real as they wanted. Ralph did not understand the hatred Jack had for him, nor did he fully comprehend why their small and simple society deteriorated. This confusion removed his self-confidence and made him more dependent on Piggy's judgment, until Piggy began prompting him on what needed to be said and done. Towards the end of the novel, Ralph was forced into independence when he lost all his followers to Jack's savagery, and when Piggy and the conch were smashed by Roger's boulder. He was forced to determine how to avoid Jack's savage hunters alone. Ralph's more responsible behaviour set him apart from the other savage boys and made it difficult for him to accept and realise the changes they were undergoing. Becoming lost in his exposure to their inherent evil, Ralph's confusion brought about the deterioration of his initial self-assurance and ordered temperament, allowing him to experience brief outbursts of his beastly self.

Piggy was an educated boy rejected by the kids of his age group on account of his being overweight. It was his academic background and his isolation from the savage boys that had allowed him to remain mostly unchanged from his primitive experiences on the island. His unattractive attributes segregated him from the other boys on the island. He was not welcomed on their first exploratory trip of the island. "We don't want you", Jack had said to Piggy. Piggy was like an observer learning from the actions of others. His status in their society allowed him to look at the boys from an outsider's perspective. He could learn of the hatred being brought out of the boys without having to experience the thirst for blood that Ralph was exposed to.

Although he was easily intimidated by the other boys, especially by Jack, he did not lack the self-confidence to protest or speak out against the indignities from the boys as the shy former choirboy Simon did. This self-confidence differed from that of Ralph's as it did not come from his acceptance by their peers nor did it come from the authority and power Jack had grown accustomed to. It came from the pride in having accumulated the wisdom that was obviously greater than that of most of the other kids at his age. Piggy not only knew what the rules were, as all the other boys did, but he also had the patience to at least wonder why the rules existed. This intuition made Piggy not only more aware of why the rules were imposed, thereby ensuring that he would abide by them even when they were not enforced.

When the boys flocked to the mountaintop to build their fire, Piggy shouted after them, "Acting like a crowd of kids"! Piggy was a very reliable person who could look ahead and plan carefully of the future. He shouted at the boys' immature recklessness, "The first thing we ought to have made was shelters down there by the beach... Then when you get here you build a bonfire that isn't no use. Now you been and set the whole island on fire". Like Ralph, his sense of responsibility set him apart from the other boys. The author used the image of long hair to illustrate Piggy's sustenance of his civilized behaviour. "He was the only boy on the island whose hair never seemed to grow". The author's description of his baldness also presented an image of old age and made Piggy seem to lack the strength of youth.

The increasing injustice Piggy endured towards the end of the novel was far greater than any that he had encountered previously. In his fit of anger, Piggy cried out, "I don't ask for my glasses back, not as a favour. I don't ask you to be a sport, I'll say, not because you're strong, but because what's right's right". This new standard of harshness brought tears out of him as the suffering became intolerable. For a brief moment, Piggy's anger at the unfairness and his helplessness robbed him of his usual logical reasoning, which returned when he was confronted with his fear of the savages. Piggy was an intelligent boy with a good understanding of their situation on the island. He was able to think clearly and plan ahead with caution so that even in the freedom of their unregulated world, his wisdom and his isolation from the savage boys kept him from giving into the evil that had so easily consumed Jack and his followers. The resulting cruelty Jack inflicted upon him taught Piggy how much more pain there was in the world.

Lord of the Flies used changes experienced by boys on an

uninhabited island to show the evil nature of man. By using different characters the author was able to portray various types of people found in our society. Their true selves were revealed in the freedom from the laws and punishment of a world with adults. Under the power and regulations of their former society, Jack's inner evil was suppressed. But when the rules no longer existed, he was free to do what malice he desired. Ralph had grown so used to the regularity of a civilized world, that the changes they underwent were difficult for him to comprehend. He became confused and less capable of thinking clearly and independently. Although he too had experienced the urge for violence that had driven Jack and the hunters to momentary peaks of madness, his more sensitive personality and his sense of obligation saved him from complete savagery. These two traits also helped to keep Piggy from becoming primitive in behaviour.

He was made an outcast by his undesirable physique and his superior intelligence. This isolation and wisdom also helped Piggy to retain his civilized behaviour. As well, he was made painfully more aware of the great amount of injustice in the world. From these three characters, it could be seen that under the same circumstances, different individuals can develop in different ways depending on the factors within themselves and how they interacted with each other.

Their personalities and what they knew can determine how they would interpret and adapt to a new environment such as the tropical island. Not everyone has so much malevolence hidden inside themselves as to become complete savages when released from the boundaries of our society. Some people will, because of the ways they were conditioned, remember and abide by the rules they had depended on for social organization and security.

Q. Effective Use of Symbolism and Symbols in Lord of the Flies?

Or

Q. Identify the Significance of Varied Symbolism and Symbols in Lord of the Flies by William Golding.

In William Golding's Lord of the Flies, the boys who are

stranded on the island come in contact with many unique elements that symbolize ideas or concepts. Through the use of symbols such as the beast, the pig's head, and even Piggy's specs, Golding demonstrates that humans, when liberated from society's rules and taboos, allow their natural capacity for evil to dominate their existence.

One of the most important and most obvious symbols in Lord of the Flies is the object that gives the novel its name, the pig's head. Golding's description of the slaughtered animal's head on a spear is very graphic and even frightening. The pig's head is depicted as "dim-eyed, grinning faintly, blood blackening between the teeth," and the "obscene thing" is covered with a "black blob of flies" that "tickled under his nostrils". As a result of this detailed, striking image, the reader becomes aware of the great evil and darkness represented by the Lord of the Flies, and when Simon begins to converse with the seemingly inanimate, devil-like object, the source of that wickedness is revealed. Even though the conversation may be entirely a hallucination, Simon learns that the beast, which has long since frightened the other boys on the island, is not an external force.

In fact, the head of the slain pig tells him, "Fancy thinking the beast was something you could hunt and kill! Ö You knew, didn't you? I'm part of you?". That is to say, the evil, epitomized by the pig's head, that is causing the boys' island society to decline is that which is inherently present within man. At the end of this scene, the immense evil represented by this powerful symbol can once again be seen as Simon faints after looking into the wide mouth of the pig and seeing "blackness within, a blackness that spread".

Another of the most important symbols used to present the theme of the novel is the beast. In the imaginations of many of the boys, the beast is a tangible source of evil on the island. However, in reality, it represents the evil naturally present within everyone, which is causing life on the island to deteriorate. Simon begins to realise this even before his encounter with the Lord of the Flies, and during one argument over the existence of a beast, he attempts to share his insight with the others. Timidly, Simon tells them, "Maybe, Ö maybe there is a beast Ö What I mean is Ö maybe it's only us". In response to Simon's statement, the other boys, who had once conducted their meetings with some sense of order, immediately begin to argue more fiercely.

The crowd gives a "wild whoop" when Jack rebukes Ralph, saying "Bollocks to the rules! We're strong ó we hunt! If there's a beast, we'll hunt it down! We'll close in and beat and beat and beat!". Clearly, the boys' fear of the beast and their ironic desire to kill it shows that the hold which society's rules once had over them has been loosened during the time they have spent without supervision on the island.

The evil within the boys has more effect on their existence as they spend more time on the island, isolated from the rest of society, and this decline is portrayed by Piggy's specs. Throughout the novel, Piggy represents the civilization and the rules from which the boys have been separated, and interestingly, as Piggy loses his ability to see, so do the other boys lose their vision of that civilization. When the story begins, Piggy can see clearly with both lenses of his spectacles intact, and the boys are still fairly civilized. For example, at one of their first meetings, the boys decide that they "can't have everybody talking at once" and that they "have to have ëHands up' like at school".

However, after some time passes, the hunters become more concerned with slaughtering a pig than with being rescued and returning to civilization. When they return from a successful hunt in the jungle chanting "Kill the pig. Cut her throat. Spill her blood," Ralph and Piggy attempt to explain to the hunters that having meat for their meals is not as important as keeping the signal fire burning. In an ensuing scuffle, Jack knocks Piggy specs from his face, smashing one of the lenses against the mountain rocks and greatly impairing his vision. Finally, after Jack forms his own tribe of savages, he and two of his followers ambush Ralph, Piggy, and Samneric, and in the midst of "a vicious snarling in the mouth of the shelter and the plunge and thump of living things," Piggy's specs are stolen, leaving him virtually blind.

Meanwhile, Jack returns to Castle Rock, "trotting steadily, exulting in his achievement," as he has practically abandoned all ties to civilized life.

The story's setting presents two more symbols that assist in showing the decline of civility on the island. A majority of the island is taken up by the jungle, which is used by many authors as an archetype to represent death and decay. In fact, since the jungle is the lair of the beast, it, too, symbolizes the darkness naturally present within humans that is capable of ruling their lives. This evil eventually spreads to almost every boy on the island, just as in the jungle, "darkness poured out, submerging the ways between the trees till they were dim and strange as the bottom of the sea". At one end of the island, where the plane carrying the boys most likely crashed, there is a "long scar smashed into the jungle" . While Golding does not include a large amount of description about the scar, the image of "broken trunks" with "jagged edges" is sufficient to give the reader an idea of the destruction caused to the island. Symbolically, this scar represents the destruction that man is naturally capable of causing and can be related to the harm the boys ultimately cause to one another, including the deaths of three boys, before they are rescued.

The degeneration of the boys' way of life is also very evident through the symbolic masks. When concealed by masks of clay paint, the hunters, especially Ralph, seem to have new personalities as they forget the taboos of society that once restrained them from giving in to their natural urges. For example, when Jack first paints his face to his satisfaction, he suddenly becomes a new, savage person. "He began to dance and his laughter became a bloodthirsty snarling. He capered toward Bill, and the mask was a thing of its own, behind which Jack hid, liberated from shame and self-consciousness". Certainly, Jack would not have acted in such a way if he had been in his home society, but behind the mask of paint, Jack feels free to act like a savage. It is also noteworthy, that the first mask that Jack creates is red, white, and black. These colors archetypically symbolize violence, terror, and evil, respectively, and in this novel, Golding uses these colors to illustrate those characteristics that are inherently present in humans. The feeling of liberation that results from wearing the masks allows many of the boys to participate in the barbaric, inhumane pig hunts. Those hunts can be interpreted as symbolizing the boys' primal urges or even anarchy. In fact, many of the boys become so engulfed in their quest for the blood of a pig that they seem to forget about their hopes of returning to civilization and neglect to keep the signal fire burning. When Ralph tries to explain how important the signal fire is, Jack and the other hunters are still occupied with thoughts of the successful, gruesome hunt in which they just participated. "ëThere was lashings of blood,' said Jack, laughing and shuddering, ëyou should have seen it!'". Also, during a later celebration over another successful hunt, the boys become carried away while reenacting the slaughter. However, the boys have become so much like savages that they are unable to control themselves, and for a moment, they mistake Simon for the beast. "The sticks fell and the mouth of the circle crunched and screamed. The beast was on its knees in the centre, its arm folded over its face". As a result of their uncontrolled urges, the boys soon kill one of their own.

Finally, one of the most memorable symbols that is used to show the violence and darkness which comes to rule life on the island is the rock, which Roger releases to kill Piggy. As an archetype in literature, a rock can symbolize strength and power, and since this rock is red, it also represents violence. It is Roger who feels strong and powerful as he stands on the ledge above Piggy. "High overhead, Roger, with a sense of delirium abandonment, leaned all his weight on the lever". When the rock lands below, it not only strikes Piggy, but it also shatters the conch shell. Up to that point, Piggy and the conch had been two of the few representations of civilization and common sense on the island. However, when the rock causes both of these to cease to exist, all order on the island is brought to an end, and the boys, who express no regrets over the death of Piggy, have fully become savages.

In conclusion, Lord of the Flies is a story that portrays the dark, deteriorating life that results from mankind's inherent capacity for evil, which is allowed to control humans when they are freed from the rules of society. Throughout the novel, Golding uses many different objects as symbols to illustrate this theme. Some of those objects would be insignificant in real life and would most likely be taken for granted. However, in Lord of the Flies, each of the previously mentioned symbols is vital to the story's theme.

Q. Complete Overview of Lord of the Flies by William Golding.

Or

Q. Discuss themes, settings and background of Lord the Flies.

Overview

Lord of the Flies became popular at the onset of the 1960s, a decade that witnessed an increase in both the number of teenagers in America and the influence of their ideas. More than thirty years after the book's publication, the situation of many modern American young adults bears significant similarities to the crisis situation of the British schoolboys whose tale is the subject of the novel.

Like the characters in Lord of the Flies, contemporary young adults in urban environments must often fend for themselves in order to survive the rugged life of the streets. Young people everywhere sometimes have trouble finding trustworthy adult guidance, while peer pressure—which compels young people to lose an individual sense of identity and morality—is pervasive. In one respect, Lord of the Flies presents a step-by-step study of how peer pressure can lead adolescents away from the values they once embraced and the people they once respected.

When the young people of Lord of the Flies find themselves the only survivors of a plane wreck, they must adjust to living in a world without adult authority and rules. They must somehow find a new way to organize a society that will ensure physical survival and social justice. The boys in Lord of the Flies must confront forces of destruction on the island and in themselves that they cannot understand. As the book continues, their makeshift government disintegrates, giving rise to a brutal gang bent on destroying those boys who have tried to form a purposeful, just society. Violence becomes the order of the day, unleashing primitive instincts.

Setting

The action of Lord of the Flies takes place during World War II on a deserted island in the middle of the Pacific Ocean. Golding deliberately borrows the setting from Coral Island in order to contrast his theme with that of Robert Michael Ballantyne's utopian novel. In Lord of the Flies, the marooned schoolboys have survived a plane crash caused by warfare; they are innocent victims of adult violence. The island at first seems to offer them sufficient food, water, shelter, and even the possibility of eventual rescue. The boys build a signal fire on the island's highest spot, hoping to attract the attention of any vessels or aircraft that might venture into the vicinity. But as the novel progresses, the island takes on a malevolent quality. An evil force seems to reside within it, threatening the boys' lives.

Themes and Characters

The principal characters of Lord of the Flies are English schoolboys ranging from young children to older adolescents. These young men represent the upper level of British society; they are members of an elite school system from which the nation draws its leaders. Ralph, one of the main characters, vividly recalls the tranquility, safety, and comfort of the life he and the others have left behind. He remembers his room at home, stocked with all his favourite books, as a place where 'everything was all right; everything was good-humored and friendly.'

At the beginning of the book, the boys organize themselves into an orderly society inspired by the regimented life of school. The youngest boys, known as the 'littluns,' look to their more mature classmates for safety. Among the older students, several leaders quickly emerge. Ralph, a decisive young man who is determined to keep the group of boys together, engages them in productive work for the benefit of all, keeps the signal fire burning, and becomes their leader. Ralph learns to rely upon Piggy, an ungainly young man who has been teased because he is overweight, asthmatic, and physically uncoordinated, but whose advice can be trusted and whose loyalty is unwavering. Simon, another member of the group, works hard at first but later slacks off. Characterized by Ralph as 'funny,' Simon undergoes a direct confrontation with evil forces later in the novel, stirring the boys into a frenzy of fear and brutal violence.

As the novel progresses, the young men divide into two groups. The larger group, which deteriorates into a savage tribe motivated by the spirit of the 'Lord of the Flies,' is headed by Jack. The original group, headed by Ralph, continues to dwindle in size and power until Ralph himself becomes a fugitive. His authority is destroyed, and he finally flees into the island's undergrowth in a desperate attempt to escape from Jack and his tribe, who are bent on murdering him.

Golding shows that societal defects reflect the flaws of human nature. He asserts that no political system can substitute for individual codes of ethics in shaping society. His theme implies that each human being must engage in a battle against both outside and inner forces of evil, taking moral responsibility not only for individual actions but for the future of society. Piggy, for example, appears to be a weakling in a physical sense but has inner reserves of moral courage; he shows that true leadership qualities are not always readily apparent but must be appreciated in whomever they appear.

The antagonist of the novel is the most elusive character; the insidious 'Lord of the Flies' seems to be a satanic presence provoking evil from outside the individual. But the 'Lord of the Flies' speaks quite plainly to Simon, informing him, 'I'm part of you.' Golding's novel suggests that the first step in the battle against evil is a war waged against some of the most powerful forces within the human soul itself.

Literary Qualities

Critics often refer to Golding's novels as religious myths

or parables, stories written to illustrate a moral point. Lord of the Flies symbolically relates Golding's idea of what happens when human beings refuse to deal with the destructive forces in their own nature. Golding defines the characters just enough to explain their various responses to the threat of the 'Lord of the Flies.' Within this group are fairly typical representatives of an English school of the time; that they have no personal characteristics beyond the ordinary serves to emphasize Golding's point that the evil infecting the boys could manifest itself in any normal human being.

Yet the novel is not merely a moral fable but a gripping adventure story. Golding skillfully leads the reader through the steps of the developing situation, from the ominous fear of the 'littlun' who dreams of 'The Beast,' to the formation of a savage tribe headed by Jack, to the hunt to find and kill Ralph. Although the transformation of the innocent schoolboys is shocking, it develops so gradually that the situation is believable. Particularly effective is the eerie and threatening manner in which the evil spirit of the 'Lord of the Flies' comes to life. By the time Simon meets 'The Beast' for himself, the reader is thoroughly convinced that it is real and more horrifying than any of the boys has imagined. The crucial scene in which the killing of a sow unleashes the savage force within the schoolboy tribe is also persuasive. Golding keeps the language simple and direct, and the dialogue accurately reflects the language of schoolboys at that time.

Some readers might think the novel ends rather abruptly with the arrival of the naval officer who rescues the boys. His response to the evidence of two murders and a group of schoolchildren turned into violent savages seems too calm. Perhaps Golding wishes to create a sense of irony through this depiction of a warrior lecturing the schoolboys on their inability to behave like proper Englishmen.

Social Sensitivity

It is significant that Golding, who comes from a social background identical to that of the schoolboys in Lord of the Flies, chooses to focus on the destructive effect of evil upon this particular group. He understands how the traditional values of respectability, order, intelligence, reason, and self-discipline have been pressed upon generations of boys in the educational system of England. Golding asserts that nothing can erase the problem of evil from human society if the individual does not directly confront the temptation to choose wrong over right.

He ensures that his novel does not imply that a particular social group, race, or class cannot be trusted. Golding's point is that, in the struggle to face the evil forces that rise from within the human spirit and threaten to overwhelm society, all men and women are equal. All are tempted to turn away from the best part of themselves and obey the most violent, degraded aspects of their personalities. To develop his theme, Golding depicts this violence and degradation in increasingly gory detail as the plot progresses and the schoolboys become savage hunters. The climactic passage describing the brutal killing of the sow is particularly disturbing for its use of sexual imagery; the murders of Simon and Piggy are also shocking, as Golding intends them to be.

Q. Write a passage on William Golding

or

Q. What do you know about William Golding

William Golding (1911-1993)-in full Sir Willam Gerald Golding English novelist, who received the Nobel Prize for Literature in 1983. The choice was unexpected, because the internationally famous novelist Graham Greene (1904-1991) was considered the strongest candidate from the English writers. In many novels Golding has revealed the dark places of human heart, when isolated individuals or small groups are pushed into extreme situations. His work is characterized by exploration of 'the darkness of man's heart', deep spiritual and ethical questions. "Twenty-five years ago I accepted the label 'pessimist' thoughtlessly without realising that it was going to be tied to my tail, as it were, in something the way that, to take an example from another art, Rachmaninoff's famous Prelude in C sharp minor was tied to him. No audience would allow him off the concert platform until he played it. Similarly critics have dug into my books until they could come up with something that looked hopeless. I can't think why. I don't feel hopeless myself." (from Nobel Lecture, 1983)

William Golding was born in the village of St. Columb Minor in Cornwall. His father, Alec, was a schoolmaster, who had radical convictions in politics and a strong faith in science. Golding's mother, Mildred, was a supporter of the British suffragate movement. Golding started writing at the age of seven, but following the wishes of his parents, he studied first natural sciences and then English at Brasenose College, Oxford. Golding's first book, a collection of poems, appeared in 1934, a year before he received his B.A. in English and a diploma in education. From 1935 to 1939, Golding worked as a writer, actor, producer, and a settlement house worker. In 1939 he moved to Salisbury, where he began teaching English and philosophy at Bishop Wordsworth's School. He married Ann Brookfield; they had two children. During World War II, Golding served in the Royal Navy in command of a rocket ship. His active service included involvement in the sinking of the German battleship Bismarck in 1940 and participating in the Normandy invasion. Demobilised in 1945, Golding returned to writing and teaching, with a dark view of the European civilization. Recalling later his war experiences, he remarked that "man produces evil, as a bee produces honey."

In Salisbury Golding wrote four books, but did not get them published. LORD OF THE FLIES, an allegorical story set in the near future during wartime, was turned down by twenty-one publishes until it finally appeared in 1954. E.M. Forster named it Book of the Years and in the late 1950s it became a bestseller among American readers. At the time of its appearance, Golding was 44, but the success of the novel allowed him to give up teaching. In the gripping story a group of small British boys, stranded on a desert island, lapse into violence after they have lost all adult guidance. Ironically, the adult world is devastated by nuclear war.

Lord of the Flies was followed by THE INHERITORS, which overturned H.G. Wells's Outline of History and depicted the extermination of Neanderthal man by Homo

Sapiens. Neanderthals are first portrayed compassionate and communal, but when they meet the more sophisticated Cro-Magnons, their tribe is doomed. The Finnish professor of paleontology, Björn Kurtén has offered in his novel Dance of the Tiger the explanation, that the Neanderthals disappeared because they fell fatally in love with their black and beautiful Cro-Magnon neighbours. In The Inheritors there is no understanding or love between these two races.

PINCHER MARTIN was story of a naval officer, Christopher Hadley Martin, who faces death after his ship is torpedoed. Like in Ambroce Bierce's 'Occurence at Owl Creek Bridge', the protagonist imagines his survival and struggle against the sea and cold-Christopher believes he is on a rock island in Mid-Atlantic. The rock he clings is metaphorically analogous to his diseased tooth. The FREE FALL was set in contemporary society. Sammy Mountjoy, the narrator, is an artist, who looks back over his past to find the crossroads of his life, and the moment he lost his freedom. Golding resigned in 1961 from teaching and devoted himself entirely to writing. He lived quietly in Corwall, gaining the reputation of a mildly eccentric and reclusive person. In 1965 he received the honorary designation Commander of the British Empire (CBE) and in 1988 he was knighted. Golding died in Perranarworthal on June 19, 1993. His last novel, THE DOUBLE TONGUE, left in draft at his death, was published in 1995. The story was set in the ancient Greece, and depicted the life of the last Delphic oracle, the Pythia, who witnesses the rise of the Roman power, and the decline of the Hellenistic culture.

THE SPIRE, which shared some motifs with Iris Murdoch's novel The Bell , concerned the construction of a cathedral spire. Jocelin, a medieval dean, has decided to erect a 400-foot spire to the top of the catdedral before his death. But its construction causes sacrifice of others, treachery, and murder; the Dean's own faith is tested. From this novel Golding's work developed into three directions: novels dealing with contemporary society without mythical substructure, the metaphysical novels in which the theme of fall from innocence into guilt was central, and sea novels imitating an 18th-century style. Golding also used in his works ideas familiar from science fiction, such as the origin of man, nuclear holocaust, and highly advanced inventions. In the play THE BRASS BUTTERFLY, based on Golding's short story 'Envoy Extraordinary', an Greek inventor Phanocles tries to get his steam engine, gun, pressure-cooker, and printing press accepted by the Roman emperor.

Among Golding's later works is the historical trilogy RITES OF PASSAGE , which portrayed life abroad an ancient ship of the line at the end of the Napoleonic Wars. It was awarded the Booker Prize. Other parts of the trilogy, narrated by young Edmund FitzHenry Talbot, were CLOSE QUARTERS and FIRE DOWN BELOW . "The author seems intent on making the ship's voyage parallel what is supposed to be Talbot's inner voyage of self-discovery, but once the ship docks, the young man is little more than the opinionated fop he was at the novel's beginning." THE PAPER MEN , condemned by reviewers as Golding's worst work, was about the battle between the world-famous English novelist Wilfred Barclay and the American academic Rick L. Turner, who has decided to write Barclay's biography. "In this book, however, Barclay and Tucker are not only poorly defined as individuals, but are also wholly inadequate as symbols. They are indeed no more than paper men." (Michiko Kakutani, in The New York Times, March 26, 1984) Golding's most widely read work, Lord of the Flies, has been translated into many languages and filmed in 1963 and 1990. It is an ironic comment on R.M. Ballantyne's Coral Island, using also the names of its characters.

The story describes a group of children, who are evacuated from Britain because of a nuclear war. Their airplane crashes on an uninhabited island, and all the adults are killed. The boys create their own society, which gradually degenerates from democratic, rational, and moral community to tyrannical and cruel. "They cried for their mothers much less often than might have been expected; they were very brown, and filthily dirty." (from Lord of the Flies) The older boys take control, a boy called Piggy, who is asthmatic and nearsighted, becomes a target of teasing and torment. Leaders emerge, two of the older boys get killed, and they begin to hunt another, just as a ship arrives. Golding's view is pessimistic: human nature is inherently corruptible and wicked. Thus the 19th century ideals of progress and education are based on false premises. Although the boys have been taught social skills, their desire to kill is unleashed when there are no strict rules of the English public-school system to control their behaviour. This is the world of freedom, that is ruled by savages and the ultimate evil, the Lord of the Flies, Beelzebub, Prince of Devils, whom the boys worship in the form of a decapitated boar's head.

Q. Critical analysis of the psychological insights in Lord of the Flies by William Golding.

Or

Q. Discuss Lord of the Flies by William Golding as 'anti-science'

As a novelist, William Golding developed a unique style characterized by simplicity and economy of expression. He deliberately refrained from excessive narration and consistent characterization. His treatment of the novel has been called 'anti-science' since he equated scientific and technological progress with dehumanization and traced the shortcomings of the modern society to the inherent negativity of human nature. His first novel, Lord of the Flies was published in 1957. The work features a group of schoolboys abandoned in an island and forced to survive without adult supervision. Initially the boys attempt to organize themselves on the lines of their parent civilization.

Later, they transform to a more primitive societal pattern dominated by blood-thirst, cruelty, aggression and rituals. The underlying theme of the work is 'end of innocence'. In many ways, the novel has a fable-orientation, conveying morals allegorically, the most fundamental being the 'darkness of man's heart'. The author's psychological insights are brought to fore by concise depiction of perverted behaviour and degrading moral standards.

The four major characters, Jack, Ralph, Piggy and Simon, represent passion, will, reason and conscious respectively. On the basis of this 'human-self' analysis, Golding explores the mutual interactions of various characters. The revelations underline the basic antagonisms of human nature. The author firmly believes men must learn to live with the chaos of existence without attempting to reshape it towards his means or ends. While man cannot alter his nature, Golding feels, he can certainly be conscious of it. And it is this consciousness, according to him, that contains the supreme achievement and delight of being a human being.

A study of the psychological insights in the Lord of the Flies clearly underlines the degeneration of virtuous characters into diabolic. Golding's reflections on the darkness in human nature emerge life-like in his analysis of the microcosm of the unknown island. The work characterizes Golding's underlying theme 'man produces evil as a bee produces honey'. In all his works the author has relentlessly pursued the objective of making man face 'the sad fact of his own cruelty and lust' and has upheld the conviction 'man is a fallen being'. The fact that man is gripped by original sin and is in an inherently perilous state justifies evil and its innate fusion with human existence.

Lord of the Flies is the story of death and the presence of destructive element in the blood's lust for blood. In Golding's own view, it is a story of the darkness in the heart of man. For adolescents and young adults, who have only recently come in contact with their self-consciousness, it is a new, intense, frightening and yet, fascinating encounter with darkness. The four aspects of human-self, as portrayed by Golding in the novel, can be likened to a phenomenological description of human nature.

Will as human self: Golding's vehicle of truth is the end of innocence experienced by Ralph, a high-spirited, confident, twelve-year old. Right from the beginning, Ralph is the only character who demonstrates his resolve for creating a democratic society. Initially, he is exultant due to the new freedom. At the end however, he longs for the tame and is bitterly at odds with others. Soon after being in the island, he finds the leadership of the community thrust upon him. He is antagonistic to Jack and intellectually inferior to Piggy. He is the quintessential symbol of democracy, torn between diverse forces. When he discovers a conch shell (a motif of authority) and blows it, he succeeds in gathering all the others. His leadership qualities are evident in his capacity to assemble others and organize meetings with confidence. Faced with disobedience, he reacts strongly. 'Choir! Stand still', so his order is obeyed. Immediately after Ralph is elected he organizes everything like; 'the choir belongs to you of course... They could be your army'. Then he says, 'listen everybody, I've got to have time to think things out'.

The humanistic view of psychological behaviour suggests that individuals are free to determine and choose their actions. Man is left free for his will and destiny. In Ralph's case he is free on will. Throughout, he displays his will for forming a democratic society despite impediments like sacrificing his close friend Piggy. Conceptually, will is defined as 'the mental power by which a person can direct his thoughts and actions or influence others'. Ralph is determined to achieve a civilized society. Civilization is a human creation, restricting the cosmic or primitive in man by bounding it within moral awareness. Till the end, Ralph runs to save his life without succumbing to the barbarians, underlining his will power. He is symbolized by the author as the strong willed politician, exhibiting leadership qualities like selfless dedication, courage, conviction, fortitude and integrity. He tries to make full use of all these faculties in bringing back control to civilized society.

Ralph's pristine status is individuation. He has a social identity, correct manners, morality and sense of justice. All these are hallmarks of civilization imbibed in him. But because of his innocent state, he uses will to proceed with civilized manners. Eventually, Jack's domination forces him to forego innocence. His loss of innocence is accompanied by the progressive destruction of his distinct conscious due to degradation of reason. Golding clearly establishes that 'will power' would be relevant only in civilized and not in primitive society. Passion as human self: Passion is connected with the character of Jack. According to psychologists, 'passion has got a division of thought and feeling'. This dichotomy is important in analyzing passion. In Jack, passion is embodied in a negative sense with Golding utilizing Jack for demonstrating the degeneration of civilization. The term 'doubling' is commonly used in psychological behaviour meaning split personalities for one person, or two relative autonomous selves. Doubling is easily applicable to Jack. His mind houses a number of primitive ideas and he can be called to possess savage traits. His features resemble those of a dictator, thirsty for power and hungry for authority.

Jack's passion for power is evident when he says; 'I ought to be chief because I'm chapter chorister and head boy'. In the Lord of the Flies, Golding takes recourse to an established literary method of examining human rights and polity through psychological insights. Nature in the tropics is sinister and threatening. The boys are led to the formation of a religion under Jack's leadership for largely personal selfish gains. Their theology is demonology and their god is devil. Jack has intuitive knowledge of the vilest elements of nature and the ways of exploiting them. He is prevented from his attempt to gain power in civilized, orderly society and takes recourse to the inherent traits of his nature i.e. dark means for gaining power. As Freud points out in his theory of psychoanalysis, human behaviour is determined by innate and immutable instincts that are largely unconscious. This is heavily exemplified by Jack. In terms of psychoanalysis, Jack is a schizoid, an irrational person suffering from delusions and withdrawing from normal social relationships. He is deluded by adult-free society and controls the savages. Passion centers on powerful emotions like drive, motivation, libido etc. The first two inspire him to leadership. Passion also induces hostility in his unconscious mind and makes it a conscious motive.

In the beginning, Jack hunts pigs for sporting. He resents killing of pigs due to the enormity of the knife and it's cutting into living flesh. Kelly defines aggression as 'the active elaboration of one's perceptual field'. Aggression arises out of the willingness to risk in order to find out 'passion' for embodiment of action. Passion, the human-self of Jack, is embodied with aggression. His passion for power drives him to diabolism. He is Golding's quintessential metaphor for underlining darkness in human beings.

Rationality as human self: The name Piggy has an irony in it. He possesses both positive and negative attributes of a weak intellectual. He rationalizes Simon's death before his own and is the only one to rationalize all events. Together with Ralph, he attempts to create an orderly society. His rationality however, is ineffective in controlling the rest. His belief that science can explain everything makes him unable to comprehend the reality of the beast. Faith in science or rationality, with a marked disbelief in the supernatural, is typical of Piggy. He is fat and ugly with thin hair that never seems to grow and suffers from asthma and weak eyes that are common affiliations of age. His physical weaknesses and other characteristics are consistent with his 'adult' role in the novel. Though he is the clear thinker, he can't enforce his will like Ralph or Jack. The boys refuse to take him seriously due to his shabby appearance.

Piggy symbolizes the force of reason among the boys. His gradual loss of sight and eventual death highlight the degeneration among the community. He is possessed with the strong urge to distinguish and order a manageable system and finds himself in conflict with the power of darkness. His wisdom could've been instrumental for achieving stability in the social order. But the leaders were reckless and thoughtless, more interested in momentary splurges rather than the steady glow of reason. When a chance for rescue goes abegging, the boys focus on hunting, a primitive activity reversing civilization, trampling Piggy's intellectual views. Piggy remains indefatigably himself till his death using logic and reason. Though physically weak, he doesn't lack mental courage. Despite Golding's faith in science and rationality, he is sarcastic of Piggy for not accepting Simon's view that evil is present in every man's heart. With Piggy's death, the remaining not only get degenerated, but completely devoid of human control that comes from rational awareness.

Conscious as human self: Simon is an embodiment of vision and forethought. This is clearly brought out when he points out that the beast that they all fear is not real and actually lies within themselves. He fails in convincing others and is eventually clubbed to death. He suffers from epilepsy, is visited by the Lord of the Flies, bears a touch of the mystic and is the voice of warning. He understands that evil can't be exonerated by pressurizing humans or by forcing them into primitive adaptations. The most self-conscious in his group, he is incapable of speaking in public and prefers solitude. In his epileptic bouts, he communicates with the Lord of the Flies and darkness. His self-knowledge imparts him the highest degree of consciousness among the boys. He is also intimately familiar with the darkness in man and is temperamentally alert to the limits imposable on a man's ego.

Q. Lord of the Flies Essay-Comparing Ralph and Jack

Or

Q. Draw a comparison between Ralph and Jack.

There are two types of people on this earth: leaders and followers. A leader is someone who acts as a guide for a person or people. Leaders manipulate followers to their cause and persuade followers to adopt their point of view. Leaders do not always strive to positively impact on the followers' lives; sometimes leaders use their skilful persuasion techniques to "force" followers to accept outrageous views. For better or for worse, leaders are incorporated into our everyday society. As politicians running a country; as a CEO managing a company; as a director filming a movie; and even as an adolescent boy governing an island.

In William Golding's Lord of the Flies, an adolescent boy does in fact govern an island. The boy's name is Ralph and he is on the island with several other boys because their plane crashed. Ralph and other boy, Jack, are the evident leaders of the group. The two boys are at opposite end of the leadership spectrum: Ralph is considerate of the other boys' opinions when making decisions, while Jack believes that he should be the one to make decisions for the group. Jack believes that he is superior to everyone on the island, while Ralph believes everyone is equal. Ralph is able to stay focused on one long-term task while Jack fulfils the day-to-day requirements of the boys. Between Ralph and Jack, Ralph is the better leader because his qualities allow him to make decisions that benefit the whole group

One very important quality of a leader is the ability to stay focused on what matters while there are many distractions about, a quality that Ralph demonstrates at the very beginning of the story. As soon as Ralph is elected as chief, he concentrates all of his newly acquired authority to being rescued. He assembles a small group of boys to go on an "expedition" to see if they actually are on an island. "If this isn't an island we might be rescued straight away. So we've got to decide if this is an island... three of us will go on an expedition and find out.". About one quarter way into the novel, Ralph becomes fed up as he finds only himself and one other boy building a shelter for the entire group."'You remember the meeting? How everyone was going to work hard until the shelters were finished?'... 'D'you see? All day I've been working with Simon. No one else. They're off bathing, or eating, or playing.'".

This shows that the he stays focused while all the other boys become distracted from the task at hand of building the shelters. Ralph's focused mind on completing the shelters kept him working and prevented him from being distracted like all the other boys. "'When the meeting was over they'd work for five minutes then wander off...'". Throughout the novel Ralph never ceases to stress the importance of the signal fire as a means of being rescued. Soon after he had been elected as chief, he focuses attention on the importance of having a signal fire and being rescued. " 'Now we come to the most important thing. I've been thinking... We want to be rescued'". "'If a ship comes near the island they may not notice us. So we must make smoke on top of the mountain. We must make a fire.'". Even after Jack had started his own tribe, stole the only means of making fire from Ralph, and Ralph's tribe consisted only of a small number of boys, Ralph still did not forget the importance of the signal fire.

"'Just an ordinary fire. You'd think we could do that, wouldn't you? Just a smoke signal so we can be rescued… now there's no signal going up. Ships may be passing. " On the contrary, Jack cannot differentiate what is important and what is not. Jack thinks that hunting is more important than being rescued, so he takes the hunters that were tending the fire to go hunting. The fire – along with the chance of being rescued – becomes extinguished as a ship passes by the island. Jack returns, and receives a deserved earful from Ralph

"'There was a ship. Out there. You said you'd keep the fire going and you let it out! They might have seen us. We might have gone home.' 'The job was too much. We needed everyone.'" When Jack forms his new tribe, they are not concerned about being rescued, all they want to do is hunt. The ability to stay focused on what matters is important for a leader because it is the only way for progress to be made that can benefit the entire group. If a leader kept on being side tracked with small, insignificant issues, then there would be no time to resolve the big, important issues that are really important and progress. Jack becomes side tracked with his hunting and forgets the very important issue of being rescued from the island. In fact, he also makes the other boys forget about being rescued from the island, making the group suffer. Ralph on the other hand, keeps his mind focused on the most important issues – being rescued and building shelter – and does not let anything get in the way. His focused mind makes decisions that benefit the entire group, which is why he is the better leader.

Being a great leader means being considerate of other peoples' opinions. Jack is not considerate of other people's opinions. During a discussion about the beast, Jack says "'We don't need the conch any more. We know who ought to say things. What good did Simon do speaking, or Bill, or Walter? It's time some people knew they've got to keep quiet and leave deciding things to the rest of us –'

This shows how inconsiderate Jack is because the conch is the only thing that lets the boys communicate their thoughts and eliminating it would mean that they do not get a say in making decisions that affects them. When Jack starts another tribe, he selfishly appoints himself as the leader – his followers do not have a say as to who leads them. As leader, he does not take into consideration the thoughts and opinions of his followers. He barks out orders and everyone follows them. "'We'll go into the forest now and hunt.' He turned and trotted away and after a moment they followed him obediently.". Ralph is the exact opposite of Jack, since he is the one who put rules in place to allow every one to speak.

"'And another thing. We can't have everybody talking at once. We'll have to have 'Hands up" like at school.'". "'I'll give the conch to the next person to speak. He can hold it when he's speaking.'... 'And he won't be interrupted. Except by me.'". These rules show that Ralph actually cares what the boys have to say . Being considerate, like Ralph, is very crucial to being a good leader because listening to everybody's opinions and beliefs ensures that final decisions can be formed to benefit the entire group. Ralph's method of considering everyone's opinions and treating people as equals allows him to make decisions that benefit the whole group, which is why he is a better leader than Jack.

An important belief that leaders must posses is that every person is equal. Jack believes that he is far superior than anybody else on the island. When the group of boys is voting for chief at the start of the novel, Jack believes "with simple arrogance" that there should be no vote and he should be appointed chief mainly because "'I'm chapter chorister and head boy.

I can sing C sharp.'". Jack constantly ridiculed Piggy when they were in the same tribe and gave no thought to what Piggy said. "Piggy took the conch... 'I don't believe in no ghosts – ever!' Jack was up...'Who cares what you believe – Fatty!'". "'Then,' went on Piggy... 'You're talking too much,' said Jack Merridew. 'Shut up, Fatty.'". This shows that Jack regards Piggy as an inferior person. Ralph shows that he regards all the boys as equals by standing up for Piggy, the most vulnerable person on the island. When Jack breaks Piggy's glasses and makes a mockery of him Ralph interferes and calls

Jacks actions a "dirty trick". "'Now I only got one eye. Jus' you wait –' Jack mimicked the whine and scramble.

'Jus' you wait – yah!'". When everyone is equal, the group benefits as a whole because people are not afraid of ridicule or persecution when they speak their minds. Their opinions can then be considered when making a decision. If decisions were made the way Jack makes them, with no consideration given to different points of view, then the decision would only benefit a select few within group. Treating people akin to the way Jack does, as "superior" and "inferior", limits the whole group's progress. The "superior" people would benefit while the "inferior" would suffer. This imbalance prevents the whole group from benefiting. Ralph's belief of equality allows him to make decisions that benefit the entire group, and that is why he is the better leader over Jack.

Q. Discuss the Plot, theme, key conflicts and moral issues in Lord of the Flies.

Or

Q. Classify the background, theme and major conflicts of Lord of the Rings by William Golding.

Background

The book begins following a plane crash that left the pilot dead and a bunch of young boys, aged five to twelve, scattered throughout a tropical island. The boys were being evacuated from England where an atomic war was taking place. When they were escaping, the plane is attacked, and the pilot parachutes away. Ralph meets up with Piggy, and they find a small conch shell. Ralph blows into the conch shell and and the boys assemble at a central point. There are choirboys and boarding school boys. They congregate to elect a leader and decide to start a fire and begin to explore the island.

Setting

Lord of the Flies takes place on an island, which Golding never gives an exact location. Although he does not tell us where the island is, he describes it in detail. He says that it has a jungle at one end, with a rocky mountain above it. At the opposite side is the lagoon where the boys go to bathe and where they first met after the crash. Near there, up the mountain, is a platform where it was decided a fire would stay lit in hope of rescue. This was in the ideal position, having a view of the ocean, therefore allowing any passing planes or boats to spot them and rescue them. It was on this mountain that the parachutist was also spotted by the boys, and mistaken for a beast. Inland, the jungle served many purposes. In the dense jungle, food was plentiful, and the plants served as a means of escape for Ralph during his run from Jack. Simon stayed there during his stage of insanity, and the used the plants to build shelter.

The boys plane was shot down during an atomic war. This set the stage for the problems that would arise on the island among the boys. Their behaviour reflects their surroundings, as they acted just like they were participating in the war. The island is a very isolated place with absolutely no contact with the outside war. The only way that they could contact an outsider was by chance, if a plane or boat happened to spot them. These boys from boarding school were in some respect lucky to land on this island, for it did have its advantages. There was food, wildlife, and fresh water. It was not their surroundings, but themselves that led to the downfall of their civilization.

Characters

Ralph: The protagonist of Lord of the Flies. He is 12 years old, tall, blond, and attractive. Ralph is a natural leader and after discovering the conch shell, he is elected as leader of the boys. Throughout the novel Ralph tries to establish order and focus on rescue. He decides that a boy can only speak at the meetings if he is holding the conch shell.

He wants to keep the fire on the mountain going so that is a plane passes, the boys can be saved. He also encourages the boys to build huts. He is very much a true human because although he tries to maintain order, he is often tempted by the indulgences of the other boys. He occasionally makes foolish mistakes, such as joining in with the hysteria of the other boys and killing Simon. When Jack forms a separate, rival group focus in on hunting and savagery rather than rescue, Ralph fights against the superstition and the terror of the other boys. When the numbers in his party begin to diminish, Ralph is left to survive on his own in the forest being chased by the transformed savage boys.

Jack: The antagonist of Lord of the Flies. He is tall, redheaded, and emerges as the leader of the choir boys. When Ralph becomes the initial leader, Jack becomes upset, for he wanted that position but instead becomes the leader of the "hunters." Jack leads the boys from civilized young men into savages through the novel. He is malicious and animalistic. As structure breaks down, Jack forms his own separate sect seperating from Ralph and the rest of the group. Jack is a cruel bully, who is constantly violent and threatens those below him. Jack is always ready to fight. Jack constantly attempts to weaken others. He breaks Piggy's glasses and leads the others towards Piggy's murder. He brings the boys into mass hysteria and eventually hunts Ralph down like an animal.

Piggy: Fat, asthmatic boy with glasses, a typical "sissy," he is scientific and skeptical. He quickly befriends Ralph and recognizes that he can express his views through Ralph. Piggy is an orphan who was brought up by his aunt. He constantly refers to the old way of life. Piggy builds the sundial. He doesn't believe in the beastie. Becausc Piggy is an intellectual who lacks social skills, he is an outsider. The boys ridicule him over and over again.

He can not do anything for himself and constantly tries to get out of work while relying on Ralph. He is the voices of reason and the link to the adult world. The taunting by the boys, escalates to beatings and having his glasses stolen. Eventually, piggy is killed by Roger.

Simon: Simon is the Christ like figure of the novel. He was skinny and had black hair. Simon was a loner who often experienced fainting spells. He would wander into the jungle to think by himself. Simon sees beyond the surface of things. The other boys were indifferent towards Simon for he was not extremely social. He helped others with necessary chores, such as building the huts and taking care of the littleuns. As the novel goes on Simon is gradually alienated. Simon becomes brave in the face of danger. He is the only character to confront the beastie and find out the truth. He believes that the beastie is only controlled in their minds. With Simon's new found knowledge of the truth he goes to explain his findings to the others. When he does, he is sacrificially killed by the boys. Simon, the selfless and harmless boy was beaten and stabbed to death by the horde of boys.

Roger: Initially a shy, quiet boy, but his taciturn nature swings in the opposite direction into a malicious murderer. He takes a liking to throwing rocks and boulders and spears at the fellow boys. Roger has no regret or sympathy after he commits his violent acts. Roger was the most savage of the boys. He engages in sadistic torture of the pig, of Piggy and the littleuns. He supports Jacks leadership in the same way Piggy backs up Ralph.

Plot

In the beginning of the novel, a plane was shot down in an atomic war carrying boys from a boarding school, on their way home. Ralph and Piggy are introduced to the reader as they meet in the lagoon. Piggy finds a conch shell and shows Ralph how to make a noise with it. Ralph uses this to call the other boys and have a meeting, setting down rules that they would live by for the remainder of their stay on the island. Ralph was declared as the ruler and Jack and the other choir boys went hunting for something to eat. This reflected their priorities, Jack hunting, while Ralph thought more rationally, and ruled the boys on the island, trying to maintain some remnants of civilization.

Some of the younger children believed that they saw a "beastie" on the island. This beast scares all of the younger children and most of the older children as well. They had many fears on this island, but needed to remember that they could not let them get in the way of what was important to them. They all decided that they needed a fire to survive on the island and came to the conclusion to use Piggy's glasses as a means of starting it. They get the fire going, but their carelessness in containing this fire burnt half of the island. This reflected their inexperience and immaturity when dealing with this serious situation that they were put into. Even though they meant well, their actions ultimately had a bad outcome.

Jack had focused on the hunting aspect of survival, while Ralph concentrated on building shelter so that they could be safe from nature. So later on, Jack went to hunt a pig while Simon and Ralph were busy building huts. Ralph and Jack argue over the importance and priorities of what had to be done. This issue began the feud that would follow throughout the novel between Ralph and Jack. While Simon is picking fruit for the younger children, he comes across a place in the jungle that he finds very tranquil.

This place would later provide the place where Simon's character would develop. A ship passed by the island one day when the signal fire was out. This carelessness was due to Jack's irresponsibility. He argues with Ralph, not taking blame for the mishap. He says that hunting is more important, and that it was not his fault that the fire had gone out. In doing this, he demonstrates his immaturity and lack of responsibility, arguing with Ralph, because of the jealousy he had for his authority. A fight breaks out and Piggy's glasses are accidentally broken by Jack.

The hunters had killed a pig, and so the boys roast it and feast on it. The next day, a meeting was held where many important issues were discussed. One of these was the validity of the beastie's existence. The point was brought up that the beastie was in fact only themselves. At this meeting, Ralph emphasized the importance of the signal fire. After this, Jack becomes even more troublesome, declaring Ralph a bad leader. Later, he would do something regarding these feelings.

A dead pilot parachutes down to the island one day. The parachutist landed on the rocks and was his parachute got caught. He is spotted and labeled the "beast from the air" by the little children. In response to this, Jack, Ralph and the others set out to hunt this "beast." While traveling, Jack finds a place that he thinks would be a good place for a fort, so they begin preparation by clearing off the ledge. Eventually, Ralph gets them back on their mission, and they continue on, in search of the "beast." After the excitement of the pig hunt, the boys gather and perform a strange tribal dance.

Meanwhile, Simon and Ralph discuss the prospects of being rescued. Simon assures Ralph that he will leave the island alive. Later, the hunters decide to go on another hunt. On this occasion though, the pig wounds Jack and is able to get away. Despite the loss, all remain happy and are caught up in mass hysteria as they reenact their savage rituals. In doing so, they almost kill Robert, who was playing the part of the pig. The leaders decide to go up the mountain to start another fire but they see the "beastie" and run back down. Soon after, a major confrontation between Jack and Ralph occurs on the beach.

Ralph is accused of cowardice by Jack and Jack moves to remove Ralph from leader of the group of boys. He is humiliated though, as none of the boys voted for his takeover. He begins to cry and runs away into the forest. He is followed by Roger and the rest of his hunters.

Realizing that they can't go up the mountain because of the "beastie", Piggy suggests that the remaining boys make a fire on the beach. The story picks up with Jack and his tribe at their new hideout at Castle Rock. They decide to have yet another hunt and kill a large sow. They cut off the pig's head as a sacrifice for the beast and paint themselves in the pig's blood. Simon, alone in the woods hallucinates and thinks the head is the Lord of the Flies, who proceeds to insult his bravery in regard to the "beastie".

Back on the beach, Jack invites the twins, Sam and Eric, Ralph, Piggy, and the littluns to feast with them. After eating, all succumb to the mass hysteria of the tribal dance and kill Simon, thinking he is the beast. Simon was actually coming to bring news that the "beastie" was a dead parachutist. Now Ralph, Piggy, Samneric, and the littluns remain alone with their huts on the beach.

Jack turns his tribe against Ralph and tells the hunters that the beast was only using Simon as a disguise. During that night, Roger and Jack invade Ralph's hut and steals Piggy's glasses to create a fire. The ensuing fight does hurt both Jack and Roger, and they fail to take the conch. Piggy, much angered by this incident desires to go to Castle Rock and make Jack give him his glasses back.

As they approach the neck, Ralph calls and assembly of all the children and tries to reason with Jack. Despite this, Jack insults Ralph again and a fight is the result. In his haste, Roger tries to hit Ralph with a large boulder and instead knocks Piggy off the cliff. In the confusion that results, Ralph is able to escape into the woods.

The entire tribe then searches to eliminate their last opposition. Ralph is forced to hide in the bushes for a long time. He is found by the others and is then closely pursued on throughout the island. He is wounded by a spear in the process. As Ralph runs onto the beach, a rescue ship is sighted and the boys seemingly revert to their former behaviour.

Major Conflicts

Ralph vs. Jack: Ralph represents order and composure in society. Eventually Jack grew tired of Ralph being in charge. He let the barbarism inside of him transform him into a savage-like creature and he went on a rampage, destroying the makeshift civilization the boys worked so hard to create.

Boys vs. Beastie: The Beastie symbolizes the Devil, and is a manifestation of all the evil inside the boys. As the boys grew further and further away from civilization, their desire to kill the Beastie grew. They went from being scared at first, to wanting to hang his head on a pole.

Boys vs. Nature: The boys went hunting many times to try to keep themselves alive. At first, Ralph was afraid to kill the sow. Towards the end, Jack's warrior identity brutally murdered the sow and hung his head on a stick.

Boys vs. Piggy: Piggy represents the weak who are often victimized. The boys tortured him because he was fat and needed such thick glasses. His torture can also be considered a lack of understanding, because the boys had likely never met anyone with problems like his. This can be seen in the boys lack of understanding of asthma, or "ass-mar".

Jack vs. Society: The barbaric quality that arises in Jack throughout the book is really a rebellion against society. He grew tired of taking orders from Ralph and participating in the democratic system that they had. This sense of anarchy must have existed inside of him before the encounter on the island began, but his experiences served to bring it out of him.

Key Issues

The Need for Civilization and Order

Laws and rules are definitely necessary to keep the darker side of human nature in line. When all elements of civilization disappear on the island, the boys revert to a more primitive part of their nature, and they turn into savages and anarchy replaces democracy. Society holds everyone together, and with out civilization and rules, the boy's ideals, values, and basic ideas of what is right and wrong are forgotten, and the evils of human nature emerge.

The Loss of Identity

The boys lose their individual identity when the older children just become known as the biguns, and the younger become known as the littluns. They are not known by their names anymore, but just as a group term. When the hunters paint their faces and kill pigs, they are losing their individualism, and becoming part of a group mentality of savagery. Two twins, named Sam and Eric, "combine" personalities as "samneric." They no longer are known as two separate individuals, but as one person who can no longer separate Sam and Eric.

Human Nature

The shortcomings in human nature will lead to an equally flawed society. Without the restraints of civilization, the behaviour of people will regress to their savage beginnings. Survival is of utmost importance. The base form of human nature will lead to anarchy, violence and death.

Lessons, Morals and Applications

William Golding wrote the novel Lord of the Flies with

the intent to include certain elements of moral behaviour for readers to absorb. he utilized specific symbols found scattered in the novel to portray his intended message to all those who read his work of Literature. The author builds his message into the novel in the form of adventure. The actions done by characters in the novel eventually create Golding's message to the reader. It can be said that Golding describes the moral of the book in relation to the scientific mechanics of society. This is found as a major theme in the book, which is actually fear. The boys on the island view this ideal in the form of the "beastie". The "beastie" is an unseen figure on the island, which is symbolized of the dead parachutist. This fear, however, represents the potential evil found in humans. Yet, this evil is only brought about amongst specific environmental conditions, which Golding synthesized in the book.

The most interesting aspect and probably the most influential characteristic of the story is found to be the age of the characters. The author successfully attempts to show how capable the aspect of evil is among human beings. However, Golding perfects this idea as he used children, who represent purity and innocence in a normal society. Through the use of children, the reader finds that barbarity and savagery can exist amongst even the smallest and most innocuous form of human beings. One can interpret that Golding is trying to represent human nature in its entirety. It is obvious that Golding is showing all levels of human capability in terms of psychology and science. The reader sees that humans exist in higher levels, such as present day activity, as well as the lowest form, which is represented by Lord of the Flies. The author creates a situation, which includes factors that are capable of forcing humans to fall into lower forms of mentality.

A very important concept of the story is the fact that in the society which was created on the island, order is a needed tool for existence. The concept of order is found to be a key issue as the society which Golding created contained no order. This book accurately shows how the absence of order results in an alteration of moral behaviour. In Lord of the Flies, morals can be seen in the form of aggressive behavioral actions. Such actions include the murder of Piggy. Obviously children would never come to such decisions or actions against one another under normal societal conditions. However, Golding creates a barbaric civilization in which children do such actions.

Lord of the Flies can be considered a classical novel. A classic in the respect that the author creates special circumstances under which abnormal actions and functions mutate into everyday activity. All of these concepts and ideals are generated by Golding to finally produce a novel of both perplexity and perfection.

Themes

William Golding says that "the theme (of the book) is an attempt to trace back the defects of society to the defects of human nature...The moral is that the shape of society must depend on the ethical nature of the individual and not on any political system."

Power

Different types of power, some used and abused. Democratic power is shown when choices and decisions are shared among many people on the island. Jack shows authoritarian power by threatening and terrifying others. Some of the boys utilize brute force, when hunting for pigs, and later hunting for Ralph.

Fear of the Unknown

The boy's fear of the unknown on the island leads to their fear of the beast. The boys cannot accept the notion of a beast existing on the island, nor can they let go of it. The recognition that no real beast exists, and that the only beast on the island is fear itself is one of the deepest meanings of the story.

Blindness and Sight

Piggy is blind to his immediate surroundings but really understands what is going on on the island. Unfortunately, the boys do not realise that Piggy sees more, and he is treated poorly and is eventually killed.

Interpretive Level

Piggy and the glasses.....Clear sightedness, intelligence.. Piggy's glasses bring "fire" to the island, which is really the fire of knowledge.

Breaking of Piggy's glasses......

the progressive decay of rational influence on the island

The conch...

Democracy and Order Simon's behaviour represents...

Christ-like Figure, pure goodness

The island... a microcosm representing the world

The beast... the capacity for evil within everyone

Roger's behaviour represents... evilness and sadism

Jack's behaviour represents... savagery and anarchy

Ralph's behaviour represents...

Democracy and civilization; the capacity for evil within everyone

Lord of the Flies... the devil, great danger

Jack represents the leader of the forces of anarchy

Roger represents the "official" torturer and executioner of the tribe

Q. Compare and contrast the Jack of Macbeth and Lord of the Flies

Or

Q. Discuss the theme of evil both Macbeth and Lord of the Flies

History has shown life's mercilessness with the strongest surviving. In this game of survival, dishonorable tactics are used to climb the ladder swiftly with aspirations of attaining the pinnacle of power. Honesty and morals must be a mere memory if personal profits are to be achieved at a rapid pace. As a result, corruption and ruthlessness grows variably with the desires and cravings that haunt a person's psyche. Both Macbeth and Lord of the Flies give insight to the fact that greed engulfs people into malicious tyrants with the characters that are portrayed within these two novels.

Thus, Jack, from Lord of the Flies and Macbeth, from Macbeth have both shown the world a crucial lesson that power and ambition are the root of all evil, as they carried out unethical action to achieve and maintain their respected goals. Each author, with immense captivation, portrays his respected characters with noble beginnings unadulterated of any corruption. Ambition has not yet overwhelmed the minds of these two respected characters, which therefore, gives them a chaste disposition. Jack from Lord of the Flies is introduced to the reader in a "holy" aura with the description of his choir; " Their bodies, from throat to ankle, were hidden by black cloaks which bore a long silver cross on the left breast" Conveying religion into Jack's first emergence shows the likely innocence encompassed in the boy's life prior to crashing on the island. The induction of Macbeth also renders an uncanny depiction of a noble general, saving his country form domination and tyranny.

" For brave Macbeth,-well he deserves that name,-disdaining fortune, with his brandish'd steel, which smok'd with bloody execution, like valour's minion carv'd out his passage till he fac'd the slave; which ne'er shook hands, nor bade farewell to him, till he unseam'd him from nave to the chaps, and fix'd his head upon our battlements." The sergeant's account of the war, gives a picture perfect image of Macbeth, as a hero that has put Scotland on his back, carrying the country to freedom. As the character progresses in the plot, their inhabitance is parallel in that they have both receive prestigious rankings amongst their societies and in essence, their lives are ideal. Each holds substantial power over some aspect of civilization. Jack is appointed Leader of the hunters, the only high rank besides Ralph, who was chosen leader.

This gives Jack elevated stature as he controls a certain portion of the boys inhibited in the island. Macbeth receives titles of nobility and influence as Thane of Glamis and is recently appointed Thane of Cawdor. With a great quantity of control being received, each character devours the power as if it were a precious jewel. This sample of power gives both characters further aspirations for additional clout, like a sharks reaction to the first taste of blood. Virtue has been forgotten and once moral men have been swallowed up by the cravings of greed with the search for more abundance of power.

Evil has seeped through each character, diminishing their moral code in the name of attaining their esteemed goals. Both state their feelings in different ways. Macbeth, seconds after hearing his new appointment states, " If good, why do I yield to that suggestion whose horrid image doth unfix my hair and make my seated heart knock at my ribs, against the use of nature? Present fears are less than horrible imaginings; my thought, whose murder yet is but fantastical," Jack although less apparent, also show his attentions to overtake all leadership. His constant disagreement with Ralph exhibits no respect and shows his aspirations of taking total command. Instead of looking over the fire, Jack deliberately disobeys the order made by Ralph and goes out hunting instead.

Ambition has driven evil spirits, which will not die until their dreams are accomplished. With the seed of power and ambition implemented into these two minds, the plant grows out of control until conscience is completely drained out. The tainted characters now obsess about their castle in the sky. In order for this dream to become reality both Jack and Macbeth listen to the dissipation that frequently rouse their minds. Macbeth in his aspirations of becoming king exterminates the life of Duncan (the present kind of Scotland) in his sleep. During this era, Crimes against the King who is to be worshipped at all times was the supreme sin to commit. Universal order has been destroyed, as Macbeth has pursued the evil that was brought on to him.

Similarly although not as severe as Macbeth, Jack pays attention to the evil that constantly penetrates his imagination. Jack goes against the beauty of nature and viciously slaughters a boar in an attempt to obtain additional supremacy. Jack has essentially ignored the very conscience that would not allow himself to do the same deed earlier at their inhabitance in the island. Even though killing a pig is not as an immense offense as the assassination of an emperor, both have perpetrated atrocious transgressions in the name of collecting enhanced dominance. Ambitions caused evil spirits to infiltrate the lives of these two prevailing characters.

In order for the unethical measures to be fulfilled, evil

manifestations are fully needed to erase the souls of the offenders. Jack just prior to the slaughter of the innocent animal put on a mask consisting of clay to conceal his virtue and expose the evil needed to perform the act. " Jack turned a half-concealed face up to Roger and answered the comprehension of his glaze. 'For hunting. Like in the war. You know – dazzle paint. Like things trying to look like something else —-' " Concealing their human temperaments, Jack and the hunters developed savagery that was initiated by evil. In an even more confounding scenario, Macbeth also utilizes evil to aid in his endeavor to become king.

The three witches who glisten with pure evil are the first to embed Macbeth with the precise actions that were needed to become the future king. Without the existence of the malevolent witches, the killing of Duncan would not have been eminent as Macbeth would have been perfectly at ease with the positions of power he had just received. An illusion of a dagger appears straight from the demons, leading Macbeth directly to Duncan's room. " Is this a dagger which I see before me, the handle toward my hand? Come, let me clutch thee; I have thee not, and yet I see the still." The hallucination tantalizes Macbeth as the encounter puts his brain in the precise state of mind for perpetrating the unlawful death of the king.

By way of the massacres carried out by both Jack and Macbeth, a line has been crossed to a world of evil. In penetrating this point, turning back to virtue and honesty is merely an impossible task. As a result, each character is embedded in a root of dissipation that will rule over their lives infinitely even after all their ambitions have been accomplished. Macbeth upon fulfilling his prerogative and ultimate dream of ruling his nation still carries the evil that lent a hand in the execution of Duncan. This evil harasses his soul as if it were a parasite leaching on with no intention of ever leaving its victim. Due to this corruption of his heart, Macbeth orders the execution of his best friend Banquo only because he feels the slightest sense of danger burdening his conscience.

This cold-heartedness grows like a snowball as the evil holds a stronger grasp of Macbeth's nature. Upon the failure of having Fleance killed, Macbeth does not even hesitate in sealing the fate of the two murderers by killing them himself. In fighting for his ambitions, Macbeth has made murders a routine, as the evil in hand seems to be perfectly normal in his eyes. Jack, also in his accomplishments loses control of all sense of right and wrong and begins to diminish the civilization on his island. Becoming progressively more cockier, Jack forms a new tribe in Castle Rock, which represents malevolence in a primitive existence. In forming this new group Jack receives the full-blown power that he has yearned for.

Unfortunately this uprooting for ambitious power closes the door for the chance of Jack redeeming himself as evil has now engulfed his intellect. In addition to the newfound evil that casts over the characters, the wickedness also manifests its self throughout their societies poisoning everybody that crosses its path. Due to this poignant fact, chaos and destruction results for each of the respected civilizations. The utopia of the island in Lord of the Flies became sheer remnants as fear and persecution was all that remained. Jack installs in the boys immense trepidation as the beast is purposely blown way out of proportion in an attempt to receive absolute obedience. The fear that is implemented gives Jack more influence, as he is now the only salvation in suppressing the dreaded "beast".

Even more disheartening in this chaotic regime is the death of Simon. An angelic figure, Simon is brutally slain as Jack led all the boys to a demonic trance that led all reason go. The trance brought out the utmost hatred as it stated, "Kill the beast! Cut his throat! Spill his blood!"Without this loathing that was spurred by the "Chief", the death of Simon who represented innocence would have been simply avertable. Correspondingly, Macbeth seeps evil into the people he rules giving them a period of downright pestilence.

" We may again give to our tables meat, sleep to our nights, free from our feasts and banquets bloody knives, do faithful homage and receive full honors; all which we pine for now." This example exemplifies the state of terror Scotland was put through, as the King creates a kingdom in his own image and since Macbeth cannot eat and sleep, the people he rules over must also suffer the same existence Ambition still put in overdrive; the two fiends go over the edge by losing every single ounce of dignity left in their vicious soul. Diminishing to the lowest form of humanity, each tyrant commits atrocious undertakings deliberately on the most innocent of the populace. Arguably the most defenseless member of the group in Lord of the Flies, Piggy's death brought supreme dishonor in Jack's reign as leader.

Although Jack did not pull the trigger in throwing the boulder, his approval alone demonstrates the evil intentions that captivated his mind. Equally malicious if not worse due the maturity that age has brought him; Macbeth sets out and kills the most vulnerable as a method of revenge. Having seen Macduff's non-attendance at his banquet as a personal insult, Macbeth commits a cowardly act by sending troops to slay Macduff's innocent wife and children. "The castle of Macduff I will surprise; Seize upon Fife; give to the edge of the sword his wife, his babes, and all unfortunate souls that trace his line. No boasting like a fool; this deed I'll do before this purpose cool." All scruples that once existed in Macbeth as a noble general has been burned by the fire of evil that now lights his nucleus.

Once dreams and ambitions of power have been achieved to reality at the costly price of their souls. Both characters now encompass full-blown hatred and can represent symbols as harsh as the devil. Macbeth and Lord of the Flies both have mesmerizing truths entrenched into the plots of the respected books. History to the present has revealed that carrying out ambition can precisely result in evil undertakings. Tyrants such as Hitler and Saddam Hussein have shown the world that these cases are not all fantasy but striving to fulfill ambitions through evil methods are ingrained in our society. The way that our modern civilization is set up Macbeth and Jack could be considered the norm.

Both men would be the ideal businessmen doing immoral

tasks that others wouldn't dare in a ruthless fashion, all in the name of the almighty dollar. Without power and ambition evil could not exist, as it would be suppressed without fuel or motive to ignite it. Macbeth and Jack have both taught us a vital lesson in life that both authors have set out to teach. Using events that were probably deep-rooted in their lives, Golding and Shakespeare have tried to shed light to the reader the hidden reality of greed and ambition. Complete onus is on us to learn from such ingenuous intellect and not make similar mistakes that will lead us in the identical road as these two tragic heroes.

Q. Discuss the impact of World War II on William Golding's Lord of the Flies

Or

Q. Examine the symbols of light and darkness in William Golding's Lord of the flies

The world had witnessed the atrocities of World War II and began to examine the defects of their social ethics. Man's purity and innocence was gone. Man's ability to remain civilized was faltering. This change of attitude was extremely evident in the literature of the age. Writers, who through the use of clever symbolism, mocked the tragedy of man's fate. One such writer was William Golding. An author who has seen the destruction of war and despises its inevitable return. Through the use of innocent and untainted children, Golding illustrates how man is doomed by his own instinct. The novel is called Lord of the Flies, and is of extreme importance to help reconstruct the current wave of revolutionary ideas that swept the twentieth-century generation.

Lord of the Flies portrays the belief of the age that man is in a constant struggle between darkness and light, the defects of human nature, and a philosophical pessimism that seals the fate of man. Golding's work are, due to their rigid structure and style, are interpreted in many different ways. Its unique style is different from the contemporary thought and therefore open for criticism. The struggle between darkness and light is a major theme in all the works of William Golding. Strong examples of this are found throughout Lord of the Flies.

The most obvious is the struggle between Ralph and Jack. The characters themselves have been heavily influenced by the war. Ralph is the representative of Democracy. Elected as the leader he and Piggy his companion keep order and maintain a civilized government. The strength of Ralph's character was supported by the power of World War II. Jack, on the other hand, represents authoritarianism. He rules as a dictator and is the exact opposite of Ralph. Jack is exemplifying the Hitler's and Mussolini's of the world. He is what the world fears and yet follows. This struggle is born at the very beginning and escalates till the very end. The struggle in the book is a negative outlook on life in the future.

One other example is the debate over the existence of the beast. The idea of a beast brings all into a state of chaotic excitement in which Ralph and Piggy lose control. Ralph and especially Piggy try to convince everyone that there is no such thing as a beast to maintain order. Jack and his choir of hunters do all to win support of the hunt and in doing so he becomes an advocate for evil. This struggle between good and evil is a fairly clear picture of the way this post-war generation viewed man and his journey through life. This is done through Golding's masterful use of allegory.

Therefor making it enjoyable for all readers. Golding himself stated that the purpose of the novel was to trace the defects of society back "to the many defects of human society." The use of children is an extremely effective way of making the purpose understandable to readers of all generations. "The idea of placing boys alone on an island, and letting them work out archetypal patterns of human society, is a brilliant technical device, with a simple coherence which is easily understood by a modern audience." This quote by C.B. Cox gives us the reason why this novel has survived so long and is so well respected. The children are left to react in ways that will test how close they will resemble modern civilization.

The group at first tries to assemble a type of demcratic government in which Ralph is elected leader. At this instant we see something that is most important. That is the reluctance of Jack to become the leader. He and his choir singers, which are dressed in black to symbolize evil, are immediately separated from the group and labeled as hunters. This gives Jack some piece of power and like the dictators of the 1930's he insists he receive more. The hunter party is Golding's triumph in giving the first glimpse of human savagery through the hunter party. As the hunter party grows in numbers the hunters have a great thirst for blood and death. This is how the beast is first seen. They become more savage and soon begin to paint their faces to show how fierce they are. The whole time Ralph and Piggy the only rational thinkers have become the greatest enemy of the party.

They begin to make chants and dances and do all to destroy any order. When Piggy is killed we see the end of rational thinking and the complete collapse of mankind's strength to remain civilized at all costs. Man has become savage and has shown a terrifying glimpse into the future of Democracy. The defect of man is revered to as the beast. The thing the boys were all running away from was what they became and it was lead by the representation of Satan himself, the red haired Jack. At certain stages in the story Golding deliberately makes us forget that these are only young children. Their drama and conflict typify the inevitable overthrow of all attempts to impose a permanent civilization on the instincts of man.

Golding along with many of the writers of the time gave pessimistic endings not only to their books but to life in general. They showed society in a sort of downward decent which could not be stopped because it is in our nature. The savagery of man is used through the use of the hunters. The pessimism is viewed through the ending.

The ending has been interpreted in many ways but most contain the same ideas. The idea that there is no hope or mankind. The story takes place in the near future during an atomic war. The children were being transported away from Britain. The world had already started to become savage and as many people in the generation said " If world war three is atomic bombs than world war four is sticks and clubs." Obviously the idea of human nature and savagery were in fact very prominent. Golding uses an excellent idea for the end of this story. The naval officer comes to rescue the children from their war with Ralph and are suprised to find how savage the "English" boys were acting. At this point we see Ralph begin to cry not for being saved but for mankind. " The naval officer, who comes to rescue them...His trim cruiser, the sub-machine gun, his white drill, epaulettes, revolver and row of gilt buttons, are only more sophisticated substitutes for the war-paint and sticks of Jack and his followers. He too is chasing men in order to kill, and the dirty children mock the absurd civilized attempt to hide the power of evil.

And so when Ralph weeps for the end of innocence, the darkness of man's heart, and the death of his true wise friend, Piggy, he weeps for all the human race." Such a tragic view of the future of mankind and their nature is a perfect window for people to understand how the impact of the war made the world rethink its ethics and how life was thought of as a punishment in the extreme sense and that there was no hope for the future except fear.

This view has since changed but not greatly as one would imagine. The basic ideas are still their and modern society may still relate to this novel. The interpretation may not be exact but from now on mankind will always weep for " the end of innocence, the darkness of man's heart, and" the most disturbing" for all the human race."

Q. Discuss the Concept of Democracy and Equality in Lord of the Flies

Or

Q. Discuss evil as a destructive influence in man with reference to Lord of the flies

The Lord of the Flies is not just a nasty story about little boys on an island. In fact it is a parable about real life and human nature. This book is about Golding's views on human society and having lived through two world wars and many others, Golding has seen how evil we can get and the continual ironic re occurrences of human errors throughout history. At first, Golding is saying that the future is gray, society is disintegrating and anarchy and violence are due to thrive once more, but the arrival of the naval officers symbolizes that there is still hope. He show this all with the continual theme that evil is present as a destructive influence in man, operating against the forces of reason and civilization.

When landing on the island, the boys were faced with freedom from rules, or as Piggy saw it, freedom from adults. On the Island, the boys had problems from the beginning. The first thing the boys did was form their own society, establishing rules and electing a chief- these were remnants of their past, and the automatic need for authority was in their blood. Both Ralph and Jack wanted to be chief and when the rest of the biguns and littluns voted for Ralph, it caused the first sign of friction between the two 'elders'. Ralph tries to deal with the problem by appointing Jack the leader of the hunters, and leader of the keepers of fire. However, even though being a good chief and making everyone happy, this solution ended up doing more harm than good. There are definitely problems with between Ralph's system of practicality, common sense and civilized life, and Jack's instinct of hatred and savagery.

Although establishing a serious foundation of rules and civilization, Ralph was pulled in another direction as well as all the other boys, he wanted to have fun going hunting, playing and building forts. Everyone deep down inside them wants pleasure. He also realized, though, the need for fire. The fire was one of the only the hopes of returning to civilization again. At first the fire seemed like fun to the boys, but when realization of the hard work for constant upkeep occurred, the boys got bored and wanted to go on and do more exciting activities. The boys lost sight of the truth and were drawn away by Jack. Jack's leadership was in the direction of pleasure. Ralph and Piggy understood the important of the fire, but the boys followed Jack and his obsession with savagery and killing. The only thing Jack cared about was meat. Jack eventually killed a pig but at the sacrifice of the fire, missing an opportunity of rescue and the return to civilization because the fire went out. But Jack didn't seem to care

"'Jack, his face smeared with clays, reached the top first and hailed Ralph excitedly, with lifted spear.

'Look! We've killed a pig-we stole up on them-we got in a circle-' "They seemed to share one wide ecstatic grin. Jack had too many things to tell Ralph at once. Instead he danced a step or two, then remembered his dignity and stood still, grinning.

Ralph spoke.

'You let the fire go out'

Jack checked, vaguely irritated by this irrelevance but to happy to let it worry him 'There was lashings of blood,' said Jack, laughing and shuddering. 'You should have seen it!' Ralph spoke again, hoarsely. He had not moved.

'You let the fire go out.'"

This shows how much Jack really cared about screwing up, representing humans in their most basic form. Thinking just about himself and not admitting to his mistake. Ralph is upset as being rescued was his top priority. As the book continues, Jack tries harder and harder to assert his total authority. More symbolization – Jack becomes leader in the forest, where it is all dark and scary, while Ralph is chief where there is light out on the open, civilized beach. By now, everyone has become completely barbaric, or natural, as they worshipped the Lord of the Flies. It is most evident now that Jack only gives orders, he doesn't take them. We see the huge differences now, -Ralph is centre-wing offering freedom of speech, democracy, steadiness and he takes advice, all the things we have used as the basis of a successful society. While Jack represents ambitious radical rule – a culmination of right-wing totalitarianism and left-wing 'democratic' monitored guidance. A very accurate image of the 20th century.

In the end Jack and his hunters kill two very good people and try to kill Ralph before all of this is stopped by the appearance of a naval officer. Maybe it is individual greed that has ripped this small bio-society apart. This whole book would have turned out differently if Jack – the savage problem maker, had thought about more than himself. I fell that the message in this book is that people are like a flock of sheep; if a few people are savage, then many are savage, if a few people are greedy, then others will definitely soon follow. If a society was made up of all saints, then we would have a system where, "each individual would contribute to the total harmonious operation of society."

William Golding told a story rich with symbolism and irony to make a point. Humans delicately depend on their use of the norm of society. People are okay and cool when under the control of society, but as the book shows,

"freedom of the human spirit means the end of moral society" Does this mean that pure equality and democracy can never be achieved?

Alternate Ending to the Lord of the Flies: Smoke grew thick as the fire spread, engulfing everything in sight. Cries of birds, animals, and boys alike echoed through the depths of the jungle. Humidity from the sun and flames grew causing distant illusion to some of the boys.

Ralph ran through the bushes, creepers and trees. Not minding about the minor hurts and pains or the cuts on his feet he passed over rocks and the hard ground. His eyes burned with the smoke from the raging inferno.

He stopped immediately once a burning tree came to his path. He turned and ducked under a fallen tree and crawled through the foliage. He kept his speed up as best he could. His heart pounded in his chest with fear, anguish and determination. Two emotions fought inside of him as he ran. Was he to give up? Everything was already out of control. Should he just stop and face death as it seemed to be..? Then the thought of Piggy and Simon came to his mind, and brought a wrenching feeling in his chest. They were the only ones who had any sense on this bloody island! But they died. Ralph wouldn't be surprised if he met the same fate... He wondered how he could continue on, or when he should he even try.

The dominant people are the one who rule this island, if you're not strong then you'll be no better than the pigs that the hunters ate. Ralph ducked under a low branch. An idle thought of how long would he be able to keep this up, crossed his mind. He had no one and wouldn't dare put the twins in danger again. He couldn't bring anyone else down because of his mistakes.

He jumped over a log and went down hill, losing his balance and tumbling a bit but quickly getting to his feet. He used his spear as walking stick, his ankle hurting from the fall. His feet caused a little splash in the small stream which ran into the river. He splashed through it before coming to dead stop. Taking a couple steps back, he saw a figure shift out from the looming palms.

Ralph felt fear blended with his anger like dark clouds colliding against each other into a swirl of hurricanes and storms. The Beast... Simon was right. Remembering the faint words that seemed to have been said so long ago, he heard from the nature boy. All those times when they, including himself have believed that he was batty...

"Jack." Ralph said. His jaw clenched and looked at the former leader of the choir boys who was now an aggressive hunter in this foreign land. This hell. His dirty hands tightened its hold on the spear. One on one. He'd beaten Jack before. He do it again. Jack watched him. Sharp blue eyes glinted like a pair of blades. The eyes of a true predator, scrutinizing his prey with hunger in those depths. He could almost feel the heart beat of the chief. The fair haired boy. A slow sadistic smile appeared on his face.

"Well, how you do you like things now, Ralph? Look where you're at with your stupid rules," Jack said coolly. Ralph met his gaze. "I know where I am... Why don't you open your eyes Jack?" Ralph gestured around them. "You call this a good island!? This good island of yours is up in flames! What this is is hell! The littluns talked about the beast. They were right. There is a beast." Ralph's eyes narrowed. "And I'm looking at him right now..." Jack's body tensed, as he approaching his prey in smooth motion. Sleek like a feline. "Simon was right. The only beast here was us."

A flicker of emotion showed through his face but then vanished as soon as it had come. Jack had never meant to hurt Simon... But Simon just got himself in that mess. It was his own fault. He should've known better than to scare them like that.

"And then Pig-"

"Fatty was just a useless lot," Jack snapped. He took another step forward, as Ralph took an automatic step back, keeping the distance from his former friend.

"Look at yourself, Jack. Savages," Ralph said with distaste. Jack kept his smile. "You're not going to run anymore leader? This is an island. I know this as much as I know my own hand." Ralph shook his head, standing his ground. Both get back into their stances they knew so well from the other practice they'd been having recently. Like two wolves, body tense, eyes focus on the other, continuing this small dance of death.

Ralph was the one who made the first shot, lunging at Jack with all he had despite his exhaustion. He hit jack with the butt of the spear. Jack countered that shot, striking Ralph with his own spear. They continued to fight, like two dominant wolves, trying to get the other pinned... or killed. Teeth were almost bared and spears were thrown at each other. Slicing skins drawing drops of blood. The clacking noise when the spears hit each other was heard. Soon the spears tossed aside, and they were rolling on the ground throwing their fists at each others face. Ralph grabbed a handful of the red hair and pulled back and force him down and off of him. He lunge at Jack. He threw severe punches as blood trickled from his hand.

Jack grabbed his throat and instantly have them rolled over. Ralph underneath him and have Ralph's head hit the smooth stones of the bottom of the river, knocking Ralph out of his concentration, making pay more attention to sparks of pain that erupted in his mind.

Water rushed passed them, soaking Jack's fair hair, carrying away the crimson blood, taking it down river. The sound of small tapping blood dripped off of Jack and landed on Ralph's face.

Ralph's eyes locked with Jack's. Emotions of annoyance, hatred and dispute reflected from them, but then faded. When exhaustion took its final shot at him, as things started to become fuzzy. Adrenaline left the youth's body as he peered up at the predator. His eyes fell shut and his voice became laced with tiredness.

"Well, what are you waiting for? Kill me already."

There was no response. Sounds of the fire crackling not far away blended in with the gentle trickling of water that passed and swept the blood, sweat, and grime from his body along with the harsh unison of the two boys.

With the painful seconds drawing and the annoyance of curiosity eating the back of his mind, he opened his eyes and looked at the wiry savage. The blood took some of the dirt from his face and trickled down onto Ralph's face. Ralph closed his eyes to avoid the small splash when the drop of blood touched right below his right eye. Looking back up at Jack, his vision was dulled with the creeping of darkness around the corner of his eyes. The blood loss was affecting him.

"What are you waiting for! Kill me!" Ralph barked, to his amazement and utter disbelief... and even fear. He saw the same smile on Jack's face, that same taunting smile that was on the pearly white skull of that pig that brought a chill down his spine drain the blood from his face. His vision got darker, as if the sun was setting. He forced his vision to focus... Or at least his hearing. The last words he heard brought fear into the pit of his stomach.

"...I have better use for you, than killing you," Jack's sneering voice whispered. Pale eyes looked at Jack one final moment before the blanket of ebony took his vision. The last thing he saw was the same chilling smile that was on the Lord of the Flies...

Q. Discuss the context of lord of the flies byWilliam Golding

Or

Q. Analyse the background setting of Wiiliam Golding's Lord of the flies

WILLIAM GOLDING WAS BORN on September 19, 1911, in Cornwall, England. Although he tried to write a novel as early as age twelve, his parents urged him to study the natural sciences. Golding followed his parents' wishes until his second year at Oxford, when he changed his focus to English literature. After graduating from Oxford, he worked briefly as a theater actor and director, wrote poetry, and then became a schoolteacher. In 1940, a year after England entered World War

II, Golding joined the Royal Navy, where he served in command of a rocket-launcher and participated in the invasion of Normandy. Golding's experience in World War II had a profound effect on his view of humanity and the evils of which it was capable. After the war, Golding resumed teaching and started to write novels. His first and greatest success came with *Lord of the Flies* , which ultimately became a bestseller in both Britain and the United States after more than twenty publishers rejected it. The novel's sales enabled Golding to retire from teaching and devote himself fully to writing.

Golding wrote several more novels, notably *Pincher Martin* , and a play, *The Brass Butterfly* . Although he never matched the popular and critical success he enjoyed with *Lord of the Flies,* he remained a respected and distinguished author for the rest of his life and was awarded the Nobel Prize for Literature in 1983. Golding died in 1993, one of the most acclaimed writers of the second half of the twentieth century.

Lord of the Flies tells the story of a group of English schoolboys marooned on a tropical island after their plane is shot down during a war. Though the novel is fictional, its exploration of the idea of human evil is at least partly based on Golding's experience with the real-life violence and brutality of World War II. Free from the rules and structures of civilization and society, the boys on the island in *Lord of the Flies* descend into savagery. As the boys splinter into factions, some behave peacefully and work together to maintain order and achieve common goals, while others rebel and seek only anarchy and violence. In his portrayal of the small world of the island, Golding paints a broader portrait of the fundamental human struggle between the civilizing instinct—the impulse to obey rules, behave morally, and act lawfully—and the savage instinct—the impulse to seek brute power over others, act selfishly, scorn moral rules, and indulge in violence.

Golding employs a relatively straightforward writing style in *Lord of the Flies,* one that avoids highly poetic language, lengthy description, and philosophical interludes. Much of the novel is allegorical, meaning that the characters and objects in the novel are infused with symbolic significance that conveys the novel's central themes and ideas. In portraying the various ways in which the boys on the island adapt to their new surroundings and react to their new freedom, Golding explores the broad spectrum of ways in which humans respond to stress, change, and tension.

Readers and critics have interpreted *Lord of the Flies* in widely varying ways over the years since its publication. During the 1950s and 1960s, many readings of the novel claimed that *Lord of the Flies* dramatizes the history of civilization. Some believed that the novel explores fundamental religious issues, such as original sin and the nature of good and evil. Others approached *Lord of the Flies* through the theories of the psychoanalyst Sigmund Freud, who taught that the human mind was the site of a constant battle among different impulses—the id (instinctual needs and desires), the ego (the conscious, rational mind), and the superego (the sense of conscience and morality).

Still others maintained that Golding wrote the novel as a criticism of the political and social institutions of the West. Ultimately, there is some validity to each of these different readings and interpretations of *Lord of the Flies*. Although Golding's story is confined to the microcosm of a group of boys, it resounds with implications far beyond the bounds of the small island and explores problems and questions universal to the human experience.

Q. Discuss the factor of Fear in The Lord of the Flies

Or

Q. How the fear of the boys made them beast

In The Lord of the Flies, fear is the cause of all destruction and violence, which leads to savagery, and disobeying of human morals. Throughout the entire book fear is what drives these young innocent boys into savagery, and what also pulls most of them away from expectable human behaviour. Without the normal rules of society helping to guide them, they become disoriented with the new surroundings, therefore freighting them into savage ways.

After the traumatic plane crash the boys became frightened because their world of comfort was no longer visible, and a dark scary place awaited their arrival. Fear inside of them became greater but the boys did not to show their fear. While struggling to get through the jungle Piggy gets caught up in tree vines, frustrated he yelled out "I can't hardly move with all these creeper things." With out even realizing it Piggy shows how his fear turns things that are beautiful in nature into things to beware. Now with the danger of many creatures/ animals, they decide to hunt. Hunt because in the mind of the hunters getting rescued is not in the future, and to survive is to kill, and to kill is to stay alive. So fear of not getting rescued sets in and the children start to hunt and destroy.

With the threat of the beastie the hunters are extra cautious so they build a fire on the beach and they hold a gathering. The fire represent the safeness of light and the gathering keeps everyone together, so as a group, are not scared. They start to dance and circle around the fire, meanwhile Simon knowing the truth about the beastie hurries to tell the boys, "The circle became a horseshoe. A thing was crawling out of the forest. It came darkly, uncertainly.

The shrill screaming that rose before the beast was like a pain. The beast stumbled into the horseshoe. Kill the beast! Cut his throat! Spill his blood! Do him in!" The beast was now turned into innocent Simon and because of the fear inside the jungle, and inside themselves, Simon was brutally beaten and killed by the other boys as the mother pig was with her young. The killing of Simon showed how fear caused disorientation in reality. Simon having no fear, was the one who had the answer. The beast is within us; there is nothing to fear. Simon used no violence and came face to face with the beast. He knew the truth.

Q. Analyse the Priorities and Hunting in Lord of the Flies

Or

Q. Discuss Jack's obsession of hunting

" We can help them find us. We must make a fire."

While the boys were making huts for shelter, Jack was off hunting instead of helping with the huts. All he cared about was that the boys needed meat, which was indeed true, but they also needed shelter.

As Ralph, Piggy and Simon are working on a shelter they are listening to, " And then," said Jack, " when I've had a bathe and something to eat I'll just trek over to the other side of the mountain and see if I can see any traces. Coming?". In the beginning, the boys got along great, but I think that it works against each other. Ralph and Jack get along so good that when things get kind of bad it just goes way bad.

"Almost too heavy."

Jack grinned back.

"Not for the two of us.".

The book starts by Ralph and Piggy meeting in the jungle of a stranded island. They wander to the beach wondering if there is any other kid on the beach. When they find a shell, "the conch", they blow into it and make a bellowing sound. At the sound of the "conch", every boy, big and small, comes to the beach. Along with a group of boys is Jack Merridew, the leader of a choir. When the assembly begins, they decide that they want a chief. The kids all believe that the boy with the "conch" should be chief. They also decide that there is no "beastie", which Jack also obsesses about hunting and takes much of his attention. Immidiatly Jack is offended and has something against Ralph, even though he seems to hide his jealosy.

When Jack's obsession for hunting overrides all other reality he decides to start his own tribe. Many of the boys choose to follow. One night when they have a feast over a dead sow of the tribe a figure considered to be the beast is beaten and stabbed with spears. It was really Simon. The ones who don't join the tribe are now the outcasts of the island.

One night Jack and two of his tribe members raid the huts of Ralph, Piggy and Samneric. They stole Piggy's glasses, which only had one glass anyway, now making him blind in both eyes. The next day Ralph, Piggy and Samneric travel to the other side of the Island to get the glasses back. They are refused the glasses, and when a rock comes plunging down the mountain, Piggy is knocked 40 feet to a rock and is carried away to the sea. Then the chase is on. Jack, Samneric and the hunters begin to chase after Ralph. While at the other end of the island a ship comes ashore and plans to take the boys to homeland. They find this out when the chase of Ralph travels to the beach where the ship has landed. The differences between Ralph and Jack cause all the confrontations. One prefers priorities, and the other prefers hunting. Both are needed but hunting needed to come second. In the end, Jack and his side wins, not only because they chase Ralph into the officer, but because he has the majority of the kids and the upper hand. Eventually, Ralph would have had to give in and either die or become Jack's slave.

In the end it all works out because they are rescued and only a couple of kids die.

Q. Who is the Antagonist and Protagonist in Lord of the Flies

Or

Q. Compare Jack and Ralph with reference to their status of Antagonist and Protagonist

Ralph is the antagonist in the story Lord of the Flies. The boys on the island choose Ralph as their chief, and he tries his best to keep the group in an orderly, civilized fashion. Ralph's main concern is being rescued and returned to a life of adult supervision. He is very persistent in keeping the fire lit at all times, and making shelters for the boys. Although must of the boys are out playing and hunting, Ralph and a few loyal others stay back to do their hard work. Whenever things become out of hand, Ralph will hold assemblies reminding the boys of where they came from.

He also listens to others opinions at these meetings, and stresses the main facts. However, as the story advances, barbaric instincts begin to develop in all of the boys except for Piggy and Ralph. There is just something about blood shed and violence that leads everyone but these two boys, into the leadership of Jack. Although Ralph experiences these hidden natures, the first time he helps slay a boar, he is quick to remember his morals. Eventually, Jack's cult becomes so strong, that they manage to add everyone into their society, even if it means killing them.

Soon, Ralph is the only one left, and the target of Jack's

society. However, Ralph is a strong moral person, and instead of surrendering in order to save his life, he stands up against the others. Ralph even manages to kick over the Lord of the Flies, which is the main symbol of evil in the book. But like must stories end, the good guy wins. The boys are all rescued and returned to civilization by naval officers. As this rescue takes place, Ralph weeps "for the end of innocence, the darkness of man's heart, and the fall through the air of the true, wise friend piggy."

Ralph isn't the only boy with strong believes on the island. Jack is always willing to fight for what he believes in. Jack Merridew is a very arrogant boy, who lusts for power. He is the leader of the choir boys, who he soon turns into hunters. The fact that the book and characters refer to Jack sporadically using his first and last time, makes Jake seem superior and powerful. When the boys choose Ralph over Jack for chief, Jack becomes furious. This is when the reader realizes that Jack desires power over everything. He is constantly contradicting Ralph, and speaks out of line in order to prove that he would make a better leader.

The first couple of times he tries to kill a pig, innocence keeps him from succeeding. However, he soon gets over this factor, and turns into a blood thirsty savage. Jack becomes a symbol of fear and evil, when he murders a pregnant sow, and rejoices about it. Hanging her head on a stick for all to see his victory. The more barbarian like he becomes, the more power and leadership he gains. Jack soon learns the main fear of the boys, which is of the beast, and uses this to control his army. Jack gets so caught up in his new morals; (dancing around chanting of murder, painting his face, and killing pigs,) that he is even able to commit murder using his bare hands to kill members of his own kind!

Q. Lord of the Flies: Is There Hope for Man?

One of the main themes in William Golding's 1954 novel Lord of the Flies is that without civilization, there is no law and order. The expression of Golding's unorthodox and complex views are embodied in the many varied characters in the novel. One of Golding's unorthodox views is that only one aspect of the modern world keeps people from reverting back to savagery and that is society. Golding shows the extreme situations of what could possibly happen in a society composed of people taken from a structured society then put into a structureless society in the blink of an eye. First there is a need for order until the people on the island realise that there are no rules to dictate their lives and take Daveers into their own hands. Golding is also a master of contrasting characterization. This can be seen in the conflicts between the characters of Jack, the savage; Simon, the savior; and Piggy, the one with all the ideas. Arguably, the most savage person on the island is Jack Merridew. The first image of Jack and his group is presented as "something dark" and a "creature" before Golding goes on to explain "the creature was a party of boys." Ironically, that is exactly what happens.

The beast turns out to be the evil within the children themselves. Jack conflicts with most of the other major characters from the beginning. He calls Piggy "Fatty" repeatedly and opposes Jack almost every step of the way. As the novel progresses, Jack becomes more domineering and assertive, slowly losing all of his former morals and civility. The one point in the novel where this happens is when Jack paints his face: "He made one c4heek and one eye socket white..." Then Jack proceeds to cover the other half of his face in red, foreshadowing his perpetual recruiting and takeover of the island. Jack ends up as the other authority figure on the island by force and by exploiting the other boys need for savagery. The need for savagery arises because of Golding's views of humans as being vicious by nature. Jack, being a leader in his own right, can not see the light of day again once he has seen the darkness of self indulgence and absolute power.

Simon, on the other hand, is not wild at all and can easily differentiate the light from the darkness. He is the quiet one, the thinker. Simon is the only one that can keep good and evil straight throughout the entire novel. He stays to himself until he is needed or feels that he can contribute something to the group. Simon never directly conflicts with anyone, although there are some children that think he is odd and only comment once he has left or while he is walking away. A reason for Simon's seclusion may be because he has epilepsy: "In Simon's right temple, a pulse began to beat on the brain." He does not want the other boys to know about his problem. If they knew about his problem then that would disclose a flaw to the group and Simon would be even more susceptible to injuries. If Jack had known and had decided to deliberately kill Simon, all Jack would have to do is wait until Simon was having an attack then have someone attack Simon while he is defenseless. Simon is the one unique character in the novel because there are not many people in the world like him. There are many Ralphs, Jacks, and Piggys but few live with the attitude of Simon.

The only character in Lord of the Flies that does not change for the worse throughout the novel is Piggy. Piggy does not always have the authority or the attention to get his ideas across, but Ralph does listen to him for the most part. Piggy first starts out with the idea to call everyone to a meeting by using the conch. Then he thinks to create a fire on the mountain to attract ships. If it was not for Piggy's idea to call the first meeting, the kids would have stayed scattered across the island: " 'You haven't seen any others, have you?' " That would have been worse because the island would end up with many small savage groups killing everyone off instead of one large group killing a few people. Piggy, in other terms, is the unifying factor on the island of chaos.

Finally, Golding's wartime novel about a group of British boys stranded on an island has become one of the major works of the 20th century. Through his expression of his viewpoints by way of Jack, Simon, and Piggy, Golding creates a society that both exemplifies man's worst fears and his strengths. The fears are Jack and his extremes while the strengths are the facts that Simon and Piggy would rather, subconsciously, die than revert back to their savage state. So maybe all hope is not lost after all.

Q. Discuss Lord of the Flies as Commentary on Our Times

Or

Q. Discuss Golding as an omniscient narrator with reference to Lord of the flies

Lord of the Flies is an excellent book filled with symbols, satire, meaningful themes, and is interesting to read as well. In The Lord of the Flies, the protagonist is Ralph, a strong, likeable blond, with natural leadership. There are multiple conflicts in the plot. The main conflict is Ralph vs. Jack, the antagonist. Ralph fights to maintain order, while Jack seduces the boys into anarchy.

Another conflict is the boys vs. nature. The boys must struggle to stay alive, and struggle against an imaginary beast, which is from fear imbedded in part of their nature. The plot parallels the metaphoric action of the story through the actions of Simon. Simon's insistence on climbing the mountain to discover what the "beast" was, his insistence to understand, is a metaphor for what the book itself does. The book dares to name the beast, the evil in man's heart, as the beast. The plot also metaphorically deals with the struggles between control and anarchy. When Ralph is in power, the forces of organization have control, while when the boys follow Jack, anarchy is in power.

Golding's style was fast moving, and smoothly flowing, but was very deliberate. He used sentence length to often express the passing of time. He used long sentences when describing the rhythm of daily life the boys got into, and used short choppy sentences when Ralph was running, and only gave bits and pieces of thoughts and detail. He also used good words choice to portray a scene. In the first scene, even though the boys are talking about how wonderful of a paradise the island is, Golding used words like "thorns" and "creeper" to tell the readers that it wasn't a friendly place. He also had great use of emotional material, or the lack of it, leaving us to feel, without the authors comments.

One place where this is seen is when the author describes Piggy's death on the rocks. He also inserted good imagery, for example, when butterflies were flying around Simon as he gazed upon the Lord of the Flies as flies buzzed around it.

Golding's point of view also added much to the story. The point of view was normally objective, but was sometimes limited omniscient, showing the thoughts of only one character at a time in a scene. This shifting was well executed and gave the story a sense of continuity. His objective point of view added much by showing us what was happening, but letting his tone show his meaning, instead of having the characters or himself say it right out.

Golding did an excellent job of characterization. First, the choice of names metaphorically mirror the novel. "Ralph" means "counsel," and he was the character who held the organized meetings and tried to keep everyone together. "Jack" means "one who supplants" or, one who takes over by force, which is the method Jack uses throughout the book to gain power. "Simon" means "listener" and is also the name of the Jesus's apostle. Simon is the one who listens to Ralph, and it also hints at the spiritual role the character plays in the novel, he is the only one who hears and understands the truth. Piggy's name has an obvious meaning, connecting him with the pigs the other boys hunt and kill.

"Roger" means "spear," and he is Jack's right hand man who uses his brute force at will. Ralph and Piggy were round developing characters. Both of them matured and developed throughout the novel. Jack was more of a flat static character, staying constant throughout the book, always in conflict with Ralph, an always hungry for power. Jack is portrayed as darkness, and Ralph as light. The point of view normally revolves around Ralph, but sometimes moves to other characters, but never Jack. This switching of point of view between Ralph and other minor characters, but not Jack, shows the authors attitude towards the two characters.

This work has many very valid themes. The first about the evil inherent in man's soul, that the defects in our society can be traced back to the defects in human nature. Another major theme is the need for civilization. Contrary to the belief that man is inherently good, and that society is evil, the novel shows that society is needed to keep the evil of man in line. Another is the loss of identity. Civilization separates man from animals and makes them think, and when that civilization disintegrates, man's identity slips away, and he resorts to a more primitive nature. This is shown in the novel by the use of masks by the boys to hide their identity, which allows them to kill, and later murder. This is also shown in the twins Sam and Eric, who's name is later slurred together into "Samneric," which shows their loss of identity. Fear of the unknown is central to the story, as the boys fear the beast. But, one of the novel's deepest meanings is the realization that no real beast exists, only the power of fear, which was the realization Simon made before he was killed, by those who still held in fear.

The main irony in this novel is that in interrupting a man hunt on the island, the navel officer takes the boys aboard a cruiser, which will be hunting an enemy in the same sense that Jack and the boys were hunting Ralph. Irony also breaks out between different scenes of the novel. One example is the beginning and the end. Ralph starts out as being fine, clean, and enjoying the prospect of being on an island with no adults, which is a dream come true, whereas the story ends with Ralph being ragged, dirty, and sobbing, having looked forward to a clean game, and lived a horrible nightmare.

It is also ironic that Golding used Ballantyne's Coral Island as a setting, and the same names as the two main characters in that novel (Ralph and Jack). This is ironic, because the morality of the world of Coral Island contrasts drastically with what Golding shows us in Lord of the Flies. He regards Coral Island morality as being unrealistic, and therefore not truly moral, and he has used it ironically in his novel to show man's true moral nature.

The symbols in the book all reinforce the theme of the novel. All of the characters themselves were very symbolic. Ralph is a symbol of civilization, he is always the one who attempts to organize and accomplish things in order to better the group, like the fire and the building of shelters. Piggy's shattering spectacles show the continual decay of rational influence as the story progresses.

The struggle between Ralph and Jack is symbolic of the struggle between the forces of civilization and anarchy, or the struggle between moral conscience and his heart of darkness. The central symbol itself is the "Lord of the Flies," which translates into "Beelzebub" in Greek, a name for the devil, whose name implies destruction, decay, demoralization, hysteria, and panic, which were all seen throughout the book, and fits well with the novel's themes. The novel is an excellent piece of commentary on our times, and on the condition of man's soul,

Q. Discuss The Lord of the Flies as Social Commentary

Or

Q. How can you say Lord of the flies is a pessimistic novel

The Lord of the Flics is an ultimately pessimistic novel. In the midst of the cold war and communism scares, this disquieting aura acts as a backdrop to the island. The Lord of the Flies addresses questions like how do dictators come to power, do democracies always work, and what is the natural state and fate of humanity and society, getting at the heart of human nature in a very male-dominated, conflict-driven way. The war, the plane shot down, and the boys' concern that the "Reds" will find them before the British, shows Golding's intention of treating the boys' isolated existence as a microcosm of the adult military world.

He uses lush description to build a setting that will contrast and reflect the boys' primitive descent. The word "scar" describes the natural feature of the land, conjuring images of redness and blood from the first paragraph. The beautiful, yet often odd, descriptions help serve as a contrast between humans and nature. The use of words like "scar" and "blood" foreshadows the future interaction between the boys and nature-the pigs, the hunt, the storm. At the same time, the beauty and the order of the natural surroundings contrast with the decline of society developed throughout the book. Integral to this setting is the fair-haired boy climbing the rocks, Ralph. When Ralph meets Piggy, we notice the obvious differences between the two-the attractive and the fat, the daydreamer and the thinker.

There is a moment when Piggy looks up at Ralph and sees the shadows on his face reversed. This reverse of shadows seems to signify the missed initial connection between Piggy and Ralph- Ralph looks through Piggy. He smiles because he feels as if he is leaping into a "real life adventure" with no adults, and Piggy interprets the smile as "a mark of recognition."

This is central to the idea of the novel: the boys recognize in each other their shared search for recognition, and their mutual lack of recognition for the truth. Piggy desperately wants to be recognized for what he can contribute to the group. Piggy finds the conch shell-he is the symbol of civilization-and Ralph does not recognize its power until Piggy explains it to him. However, Piggy cannot blow the conch because of his asthma. Piggy has the ideas but cannot carry them out. He is the intellectual, the man with powerful ideas who gets no respect. Things begin to happen only after Ralph, the attractive leader, puts Piggy's ideas into action. The conch becomes the symbol of Ralph's leadership, even though Piggy procured it. This relationship between Piggy and Ralph contrasts with the introduction of Jack Merridew. Compared to Ralph's still attractiveness, Jack is ugly, has flaming red hair, and a black cloak that swirls behind him. Ralph seems to recognize him as both a comrade and a competitor. Despite all the darkness in his introduction, Jack cannot kill the first pig. Society still controls him at this point, allowing him to become friends with Ralph. Still, he inspires a premonition that next time there will be no mercy.

We can see this contrast between Ralph and Jack develop. Jack is the hunter and cannot focus on anything else, least of all the rescue fire. Jack thinks only of the pig-pig over rescue, pig over shelter. Ralph cannot bridge the gap and neither can Jack-the gap of hunt versus shelter, primitive thrill versus humbling domesticity. Once again, Ralph has problems with recognition. He does not recognize the nature of Jack even when he confronts him. He is not recognizing the deeper problems, the fear of "the beast" and the inhumanity of humanity, when these problems appear before him. Instead, Ralph remains concerned with the others' irresponsibility.

Jack uses clay to disguise his face and trick the pigs. When Jack does this he changes the visual representation of himself, moving further from society and rendering himself unrecognizable. Both Ralph and Jack still have some connection to the past, but Jack is moving away from it, moving to create his own world governed by the laws of hunting and survival.

Without any adults on the island, the boys must learn to govern themselves; however, problems ensue. Piggy tries to find out each of the boys' names but cannot. The youngest, the least influenced by society, are the first to run away, the first to show the breakdown of societal control. This problem continues in Ralph's speech-no one seems to understand the importance of being rescued. Just as he suggested the vote earlier, Ralph continues to act as the democratic leader who tries to organize their civilization with a series of roles and rules and gives everyone a chance to speak. In this way, Ralph begins to show some of his shortcomings. He does not know how to think, at least not like Piggy, and more importantly, he does not understand the effects of fear. Ralph keeps thinking that fear of "the beast" is not really important. Ralph fails to understand that he should be more afraid of "the beast" and that Jack uses fear to lead. He must at least acknowledge the fear if he intends to lead. His ideas of importance differ from the boys and he does not understand their fears. Ralph, signifying democratic leadership, leads without respect to human nature and fails.

Although in words the boys are still following Ralph, in action they follow Jack. Ralph begins to shirk from leadership and Jack seizes the power. We see two sides of Ralph. One half wants civilization and the comforts of home. Yet, Ralph has grown used to the dirty primitive conditions of the island and has come to consider them normal. Ralph is perfectly human and thus perfectly flawed. He rushes in with the other boys in the reenactment of the hunt with Roger, also trying to get a piece of "that brown, vulnerable flesh." He wants the boys to recognize his attempt to hunt. In theory, this should make Ralph the natural leader. He is enough like the other boys that they can relate to him, but also recognizes his own power to lead.

If this is true, why does Ralph fail as a leader? First, he

does not see the importance of his sensitive human qualities. Rather than using his perceptiveness and primitive instincts to lead, he battles against his own nature, attempting to make himself and the other boys civilized. Ralph gives up his power to Jack almost willingly. He stays behind, afraid of his own instincts, afraid to take responsibility.

The first major turning point in not only the power shift from Ralph to Jack, but ultimately in the novel, occurs in chapter 4: The hunters' first kill coincides with the first chance for rescue. The two events are linked-the boys give up the chance for rescue for the chance to kill. Their value system, what they consider truly important, has shifted significantly.

The fire burning out of control is another example of the power that the boys have to rule themselves, the power that causes their destruction just as the fire destroys the island. This is the beginning of the destruction of the island. In a previous chapter the boys roll stones down the mountain, declaring ownership. Ownership becomes destruction, and the degradation of the natural world through burning fires or killing pigs mirrors the breakdown of the boys' socialized humanity. We also get a closer view of Roger in this chapter, who throws stones near one of the younger boys, Henry. This is extremely significant. Roger aims a few yards away from Henry, still following the laws of society. Civilization forces him to limit his primitive violent instincts, but these constraints no longer fetter him by the end of the novel.

The irony between "civilization" and life on the island continues into chapter 6. "The Beast from Air" is the "sign" they receive in the form of a dead parachutist apparently killed at war. Piggy and Ralph were just yearning for what they considered the perfection of adult civilization, but just as the boys are fighting on the island, the men in the outside world also continue to fight. Even as Piggy and Ralph think to themselves that civilization is good, their only knowledge of civilization or "the outside world" proves terribly flawed.

By this point, the power dynamic has shifted. Jack gives the boys their only option. As the best hunter, only he can save them from "the beast." He leads them on a hunt, but instead of finding an actual beast on the mountain, they unleash "the beast" within themselves, attacking a nursing sow with lust and fury. Roger, cruel and sadistic in nature, impales the sow with almost demented excitement. The boys "sharpen a stick at both ends" and leave the sow's head as a sacrifice to "the beast," a sacrifice that takes on the symbolic role of the beastly urges they have succumbed to within.

Simon, the idealistic and religious character, understands the inner beast before anyone else, having a stronger connection to nature than his island-mates. Simon watches the sow's head as he sits alone in the clearing and has the onset of a seizure, during which he begins to realise the truth of humanity, namely that everything is a "bad business." He is struck by the recognition, the "ancient, inescapable recognition" of this evil force. He achieves the recognition that all the boys fumble with, seeing "the beast" or "the Lord of the Flies" for what it is: the fear and evil inside themselves.

The Lord of the Flies is not the sow at all, but rather the creature that has been created as a physical representation of the human beast. Simon finds the parachutist tangled in the rocks and cuts him free. He attempts to free the boys from what they thought was the beast, but "the beast" is in them, in the dance. When the storm breaks in chapter 9, it mirrors the rising climax and Simon is killed in the boys' frenzied "dance." The boys kill Simon because they misrecognize him as "the beast."

The shift from reason and democracy to irrational dictatorship is complete. The hunters' decision to steal Piggy's glasses over the conch signifies this shift. In a dictatorship, they have no need for an object that allows all to speak. But Golding also implies that the boys are willing subjects under Jack's rule. They follow him almost blindly, mutely. No one challenges Jack other than Piggy and Ralph. And the former symbols of power all ultimately end up destroyed. The boys ignore Ralph's conch signal: the rejection of the conch is a rejection of the rules of society. The shell remains the symbol of society, but when the shell is destroyed that which it signifies is also shattered, and Jack is secure in his role as chief.

Roger, the former "stone thrower," becomes his full role as an executioner when he kills Piggy with "a sense of delirious abandonment" by heaving a boulder onto him. The boys have removed themselves from all semblance of civilization. They hunt Ralph like an animal. Roger sharpens a stick at both ends. Even after Ralph finds the sow's skull on the stick and destroys it, the symbol of savagery, "the beast" still exists. Ironically, it is the fire that Jack sets to smoke Ralph out of the undergrowth that destroys the island but ultimately signals a Navy cruiser.

The fire, once signifying rescue and later used for destruction, becomes both. The novel ends in the adult perspective. The officer is uncomfortable thinking about the savagery of the boys, and looks off to his cruiser in the distance while Ralph weeps for "the end of innocence, and the darkness of man's heart." Golding is making a point about the hypocrisy of the civilization. In reality, the world is just a larger version of the island. The officer's comment on "the Coral Island" is also ironically significant in elevating The Lord of the Flies from a book about a group of lost boys on an island to a beautifully symbolic work of social commentary. The view presented is dark and pessimistic, making its readers look deep inside their own human nature and at the structure of society in a frighteningly different light

Q. Analyse The Metamorphosis of Characters in Lord Of The Flies

Or

Q. Discuss the characters of Lord of the flies

In his novel, Lord Of The Flies, William Golding used a group of boys stranded on a tropical island to illustrate the malicious nature of mankind. Lord of the Flies dealt with changes that the boys underwent as they gradually adapted to the isolated freedom from society. Three main characters depicted different effects on certain individuals under those circumstances. Jack Merridew began as the arrogant and self-righteous leader of a choir. The freedom of the island allowed him to further develop the darker side of his personality as the Chief of a savage tribe. Ralph started as a self-assured boy whose confidence in himself came from the acceptance of his peers. He had a fair nature as he was willing to listen to Piggy. He became increasingly dependent on Piggy's wisdom and became lost in the confusion around him. Towards the end of the story his rejection from their society of savage boys forced him to fend for himself. Piggy was an educated boy who had grown up as an outcast. Due to his academic childhood, he was more mature than the others and retained his civilized behaviour. But his experiences on the island gave him a more realistic understanding of the cruelty possessed by some people. The ordeals of the three boys on the island made them more aware of the evil inside themselves and in some cases, made the false politeness that had clothed them dissipate. However, the changes experienced by one boy differed from those endured by another. This is attributable to the physical and mental dissimilarities between them.

Jack was first described with an ugly sense of cruelty that made him naturally unlikeable. As leader of the choir and one of the tallest boys on the island, Jack's physical height and authority matched his arrogant personality. His desire to be Chief was clearly evident in his first appearance. When the idea of having a Chief was mentioned Jack spoke out immediately. "I ought to be chief," said Jack with simple arrogance, "because I'm chapter chorister and head boy." He led his choir by administering much discipline resulting in forced obedience from the cloaked boys. His ill-nature was well expressed through his impoliteness of saying, "Shut up, Fatty." at Piggy. However, despite his unpleasant personality, his lack of courage and his conscience prevented him from killing the first pig they encountered.

"They knew very well why he hadn't: because of the enormity of the knife descending and cutting into living flesh; because of the unbearable blood" Even at the meetings, Jack was able to contain himself under the leadership of Ralph. He had even suggested the implementation of rules to regulate themselves. This was a Jack who was proud to be British, and who was shaped and still bound by the laws of a civilized society. The freedom offered to him by the island allowed Jack to express the darker sides of his personality that he hid from the ideals of his past environment. Without adults as a superior and responsible authority, he began to lose his fear of being punished for improper actions and behaviors. This freedom coupled with his malicious and arrogant personality made it possible for him to quickly degenerate into a savage. He put on paint, first to camouflage himself from the pigs. But he discovered that the paint allowed him to hide the forbidden thoughts in his mind that his facial expressions would otherwise betray.

"The mask was a thing on its own behind which Jack hid, liberated from shame and self-consciousness". Through hunting, Jack lost his fear of blood and of killing living animals. He reached a point where he actually enjoyed the sensation of hunting a prey afraid of his spear and knife. His natural desire for blood and violence was brought out by his hunting of pigs. As Ralph became lost in his own confusion, Jack began to assert himself as chief. The boys realizing that Jack was a stronger and more self-assured leader gave in easily to the freedom of Jack's savagery. Placed in a position of power and with his followers sharing his crazed hunger for violence, Jack gained encouragement to commit the vile acts of thievery and murder. Freed from the conditions of a regulated society, Jack gradually became more violent and the rules and proper behaviour by which he was brought up were forgotten. The freedom given to him unveiled his true self under the clothing worn by civilized people to hide his darker characteristics.

Ralph was introduced as a fair and likeable boy whose self-assurance made him feel secure even on the island without any adults. His interaction with Piggy demonstrated his pleasant nature as he did not call him names with hateful intent as Jack had. His good physique allowed him to be well accepted among his peers, and this gave him enough confidence to speak out readily in public. His handsome features and the conch as a symbol of power and order pointed him out from the crowd of boys and proclaimed him Chief. "There was a stillness about Ralph as he sat that marked him out: there was his size, and attractive appearance; and most obscurely, yet most powerful, there was the conch". From the quick decisions he made as Chief near the beginning of the novel, it could be seen that Ralph was well-organized. But even so, Ralph began repeatedly to long and daydream of his civilized and normal past. Gradually, Ralph became confused and began to lose clarity in his thoughts and speeches.

"Ralph was puzzled by the shutter that flickered in his brain. There was something he wanted to say; then the shutter had come down". He started to feel lost in their new environment as the boys, with the exception of Piggy began to change and adapt to their freedom. As he did not lose his sense of responsibility, his viewpoints and priorities began to differ from the savages'. He was more influenced by Piggy than by Jack, who in a way could be viewed as a source of evil. Even though the significance of the fire as a rescue signal was slowly dismissed, Ralph continued to stress the importance of the fire at the mountaintop. He also tried to reestablish the organization that had helped to keep the island clean and free of potential fire hazards.

This difference made most of the boys less convinced of the integrity of Ralph. As his supporters became fewer and Jack's insistence on being chief grew, his strength as a leader diminished. But even though Ralph had retained much of his past social conditioning, he too was not spared from the evil released by the freedom from rules and adults. During the play-fight after their unsuccessful hunt in the course of their search for the beast, Ralph for the first time, had an opportunity to join the hunters and share their desire for violence. "Ralph too was fighting to get near, to get a handful of that brown, vulnerable flesh.

The desire to squeeze and hurt was over-mastering". Without rules to limit them, they were free to make their game as real as they wanted. Ralph did not understand the hatred Jack had for him, nor did he fully comprehend why their small and simple society deteriorated. This confusion removed his self-confidence and made him more dependent on Piggy's judgment, until Piggy began prompting him on what needed to be said and done. Towards the end of the novel, Ralph was forced into independence when he lost all his followers to Jack's savagery, and when Piggy and the conch were smashed by Roger's boulder. He was forced to determine how to avoid Jack's savage hunters alone. Ralph's more responsible behaviour set him apart from the other savage boys and made it difficult for him to accept and realise the changes they were undergoing. Becoming lost in his exposure to their inherent evil, Ralph's confusion brought about the deterioration of his initial self-assurance and ordered temperament, allowing him to experience brief outbursts of his beastly self.

Piggy was an educated boy rejected by the kids of his age group on account of his being overweight. It was his academic background and his isolation from the savage boys that had allowed him to remain mostly unchanged from his primitive experiences on the island. His unattractive attributes segregated him from the other boys on the island. He was not welcomed on their first exploratory trip of the island. "We don't want you", Jack had said to Piggy. Piggy was like an observer learning from the actions of others. His status in their society allowed him to look at the boys from an outsider's perspective. He could learn of the hatred being brought out of the boys without having to experience the thirst for blood that Ralph was exposed to.

Although he was easily intimidated by the other boys, especially by Jack, he did not lack the self-confidence to protest or speak out against the indignities from the boys as the shy former choirboy Simon did. This self-confidence differed from that of Ralph's as it did not come from his acceptance by their peers nor did it come from the authority and power Jack had grown accustomed to. It came from the pride in having accumulated the wisdom that was obviously greater than that of most of the other kids at his age. Piggy not only knew what the rules were, as all the other boys did, but he also had the patience to at least wonder why the rules existed.

This intuition made Piggy not only more aware of why the rules were imposed, thereby ensuring that he would abide by them even when they were not enforced. When the boys flocked to the mountaintop to build their fire, Piggy shouted after them, "Acting like a crowd of kids" ! Piggy was a very reliable person who could look ahead and plan carefully of the future. He shouted at the boys' immature recklessness, "The first thing we ought to have made was shelters down there by the beach... Then when you get here you build a bonfire that isn't no use. Now you been and set the whole island on fire". Like Ralph, his sense of responsibility set him apart from the other boys. The author used the image of long hair to illustrate Piggy's sustenance of his civilized behaviour. "He was the only boy on the island whose hair never seemed to grow".

The author's description of his baldness also presented an image of old age and made Piggy seem to lack the strength of youth. The increasing injustice Piggy endured towards the end of the novel was far greater than any that he had encountered previously. In his fit of anger, Piggy cried out, "I don't ask for my glasses back, not as a favour. I don't ask you to be a sport, I'll say, not because you're strong, but because what's right's right". This new standard of harshness brought tears out of him as the suffering became intolerable. For a brief moment, Piggy's anger at the unfairness and his helplessness robbed him of his usual logical reasoning, which returned when he was confronted with his fear of the savages. Piggy was an intelligent boy with a good understanding of their situation on the island. He was able to think clearly and plan ahead with caution so that even in the freedom of their unregulated world, his wisdom and his isolation from the savage boys kept him from giving into the evil that had so easily consumed Jack and his followers. The resulting cruelty Jack inflicted upon him taught Piggy how much more pain there was in the world.

Lord of the Flies used changes experienced by boys on an uninhabited island to show the evil nature of man. By using different characters the author was able to portray various types of people found in our society. Their true selves were revealed in the freedom from the laws and punishment of a world with adults. Under the power and regulations of their former society, Jack's inner evil was suppressed. But when the rules no longer existed, he was free to do what malice he desired. Ralph had grown so used to the regularity of a civilized world, that the changes they underwent were difficult for him to comprehend. He became confused and less capable of thinking clearly and independently. Although he too had experienced the urge for violence that had driven Jack and the hunters to momentary peaks of madness, his more sensitive personality and his sense of obligation saved him from complete savagery. These two traits also helped to keep Piggy from becoming primitive in behaviour.

He was made an outcast by his undesirable physique and his superior intelligence. This isolation and wisdom also helped Piggy to retain his civilized behaviour. As well, he was made painfully more aware of the great amount of injustice in the world. From these three characters, it could be seen that under the same circumstances, different individuals can develop in different ways depending on the factors within themselves and how they interacted with each other. Their personalities and what they knew can determine how they would interpret and adapt to a new environment such as the tropical island. Not everyone has so much malevolence hidden inside themselves as to become complete savages when released from the boundaries of our society. Some people will, because of the ways they were conditioned, remember and abide by the rules they had depended on for social organization and security.

Q. Analyse Character Development in Lord of the Flies

Or

Q. How Golding has showed "innocence is perhaps the most important thing in the world that no one ever has forever"

The ability to create characters of depth plagues many a contemporary writer. Many of those writers should look to William Golding for expertise on this issue. Golding diverges from the path of contemporary authors and sets an example of how character development should be accomplished in his novel, Lord of the Flies. Golding's Ralph exemplifies this author's superior style of character development in this novel.

At the commencement of the novel, the author introduces Ralph as an innocent boy far from adulthood. Almost immediately, Ralph is described as a "fair boy." This phrase indicates a stereotype of the perfect child—blonde hair and blue eyes with blemish-free skin—which the author manipulated to show innocence. Also, Golding used this to give the reader a feeling of Ralph's position on the scale of maturation. It guides the destination of the novel and how much Ralph needs to grow to attain complete maturity. Ralph's innocence is further implied when he says his daddy is "a commander in the Navy" and that "when he gets leave, he'll come rescue us." Clearly, Ralph's comments call attention to his inability to view matters, especially his current situation, realistically, and to show Ralph's simplistic thinking, as well. Later in the novel, Ralph views Piggy as a fat bore with "ass-mar" and "matter-of-fact ideas." Ralph is still at the point where he believes that he is on a schoolyard playground where teasing and handstands are an acceptable practice. Similarly, Ralph's thoughts are intended to show what a sheltered child he has been all his life. Thus far, Golding developed Ralph so that the reader interprets him as an ideal child without any indication of maturity. The author will build upon this to transform Ralph as a character and as a person.

As the climax approaches, Ralph begins to mature slightly as chaos erupts. After Ralph discovers that a ship passed while the fire was out and Jack is culpable, Ralph confronts him and rather than acquiescing to Ralph, Jack takes out his anger, physically on Piggy, the only person at that time intimidated by Jack. Ralph responds by saying Jack's tantrum is a "dirty trick" and tells them to light the fire. All this infers that Ralph is becoming less gregarious and a bit more serious. He shows maturity when he takes up for the underdog and does not go along with the majority. Golding used this to show that the trials of the island's events are starting to become more apparent to Ralph and that perhaps he is acting more like the leader he was elected to be. Now, Ralph decides the group must have an emergency meeting to discuss the events that have taken place on the island and thinks to himself, "This meeting must not be fun, but business." For obvious reasons, this means a great deal to the plot by showing Ralph's "adult side," but likewise, the author wants to show how far Ralph's leadership abilities have come since the onset of the novel. These thoughts also separate him from the others because they do not have the ability to be serious on the island. Farther along, Ralph notices the signal fire is out once again by declaring to the whole group, "There's no signal showing. There may be a ship out there. Are you all off your rockers?" Ralph is beginning to deviate from the majority of the group, consisting of primarily hunters now. Golding knows that innocent children do not do this and therefore includes it into the novel to emphasize how Ralph alone is beginning to attain adulthood. The climactic events are imminent as Ralph becomes more assertive and authoritative than ever, and closer to his loss of innocence.

During the events that surround the devastation of the island, Ralph shows that he is more of an adult than any of the "barbarians" roaming the island. After being a part of Simon's death, Ralph revisits the event in his head and cannot believe that he was part of a "murder." Ralph is the only character on the island to view Simon's death as illicit, hence demonstrating further maturation. Golding manifests this because he wants his readers to fully understand Ralph's journey from the day of mirth when he exclaimed, "no grown-ups." Farther along, while speaking to Piggy, Ralph wants to go to Castle Rock looking like they "used to, washed and hair brushed." He then adds that they "aren't savages really and being rescued isn't a game."

This remark almost sounds like sarcasm after reading the earlier chapters and that Ralph is saying them is almost ludicrous. The author is quickly maturing Ralph as a real child might mature if given his circumstance. Many contemporary authors would be unable to develop Ralph as realistically as Golding has. Later, as Ralph tries to escape the vengeance of the hunters, he lies "there in the darkness" realizing he is "an outcast" and rationalizes this by verbally saying to himself,

"Cause I had some sense." At this point in the novel, Ralph has accomplished the mighty task of becoming an adult and furthermore, will never have a childhood similar to the one he had before the "scar," before Piggy and Simon, and especially before Jack. Ralph's childhood is replaced now by a maturity many adults never attain, thus setting him far ahead of the rest. Golding culminated the novel with the destruction of the island and where "Ralph wept for the end of innocence, the darkness of man's heart, and the fall through the air of the true, wise friend called Piggy." Only mature adults remember true friends, weep for the end of innocence, and are capable of destroying an island. Golding intended the maturity to come fast in the end as it would come in life and to show that Ralph is now an adult.

In conclusion, Golding showed his readers what most of the world does not realise, that innocence is perhaps the most important thing in the world that no one ever has forever. The novel shows society how imperative it is to embrace, not hurry along, youth. Golding does a superior job at this by developing Ralph into a young man unlike any other author can do. He accomplishes this by harnessing the power of literature for the goodness of humankind and not for any other reason. It is for all these reasons that William Golding should be remembered as a master of character development that most contemporary authors ought to look to.

Q. Comment on The Very Unhappy Ending of Lord of the Flies

Or

Q. How Lord of the fires includes the notion that the boys are a microcosm of society.

William Golding's Lord of the Flies indeed has a happy ending in the literal sense. The boys are rescued as their foolish cruelty reaches its apex by the loving, caring, and matured outside world. On the other hand, by whom and what are the boys rescued? Symbolically, the "happy ending" is exactly the opposite. Far from sacrificing artistic excellence, Golding's ending confirms the author's powerful symbolism.

Readers know ample about the boys society and where it

heads long before the "rescue." Ralph will be killed and to remain a perpetual gift to the "beastie." The boys' xenophobic view of the beastie is ironically unfounded because the beastie emerges from within the boys: they themselves are the dangerous and scary monsters for all to fear, and they kill the first person to suggest so (Simon).

Although the parachutist may symbolize civilization's archetypical fall, he is only a "beastie" insofar as civilization is to be feared. (The boys' fear of the beastie may, then, be well-founded, but only symbolically). As action progresses, readers see no signs of a veer from the boys' self-destructive course. Shortly before the boys' "rescue," they expect the boys to perish either from the fire (which actually ends up saving Ralph), a tragedy of the commons, or internal war. Golding could either have extended the book to its predicted bloody end, or he could have changed course. The surprise course of action becomes Golding's central theme.

Golding's theme is not just the obvious evils of the boys' society; it includes the notion that the boys are a microcosm of society. While readers may be able to ascertain his theme immediately prior to the ending, the connection to the real world is weak and underdeveloped. Critics who claim that something was sacrificed for the sake of a "happy ending" fail to understand Golding's thesis: the boys are allegorical of society as a whole, yet are "rescued" by that very society which they symbolize. In a sense, the boys swap one war for another. Instead of being at war with other children, they re-join a society which is at war lead by adults who are supposedly more mature than the boys. Like the island, the world is an isolated entity, but no one can rescue the world. Golding's boys are symbolic of the world, but he cannot juxtapose the world and the boys without the rescue.

Moreover, the "rescue" provides the logical continuation of Golding's loss of innocence theme by cementing the parallels between the boys and society. The boys' killing of a mother sow was, at least, shocking, but similar events occurred in Golding's time: Hitler's Holocaust and blitz of Austria, Czechoslovakia, and Poland; the Japanese Rape of Nanjing and

"Hidden Holocaust;" and Britain's brutal imperialistic exploits. The loss of innocence represented by the sow's murder leads to brutal killings, much like Hitler's anti-Semitism lead to the brutal killing of nations. The military "rescue" brings the symbolism full circle by fusing the symbolism. The boys may be rescued, but no one can rescue the earth should savagery go out of control as on the island.

Another parallel is rather inverse. The boys are on a paradise island, but they dirty themselves as they become more vicious. The officer who rescues the boys, however, has a clean white uniform complete with medals and epaulets. As the boys become dirty, they become savage, but as adults become savage, they are awarded cleaner uniforms. Golding again asserts that adult society is little more than a clean, orderly-appearing version of the boys' savage island.

Golding's ending, then, is not an escape, but the capstone of his allegory. He welds the boys' symbolism to that of the outside world. He presents an ironic ending which beseeches readers to recognize their own helpless quagmire of 'clean' savagery. Golding does not have a "happy ending" for the sake of either happiness or an ending, but for the purposes of powerful symbolism.

Golding's conclusion serves a final purpose. Golding creates dramatic irony with the officer's blunt ignorance of the boys' savagery. Perhaps he is at a loss for words, but the officer treats the boys as if they were playing a backyard game. "Jolly good show, like Coral Island," he remarks, followed by the inquiry, "You're all British, aren't you?". The officer thinks that the boys have formed an enlightened, orderly society like in the novel Coral Island, but he fails to realise that even the British, "the best at everything," can fall into the trap of brutish war. The officer shreds readers' stereotypes of themselves as superior to war because he shows that war is a virus which can infect everyone. In short, Golding's ending is as symbolic as it is unhappy. The ironic rescue transcends the remote island to affect readers, especially the British, to recognize their potential for evil. The naval officer points to how far the boys have fallen and why their "rescue" wasn't really so happy.

Q. Comment on the True Portrayal of Children in Lord of the Flies

Or

Q. Discuss the behaviour of children in Lord of the flies

In the novel The Lord of the Flies, by William Golding, one can see how children react to certain situations. Children, when given the opportunity, would choose to play and have fun rather than to do boring, hard work. Also, when children have no other adults to look up to they turn to other children for leadership. Finally, children stray towards savagery when they are without adult authority. Therefore, Golding succeeds in effectively portraying the interests and attitudes of young children in this novel.

When children are given the opportunity, they would rather envelop themselves in pleasure and play than in the stresses of work. The boys show enmity towards building the shelters, even though this work is important, to engage in trivial activities. Af ter one of the shelters collapses while only Simon and Ralph are building it, Ralph clamours, "All day I've been working with Simon. No one else. They're off bathing or eating, or playing.". Ralph and Simon, though only children, are more mature a nd adult like and stray to work on the shelters, while the other children aimlessly run off and play. The other boys avidly choose to play, eat, etc. than to continue to work with Ralph which is very boring and uninteresting. The boys act typically of m ost children their age by being more interested in having fun than working. Secondly, all the boys leave Ralph's hard-working group to join Jack's group who just want to have fun.

The day after the death of Simon when Piggy ! and Ralph are bathing, Piggy points beyond the platform and says, "That's where they're gone. Jack's party. Just for some meat. And for hunting and for pretending to be a tribe and putting on war-paint.". Piggy realizes exactly why the boys have gone to Jack's, which would be for fun and excitement. The need to play and have fun in Jack's group, even though the boys risk the tribe's brutality and the chance of not being rescued, outweighs doing work with Ralph's group which increase their chance s of being rescued. Young children need to satisfy their amusement by playing games instead of doing work. In conclusion, children are more interested in playing and having fun than doing unexciting labour.

When children are without adults to look to for leadership, they look for an adult-like person for leadership. At the beginning of the novel, when the boys first realise they are all alone, they turn to Ralph for leadership. After Ralph calls the first meeting, Golding writes, "There was a stillness about Ralph as he sat that marked him out: there was his size, and attractive appearance, and most obscurely, yet most powerfully, there was the conch. The being that had sat waiting for them.". The boys are drawn to Ralph because of his physical characteristics and because he had blown the conch. The fact that there are no adults has caused the boys to be attracted to Ralph as a leader.

The physical characteristics of Ralph remind the boys of their parents or other adult authority figures they may have had in their old lives back home. There is also the conch that Ralph holds which may remind the boys of a school bell or a teacher's whistle. Finally, at the end of the novel, the boys turn to Jack to satisfy their need for some much-needed leadership. When the boys are feasting on the meat of a freshly killed sow, the narrator says: Jack spoke 'Give me a drink.' Henry brought him a shell and he drank. Power lay in the blown swell of his forearms; authority sat on his shoulder and chattered in his ear like an ape. 'All sit down.' The boys ranged themselves in rows on the grass before him. Jack now has full authority over the other boys. The boys look to Jack for his daunting leadership which intimidates them. Jack is very forceful and his ways most likely remind the boys of authoritative figures in their pastwho may have strapped, beaten or used other forms of violence when disciplining the children.

Therefore, the children when left without adult authority figures turn to others who can replace that adult authority figure. In addition to seeking adult-like authority figures, children lose their innocence and stray towards savagery when not around adult authority. When the boys have been on the island for a short time, they start to show more violence, but when they realiz e what they have done they become contrite, embarrassed by their actions. After Maurice destroys Percival's sandcastle and some sand gets in Percival's eye, the narrator writes: Percival began to whimper with an eyeful of sand and Maurice hurried away. In his other life Maurice had received chastisement for filling a younger eye with sand. Now, though there was no parent to let fall a heavy hand, Maurice still felt unease of wrongdoing. Maurice has hurt Percival but feels bad about it because in his past life he would have been punished for it.

Without adults, Maurice is turning towards barbarianism has not been away from the order and discipline of his previous life to be considere d a savage. Children misbehave when not around adults because there is no one to discipline or punish them. Yet, for a brief time after the children have been away from adults, the children will feel remorseful. Also, after the boys have been absent fr om structured discipline, they become blatant savages and retain absolutely no innocence. When Piggy and Ralph visit Castle Rock to get back Piggy's glasses, Golding says: Roger, with a sense of delirious abandonment, leaned all his weight on the lever. The rock struck Piggy. Piggy fell forty feet and landed on his back across that square across that square red rock in the sea. His head opened and stuff came out and turned red.

Without apprehension, Roger performs the horrible and violent act of killing Piggy. Roger has now been without adults to discipline him for quite a long time and his actions have become more intensely brutal. The boys have been unpunished for so long tha t they continually become more and more violent and thus, have made the final step to becoming all out savages. Typically, children are reprimanded for their misbehavior and as they mature, what is right and what is wrong becomes embedded in their brains to the point where they almost never stray towards uncivilized behaviour. Clearly children can quickly forget what is right and what is wrong, especially when being away from adults for an extended period of time, often resulting in a loss of innocence. Lastly, at the end of the novel when around the naval officer arrives, the boys return to their old ways of being orderly and civilized. When Ralph is chased onto the beach by Jack's tribe and finds the naval officer, the na! rrator says, "A semi-circle of little boys, their bodies streaked with coloured clay, sharp sticks in their hands, were standing on the beach making no noise at all.".

The previously wild savages are now quiet little boys in an orderly semi-circle. With the arrival of an adult authority figure from the outside world, the boys are beginning to return to the decorum of their innocent, more childlike past. The boys are in a semi-circle instead of in a pack of savages, they are coloured with clay ins tead of gaudy war-paint, they are holding sticks instead of spears and they are absolutely as quiet as they would have been around adults in their previous lives. Children are usually more ordered, disciplined and civilized under adult supervision just a s the boys are the instant they see the naval officer. To summarize, when not around adult order, discipline and punishment, children become very much like savages and lose most of their innocence.

In conclusion, in the novel The Lord of the Flies, Golding succeeds in showing the actions, decisions and thinking of young children. Children would choose to play and have fun rather than work. When children need to look for leadership and there are no adults around to provide this, children look for another child who has adult-like qualities for leadership. Children are disobedient, violent and lose their innocence when there are no adults to supervise them. A child's life is a long and winding road in which they can be sidetracked quite easily

Q. Discuss the Philosophical and Political Aspects of Lord the Flies

Is easy enough to make a broad generalization about philosophical, political or even religious interpretations on each book (even if we consider religion in some way vinculated to philosophy), but in reality the issue is an extremely complex one. It would be so comfortable to reduce a story to a mere source of external references and to lose all the nuances that make literature a special phenomenon This not only happens in literature; for example, in children's films, where the content is supposed to be political unexisting, there always appears somebody who tries to give the movie a second political reading, trying therefore to measure its value by any subjective comment. It would appear then that some creations do not have enough interest if viewed from a neutral point of view.

The fact of the matter is that literature is not a mere moral eulogistic topic. In this essay we shall try to contrast several interpretations, mainly focusing on philosophical and political aspects, including religion if necessary.

A number of key issues arise from the simbology of the book. The story is an allegory traced with great skill and allows the reader to give the book second readings.

Firstly, we would like to explain some possible meanings of the islands as a metaphor. When framing the book on an island, the author's purpose is to freely experiment with the characters and the role they shall take within the book. This virgin territory can be identified with the primary idea of all times. In fact, the story illustrates the corruption of mankind since a kind of the Rousseaunian Natural Man disappeared due to the establishment of some sort of social -or, what is the same for the french philosopher- anti natural order.

As for the will of being rescued that the children have, one may observe that a real, but unconscious anxiety to escape from terrenal world could be deduced from a strictly religious point of view; therefore the island is a secluded portion of a bigger world that waits outside.

Another point of a view could be synthesized as follows: the author extrapolates a group of children from high class school to a wild and unexplored territory. We could blend the kid's origins with their final destination, in this case a desert island dwelled by a supposed beast. If these children come from a well based class they have to be the living example of moral, religious and political correctness. This purity, not only because of being children but also because those circumstances could be identified with the so called innate leniency that some philosophers maintain. When you find out that these lenient children fall into total depravation, you question yourself if real goodness in mankind is rather dubious.

Existentialism fits too with the idea of escaping from routine. A great effort is made to that purpose, but when the unavoidable frustration that appears as a result of that fight make strength fade away; as the fire in the novel finally disappears. In addition to this, we shall consider an island as a symbol of loneliness, of solitude; escaping is sometimes an impossible task. This existentialism tortures and leads anyone to void. Some may desire to escape from the island which bears human condition.

Human condition is depicted through the main characters in the novel. Each one embodies a determined social stereotype which will be later on deeply explained. This existentialist dissatisfaction is a factor which endarkens human kind like other factors such as the kind of fear which is dealt through the book, being this one of the main causes of chaos. Those parallelisms, being some of them adventured, are valid too exposing two questions which take far beyond this point: to what extent is cruelty a mere result of circumstances or a genuine feature in mankind.

We shall now shortly analyse the novel. The will of being rescued will unite all the children with a same purpose. They pursue a determinate objective. For this purpose, a first rudimentary political and social order is established. We would like to trace a parallelism between the situation of the kids when their plane crashed and the so called Natural Man conceived by Rousseau. The Natural Man was an idealized savage who lived in harmony with his instincts and enjoyed communion with nature. Once the social order appeared, the corruption of his condition begun, and the consequences of a degraded order derived into a different kind of savagery: social savagery, a kind of paradoxical parable. The plot in the novel describes with special care how the democracy of the shell generated enough envy and conflicts to finally fracture their attempt to organize themselves under a rational thought.

An elementary hierarchy was established at the same time

with a first order. Apart from that those who reincarnate some kind of power that will be later outlined, the mass is curiously seen as a bunch of hypocrites. Only a few worked hard when constructing the shelter; the majority did not make great efforts and hid in the anonymous existence of plurality. Based on people whose main interests are not as solidary as we would like to think, social order is then seriously threatened.

The fire has a crucial importance as it represents the common will of abandoning the island. In fact, the knot of the novel starts when Jack is ashamed by Ralph, for being the guilty of its extinction in the very moment a boat was sailing at a long distance. Jack's success on hunting the pig is endarkened by his carelessness: the seed of rivalry and hate between the two characters is going to change the events into a tragedy.

The fear which the beast provoked in them is also a factor which we must point out. Imagination and myth take place in the illusory description of the creature which Sam and Eric invent. This has something to do with the hieratism of some religions whose main idea is the existence of a terrible supernatural justice that won't have mercy on mankind: the idea of God is conceived -this idea is stronger in some religions than in others- as an implacable entity whose source of power is terror. Anyway, those beliefs have at least a reward: the comprehension of the world and of the universe. For some civilizations it could be a worthwhile compensation, but we should not forget the coercive power that a premeditate use of terror (maybe even its creation) has within the high spheres of power.

We can find an example on Jack's use of fear to achieve his purposes. therefore, the group's fear towards an unknown beast will end up driving all the group into Jack's fascist hands: in other words, the the primary ideas and events which united the group, are finally disintegrated. Jack will not only use fear but also leadership to recover his pride and his prestige within the group. This pride grows when the tribe is formed. So, to reinforce his pride Jack hides his own image behind a mask; a mask which has something to do with the fascist imaginery, like the paint of the faces. The paint institutionalizes the group and makes personal identity disappear. In all those societies marked by dictatorial there is an uniformity in how people think, dress and react towards certain stimuli; and the same thing happens with the tribe itself.

In contrast, the first established order in the text could be related to a democratic one. But in this system is more uncomfortable to give way to your unhappiness and disconformity: you have to think and you need to collaborate within the system trying to find all the mistakes in it. A fascist order justifies by itself (as the term and the particular circumstances of its creation indicate) providing you with methods to canalize your insatisfaction: hostility, hate, easy thoughts... although its ideals are always used to favour interests which are far from those of the community; as it happened in the novel,, where Jack is the selfish tyrant of the tribe. As an example, we have the members of the group servilism, which is not totally imposed: they find pleasure in being committed to the lidded and his safe but at the same time irrational order.

In the one hand it is worth stating at this point that the most outstanding key issue lays in Simon's savage killing. He represents the search for the truth, but even the truth has not enough power to be heard in such an unbridled atmosphere. What deserves especial consideration is the similarity between Simon and Christ's figure. Simon is the only character depicted in the novel who will have enough courage to search and confront the beast, finding the logical solution to this enigma (more concretely, the parachute's mechanism).

And on the other hand, irrationality and reason are in conflict in the book, and they are solved through someone's killing, the tribe's scope goat, which also represents adulthood and awareness; in this case it will be Piggy.

We can stand a premonition of Simon's death through the Lord of the Flies' message. It can be considered as an advice of the potential danger implied on the possession of truth. Ignorance is praised as a condition to enjoy life without getting in trouble; so Simon is encouraged to leave that forbidden place and play with the other children. The Lord of the Flies reveals itself as the main cause which will not allow them to abandon the island. This powerful symbolic connotation is directly explained by the text, although in an abstract and obscure way.

Once Piggy and Simon are dead, reason is out of the island. There is still one representative character of the initial order, but he is persecuted and his credibility no longer exists. Therefore he will be tracked and hunted as a pig unüil the officer arrived.

The plot is solved with the coming of the only adult figure which the story portraits, although the matters arised in the book are not given a concrete answer. A big interrogation is still in the air, but the fact that the end of this book is not as metaphorical as the rest of the book will allow us to make our own conclusions freely.

So,. is the book a great interrogation which solves small questions? From a religious point of view, the arrival of the soldier represents an ideal of salvation which is only comparable to God's mercy, but we think the end is not a clear metaphor but a pretext to avoid the responsibility of solving those questions. Even the author himself could not be able to solve it; his main achievement consists in giving a clear, bright, and representative allegory. Maybe to be wise is to make the good question rather than the right answer.

It is essential to realise that the merit of the allegory is the relation established between characters and those ideals which they incarnate. Let us begin by saying that firstly we shall outstand the crucial characters, passing later on to a further insight into those characters which we consider less active in the events.

Ralph represents leadership, charisma and reason as an attitude. He often needs Piggy's help to express clearly what his purposes are. The relation between these two characters defines the authority of the democracy of the shell. Ralph is balanced enough to compilate a sensible character with his like for adventure. His humanity is perhaps one of his most suggerent characteristics: he could not bear sleeping alone in the night even when being persecuted by the children's tribe and decided to hide near the Castlerock. The beast, an illusory creation, was less frightening to him than the imminent danger of his own hunting.

Piggy embodies the voice of adulthood. He is laughed at by everyone, a fact which is in clear contrast with his early cleverness to point out ignorance and unconsciousness. His appearance as rejected as his intelligence. As the story goes on, fear and hatred acquire a relevant importance. He is the perfect complement of Ralph for maintaining an order which later disappears. He also has a tool which is essential for everyday life and protection of the community: his glasses, which are firstly used to make fire and later on became an object which triggers a major conflict. Science and its use is therefore partried in the fight for Piggy's specs.

Jack symbolizes the triumph of instincts as a consequence of destabilization. At the beginning of the story he is reasonable and worried about his own and the group's rescue. But his envy grows after being ashamed and he finally uses the children's fear for his own purposes. As a result, he will obtain what he desires, being therefore dominated by egoism.

It is strange that the only symbol of uncomformism is a character whose actions are considerably the causes of the disaster. Uncomformism should not be considered as a negative factor since it is a brain-teasing factor which can provide solutions in many aspects in life. We think the author blends rebellion with a kind of destructive disdain. The degeneration of Jack's character makes us miss a more dignified conception of the search of any possible alternative.

Jack also reminds us of one of the fallen angels; so it is easy to make a comparison between his corruption and the story of Satan, the first fallen angel.

But if we are searching for a figure who can be seen as the reincarnation of the forces of evil we have there in mind Roger. In spite of his quiet character, he is a blood-thirsty kid who enjoys hunting and hurting people, finding special pleasure when killing Piggy. He unconsciously downloads responsibility in Jack.; but if Jack tends to represent the evil figure, Roger represents evilness as an abstract force. The relation Jack and Roger hold could be compared to that of Ralph and Piggy. If Piggy symbolizes the voice of reason, Ralph's charisma makes his reasonable proposals come to light. Roger is also the executive power, the indispensable authority which stands beside the leader doing the dirty work; but a secret yearning of power is observed when mistreating Sam and Eric.

Simon is the opposite of Roger, a strange and secluded one, like the artist which trusts in solitude to develop inspiration and deep thinking. He could be seen as the philosopher who sacrifices enjoying any pleasure for making complex intelligent efforts. As Christ helped the disfavoured, Simon took delight in taking care of the "littluns". His like-mindedness with the children leads him to search and discover the enigmatical truth.

Simon and Eric are also interested in the good working order, since they need an amity with the group similar to the one that the two brothers maintain. The strength of their union is idealized to the extent of being considered an only person. It is so explicit that the kids on the island even call them by a single name: Samneric.

We can also outstand other features in their character like being subdued to the leader. Firstly they accept the order of the shell, but later on their lives overcome their honour and they finally betray Ralph. Their betrayal is due to their innocence, but their act could be seen within the adult world as a sign of cowardliness and interest.

The adult world appears finally in the book with the coming of the officer, an officer which is taking part in a real war. He is surprised of finding a burning island, but he is still proud of being a soldier who also contributes on a nuclear war which is destroying the whole world. So therefore we are dealing with mankind's hypocrisy; an hypocrisy which Ralph shows too when he does not want to recognize being implied on Simon's murder.

Perhaps the reason to be learned from this book is that we all hide a tyrant, or an evil, or a dark instinct which must be sacrificed in favour of living in society. Maybe those features are natural; but the human being is also social by nature, and so the fatal conflict could be intrinsic and unavoidable within ourselves. 'The Lord of the Flies' could not be a great question but a mere explanation of what we are. An explanation of human history and a pessimist message for those who believe in utopia. Anyway, if pessimism is an obstacle, it is also a challenge to be faced; and by facing trouble, if you are not destroyed, you will surely check out that there is a lot of truth in this simply, known but overwhelming phrase: whatever does not kill you makes you stronger.

Q. Discuss the character of Simon

or

Q. Analyse Simon as a symbol of holiness

Throughout The Lord of the Flies, the author shows how different Simon is from the rest of the savages on the island. He is much more innocent and pure than the others and has a religious demeanor. Light, very commonly a symbol of holiness and purity, is used quite often during Simon's "funeral". In the last four paragraphs of chapter nine, "A view to a death", Golding makes clear the use of light imagery to suggest the apotheosis of Simon.

During chapter nine, the sky and water are used to convey a sense of innocence during Simon's glistening funeral. For example, the air becomes clear as the rain ceases, indicating a calm and peacefulness. When the "silver tide" comes in and washes away his blood and "streaks of phosphorescence" mend his battered body, it is as though Simon's body is being prepared for ascension into heaven. "Lamps of stars," "bright constellations," and the moonlight provide much radiance. In addition there are brilliant flashes of lightning from the still lingering storm. The luminous sky provides light while the clear, silver water works on restoring Simon's body after he has been savagely killed.

Simon's body and the creatures around it also show his holiness. Light images of the creatures that surround Simon glorify his body, and as light falls on his corpse he is transfigured into an icon of expiation. Also, the water covers

Simon in a "coat of pearls" and "creatures" (interpreted to symbolize angels) begin to spread a layer of silver over him. The apotheosis of Simon is complete, as he becomes completely silver. As Simon's body is carried out to sea, the angels create a halo (phosphorescence) around his head and attend to his wounds. Simon indeed was the purest and most innocent boy on the island; his character a true symbol of religiousness. At the end of the story this becomes very obvious as Golding uses light imagery for an eloquent funeral to properly end Simon's life. The book Lord of the Flies, is about, a few boys who crash land on to an island, and have to fight off against the elements, and against human nature for basic survival. Golding compares many characters over the passage of time.

For a certain excerpt, he compares two characters Jack and Simon. Jack is the leader of some school Choir boys, knowing this, your first impression of him would be a mature, well behaved, disciplined young man. As the story progresses Golding describes him as more of a savage, and animal like person (doglike, on all fours, ape like.) Golding also describes another character, some one who may seem the exact opposite of Jack, Simon. Through his actions and descriptions, you would notice that Simon is described as having ?blended with nature.? Simon is described to be one with nature. An example Simon walks ?with an accustomed tread through the acres of fruit trees.? Simon passes through the vines, without much of a problem while others suffer to make it through.

Simon and Jack both have one thing in common. They after a while both become part of nature on the island, each in their own special way. Jack becomes part of the island in a negative way, by becoming a hunter, a savage, a civilized person gone primitive, and he always wants to kill. On the contrary Simon, becomes part of the island in a positive way, he has become some sort of meditation person and he always has positive thoughts and unlike Jack he never carries any bad vibes.

Q. Discuss The Lord of the Flies: Biblical Allegory or Anti-Religious Critique?

Or

Q. Comment on The Lord of the Flies allusions to Judeo-Christian mythology.

One of the major points of debate between critics who have studied Lord of the Flies is the significance of the substantial number of allusions to Judeo-Christian mythology. While many scholars have argued that these references qualify the novel as biblical allegory, others have suggested that the novel's allusions to the Old and New Testaments turn out to be ironic and thus criticize religion. A careful reading of Lord of the Flies should take into account not only the abundance of biblical images and themes in the text, but also the ways in which religion and religious themes are used.

In particular, the biblical account of good and evil is invoked-but the account in the novel is not quite the same. Take, for instance, the narrative of Eden. The early chapters of the novel, the island itself resembles the Garden of Eden from Genesis, with its picturesque scenery, abundant fruit, and idyllic weather. Accordingly, the boys are symbolically linked to Adam and Eve before the fall. Ralph's first act after the plane crash is to remove his clothes and bathe in the water, a gesture that recalls the nudity of the innocent Adam and Eve and the act of baptism, a Christian rite which, by some accounts, renews in the sinner a state of grace.

Naming also becomes important in Genesis, reflected in the novel as the boys give their names. Golding extends the Edenic allusion when he presents the contentment of island life as soon corrupted by fear, a moment that is first signified by reports of a creature the boys refer to as "snake-thing." The "snake-thing" recalls the presence of Satan in the Garden of Eden, who disguised himself as a serpent. But unlike Adam and Eve, the boys are mistaken about the creature, which is not a force external (like Satan) but a projection of the evil impulses that are innate within themselves and the human psyche.

Still, it is the boys' failure to recognize the danger of the evil within themselves that propels them deeply into a state of savagery and violence. They continue to externalize it as a beast (again "Lord of the Flies" and "the Beast" are used in religion to refer to Satan), but they become more and more irrational in their perception of it, and they end up developing alternative religious ideas about the Beast and what it wants and does. Although Satan in the Genesis account also has been read as a reflection of evil within human nature, readers usually consider Satan an external force. Original sin enters human nature because of Satan. Without a real Satan in the novel, however, Golding stresses the ways that this Eden is already fallen; for these boys, evil already is within them waiting to be discovered.

On the positive side, Simon's story is that of a prophet or of Jesus Christ. Simon is deeply spiritual, compassionate, non-violent, and in harmony with the natural world. Like many biblical prophets and like Jesus, he is ostracized and ridiculed as an "outsider" for what the others perceive as his "queer" or unorthodox behaviour. Critics also have noted that Simon's confrontation with The Lord of the Flies resembles Christ's conversation with the devil during his forty days in the wilderness as described in the New Testament gospels, and critics have noted parallels between Simon's murder and Christ's sacrifice on the cross. But Simon's revelation is more of a debunking and a turn to the secular, rather than a prophetic condemnation of evil or a call to the higher things. His revelation is that the beast does not exist but is just a dead human.

Q. Discuss the Concept, Identity, and Manifestations of the Beast in Lord of the Flies

or

Q. Analyse humankind work in the struggle to keep it from becoming the dominant force in our lives.

Golding uses the boys' fear of a mythical beast to illustrate their assumption that evil arises from external forces rather than from themselves. This fearsome beast initially takes form in their imaginations as a snake-type animal that disguises itself as jungle vines; later, they consider the possibility of a creature that rises from the sea or the more nebulous entity of a ghost. When they spot the dead paratrooper who has landed on the mountain, the boys feel sure that they have proof of a beast's existence. In fact a beast does roam the island, but not in the form the boys imagine.

Golding wanted to illustrate in this novel the dark side of human nature and make the point that each member of humankind has this dark side. The boys conceptualize the source of all their worst impulses as a beast, some sort of actual animal or possibly supernatural creature inhabiting the island. Yet all along the boys take on the persona of the beast when they act on their animal impulses. There is no external beast.

Golding conveys the beast's identity through the literal actions of Jack and his tribe and through the abstract concept conveyed in Simon's vision. Simon's revelation about the beast comes upon him after he witnesses the sow's death and beheading. As an observer instead of a participant, Simon is able to comprehend the brutality of the act. The sow's head becomes covered with flies, creatures that lack the capacity to feel compassion for or empathy with the dead sow, occupied entirely by their need to eat and multiply. That compassion is one of the key dividers between humanity and animality; tellingly, Jack lacks compassion for the littluns and the vulnerable Piggy. Soon his hunters lose their compassion as well, seeking only to hunt meat and increase the numbers of their tribe or kill those who will not join.

When Simon hallucinates that the staked head is speaking to him, his perception of the other boys as the island's true threat is confirmed. The Lord of the Flies confirms that "You knew, didn't you? I'm part of you? Close, close, close! I'm the reason why it's no go? Why things are what they are?"

Note that the literal translation of the Greek word Beelzebub, a term used for the Judeo-Christian idea of Satan, is "lord of the flies," and flies feast on dead animals and excrement. When Simon asks the assembly "What's the dirtiest thing there is?" he looks for the answer "evil" but also included in that answer is decay and death. Ironically, Jack's excretory answer is partially correct.

Jack provides more insight into the beast's identity when he asserts that "The beast is a hunter," unwittingly implicating himself as part of the problem, a source of the boys' fears. His lust for power and authority causes him to commit and encourage savage acts against his own kind — an accurate measure of his depravity. Sitting in front of his tribe, "Power... chattered in his ear like an ape." The figurative devil on his shoulder is his own animality, looking to master other creatures.

Golding pairs the devolution of Jack's character with Simon's hallucinatory revelation to paint a complete picture of humankind's dark side — that which the boys call "the beast."

Part of Golding's intent was to demonstrate that the evil is not restricted to specific populations or situations. On the island, the beast is manifest in the deadly tribal dances, war paint, and the manhunt; in the outside world that same lust for power and control plays out as a nuclear war. Prior to the war, some of the boys, such as the perpetually victimized Piggy, experienced the brutality of others on the playground, an environment often idealized as the joyous site of a carefree childhood. Within civilized society the beast expresses itself in various ways: through acceptable venues such as the military; in unacceptable forms such as madness or criminality, which carries punitive repercussions; or concealed in the maneuvers of politics and other nonviolent power plays. In *Lord of the Flies* Golding illustrates that evil is present in everyone and everywhere; humankind's work lies not in the impossible mission of eradicating it but in the struggle to keep it from becoming the dominant force in our lives.

Q. Discuss Golding's Use of the Fable Structure in Lord of the Flies

A fable is a short fictional story intended to teach a moral lesson. Best known are Aesop's fables, which feature talking animals as the main characters and end with such truisms as "slow and steady wins the race." The one-dimensional characters and simplistic story line of a fable leave little room for argument with the concluding proverb. It is ironic, then, that Golding considered *Lord of the Flies* a fable, because his novel allows much room for speculation.

Instead of using cartoonish talking animals, Golding

teaches his lesson with fully developed human characters representing the dominant motifs. As the characters interact with each other and with their environment, so do the forces they represent. Using the characters to embody these forces allows Golding the opportunity to compare and contrast with rich shadings of meaning rather than with simplistic oppositions. Unlike Aesop's animals, human beings act in ways that frequently conflict with the values they consciously hold, as is the case with Golding's protagonist Ralph. Because Ralph finds himself participating in the same savage behaviour he condemns in the other boys, he presents a realistic picture of a humane person resorting to brutality under unusual circumstances.

Other characters also bring ambiguity to the motifs they embody. Piggy, for example, represents the scientific rationalist whose knowledge and intellect far exceed that of the other boys. Yet for all his intelligence, he cannot figure out how to speak so that the others will listen.

Golding does seek to provide a lesson in morality, but the lesson lacks the straightforward and decisive tone of the proverb that concludes most fables. At the end of Golding's fable, the reader has learned not that evil is confined to the militaristic portion of the population as epitomized by Jack; the pacifist Ralph participated in some of the brutal tribal activities. Neither has the reader learned that science or even simple common sense will save humanity from itself; Piggy is ridiculed throughout and then killed. Mystical revelations or visionary insight into the human condition will not save us; consider the fate of the saintly Simon. Instead the reader learns that evil lives in us all, and there is no proverb to remedy that situation. By invoking the complexity that underlies human nature, Golding's tale brings depth to the fable structure and presents a complex moral lesson as well.

Bibliography

- The 100 Most Frequently Challenged Books of 1990-2000. American Library Association (2007). Retrieved on 2007-03-27.
- The Complete List: TIME Magazine ALL TIME 100 Novels. TIME (2005). Retrieved on 2007-05-12.
- Fenlon, John Francis. (1907). "*Beelzebub*" Catholic Encyclopedia. Vol. 2. New York: Robert Appleton Company. Retrieved: May 29, 2008
- *Johnson, Arnold* (1980). Of Earth and Darkness. The Novels of William Golding. Missouri: University of Missouri Press, 132.
- Green Paint: Mysteries of William Golding's Lord of the Flies" Great War Fiction
- Wagner, Thomas M. (2006). Robert A. Heinlein: Tunnel in the Sky. SF Reviews.net. Retrieved on 2007-03-27.
- Stephen King (1947). Authors' Calendar (2003). Retrieved on 2007-03-27.
- Bailie, Stuart (1992-06-13). Rock and Roll Should Be This Big!. NME. Retrieved on 2007-11-28.